Prosecutors in the Boardroom

Prosecutors in the Boardroom

Using Criminal Law to Regulate Corporate Conduct

EDITED BY

Anthony S. Barkow and
Rachel E. Barkow

NEW YORK UNIVERSITY PRESS
New York and London

NEW YORK UNIVERSITY PRESS
New York and London
www.nyupress.org

References to Internet websites (URLs) were accurate at the time of writing. Neither the author nor New York University Press is responsible for URLs that may have expired or changed since the manuscript was prepared.

Library of Congress Cataloging-in-Publication Data
Prosecutors in the boardroom : using criminal law to regulate corporate conduct / edited by Anthony S. Barkow and Rachel E. Barkow.
p. cm.
Includes bibliographical references and index.
ISBN 978-0-8147-8703-8 (cl : alk. paper) —
ISBN 978-0-8147-0937-5 (ebook : alk. paper)
1. Corporation law—United States—Criminal provisions.
2. Prosecution—United States. I. Barkow, Anthony S. II. Barkow, Rachel E.
KF9351.P76 2011
345.73'0268—dc22 2010047467

New York University Press books are printed on acid-free paper, and their binding materials are chosen for strength and durability. We strive to use environmentally responsible suppliers and materials to the greatest extent possible in publishing our books.

Manufactured in the United States of America
10 9 8 7 6 5 4 3 2 1

As with everything, for Nate

Contents

Acknowledgments

This book could not have been completed without the tremendous efforts of many people. The editors would like to thank several in particular.

First and most obviously, we must thank the book's contributing authors. As a compilation, this book is only the sum of its parts. We are fortunate and grateful to have worked with such an incredibly talented and diligent group of scholars. These scholars also deserve thanks for participating in the Center on the Administration of Criminal Law's inaugural annual major conference, "Regulation by Prosecutors," where many of the ideas in the book first emerged. Additional thanks also go to the scholars who served as moderators at the conference and spurred a great discussion and all the practitioners who participated in the conference as speakers.

David B. Edwards ('08), Attorney-in-Residence at the Center in 2009 and 2010, deserves special thanks. Dave was absolutely indispensable to the publication of this book. He edited every page of it in one way or another, often several times. He formatted the entire book. He made helpful substantive contributions to each part of it. It could not have been published without him, and is a much better book because of him. Jing-Li Yu, David's successor, also deserves special thanks.

Many New York University School of Law students who worked as Center fellows also made significant contributions. We thank Julia Fong Sheketoff ('10), Laura J. Arandes ('11), Mahalia Annah-Marie Cole ('11), Kelly Geoghegan ('11), Alexander Li ('12), Karl Mulloney-Radke ('12), Meagan Elizabeth Powers ('11), Jason A. Richman ('11), Elizabeth-Ann S. Tierney ('11), and Alicia J. Yass ('11). Two Harvard Law School students who worked as Center summer fellows, Mark Savignac and Tom Ferriss, also provided first-rate assistance; we owe a special thanks to Mark for his work on the introduction.

Thanks to Barry Friedman and Noah Feldman for their help in navigating the world of book publishing.

Finally, neither the Center nor any of its activities, including this book, would have been possible without the generous support of Dean Ricky Revesz and of the Ford Foundation. We thank both for making possible this endeavor.

You can read about the Center and its work at www.prosecutioncenter.org.

Introduction

ANTHONY S. BARKOW AND RACHEL E. BARKOW

The simple account of America's system of separated powers has legislators responsible for making laws, the executive branch (and prosecutors within it) charged with enforcing the laws, and judges with the power to adjudicate any disputes by declaring what the law commands. Two aspects of our modern government that have disrupted this paradigm—judicial and agency policymaking—have become scholarly obsessions. But there is another, equally strong challenge to the traditional separation-of-powers framework that has received far less attention: prosecutors who regulate.

The constitutionally limited role of the prosecutor is to "take care that the laws be faithfully executed"—that is, to enforce the policies laid down in laws enacted by the legislature. Whether this was ever true, it is certainly not the case today that prosecutors are merely enforcing preestablished rules. Armed with expansive criminal codes and broadly worded statutes, plus the ability to threaten harsh and often mandatory sentences, prosecutors have so much leverage in negotiations with defendants that they have, for all practical purposes, taken on the role of adjudicator as well. The prosecutor alone sometimes decides a defendant's liability and sentence.

This adjudicative authority gives prosecutors leverage to engage in lawmaking power as well. Because criminal laws themselves are broad, power is delegated to prosecutors to define what those laws mean, establish what conduct within the broad parameters of the law they wish to target, and dictate how that conduct should be punished. This power is akin to that of administrative agencies to define the meaning of regulatory statutes.[1] One could argue, however, that, despite its scope, this kind of regulatory power is inherent in executive power. The power to charge will necessarily include some policymaking given the necessary breadth in the way laws are written.

But prosecutorial regulatory power has gone further than the incidental power to regulate that comes with enforcement discretion. In the area of corporate crime in particular, prosecutors have gone beyond law interpretation and the pursuit of punishment for what they believe to be past violations of existing criminal laws. In this context, prosecutorial goals are sometimes more grand, with prosecutors seeking to reform the way companies do business going forward.

As with prosecutions against individuals, prosecutors gain this power because of their ability to exact a high price if a defendant opts to exercise its trial rights. Indeed, with companies, the threat is even more pronounced. First, American law embraces the doctrine of *respondeat superior*, under which corporations may be criminally liable for the actions of low-level employees taken in the course of their employment, even where these actions contravened stated company policy and, in some states, did not actually benefit the corporation. Second, a firm's success—particularly in finance-related industries in which integrity is important—is often dependent on the strength of its reputation. Thus, when a firm is implicated in criminal wrongdoing, it stands to lose far more than a monetary fine: the mere fact of indictment may cause a loss of consumer and investor confidence, resulting in collateral losses to the firm far outweighing its legal liability and without regard for the ultimate verdict.

No other case demonstrates these collateral effects as well as the prosecution of the accounting firm Arthur Andersen LLP. While the Securities and Exchange Commission ("SEC") was investigating Enron, Andersen employees shredded documents pertaining to Andersen's audit of Enron's books. After reportedly refusing to enter into an agreement with prosecutors,[2] Andersen was indicted in federal court for obstruction of justice. The indictment badly damaged Andersen's reputation, causing many clients to abandon the firm, and its eventual conviction led to the loss of its auditing license. Although a unanimous Supreme Court later overturned the conviction, the original indictment and conviction had already crippled Andersen beyond recovery and resulted in the loss of 75,000 jobs.[3]

Andersen's fate can never be far from the minds of prosecutors and corporations accused of criminal wrongdoing. Many firms have taken away the lesson that avoiding criminal charges and the disastrous collateral consequences they bring is worth just about any price exacted by prosecutors. Prosecutors, for their part, would prefer to avoid the hard choice of either letting companies off the hook or indicting them when it could mean another Andersen-like collapse and substantial harm to innocent shareholders and employees.

Thus we have entered a new era in which prosecutors and firms have embraced a third option: regulation by prosecutors. Prosecutors have increasingly reached agreements with companies that allow the companies to avoid indictments so long as they meet the prosecutors' regulatory terms.

The agreements go by different names. In the federal system, they consist of nonprosecution agreements ("NPAs") and deferred prosecution agreements ("DPAs"). In some states, they are known as settlement agreements. When the agreements require companies simply to obey the law or pay for prior bad acts, they are not particularly noteworthy because they are incidental to the traditional exercise of executive power.

But in many of these agreements, prosecutors impose affirmative obligations on companies to change personnel, revamp their business practices, and adopt new models of corporate governance. These dictates are often sweeping, and some prosecutors have imposed them on industries, not just isolated companies. They resemble, in significant respects, the structural injunctions courts have imposed in areas like prison and school reform[4] and the regulations promulgated by administrative agencies.

Recent efforts by the New York Attorney General's ("NY AG") Office exemplify this type of prosecutorial regulation. Indeed, former Attorney General and Governor Eliot Spitzer once referred to himself as a "prosecutor-slash-regulator" and explicitly set out to change "the way Wall Street operates." During his tenure as attorney general, Spitzer sought to reform the investment banking, mutual fund, and insurance industries by reaching agreements with the top firms to alter their business practices. In the investment banking industry, Spitzer confronted a conflict of interest between research analysts and investment bankers at the nation's top investment firms after discovering that stock recommendations by analysts were influenced by whether the company issuing the stock had promised to give its banking business to the analysts' firms. The settlement with the investment firms included not only a mandate for separation of their research analysts from their investment bankers but also a five-year commitment to contract with independent research firms to provide information to the firms' customers. In his settlement with the mutual fund industry, where brokers were promoting in-house funds without disclosing that they received higher commissions for selling those funds, Spitzer even tackled the companies' fees, requiring them to lower their fees by 20 percent for five years.

Spitzer's successor, Andrew Cuomo, has entered into comparable settlements with health care and student loan providers. Soon after replacing Spitzer, Cuomo began an investigation into the health care industry's in-network doctor ranking programs, resulting in an agreement establishing a new code of conduct for ranking doctors that requires health care companies to disclose more information on how doctors are ranked and the rankings' ties to quality of performance and cost efficiency. Additionally, after Cuomo uncovered various deceptive and illegal practices in the student loan industry, schools and lenders, under threat of prosecution, adopted a College Loan Code of Conduct that specified new practices to govern their behavior going forward.

While the NY AG's Office arguably provides examples of the most sweeping regulations imposed by prosecutors, the NY AG is not the only prosecutor seeking to regulate companies. Federal prosecutors in numerous districts have been active as well. Recent years have shown a dramatic increase in the use of DPAs and NPAs by federal prosecutors, rising from a mere eleven agreements negotiated between 1993 and 2001, and twenty-three agreements between 2002 and 2005, to sixty-six agreements between 2006 and 2008.[5] The increasing number of agreements spans a multitude of businesses, including the telecommunications, banking, medical, and fashion industries, and charges a variety of misconduct, including accounting, securities, and tax fraud, bribery of foreign officials, and theft of government property. These agreements, like their New York counterparts, go well beyond a simple insistence that companies cease disobeying the law. Consider in this respect agreements reached by Christopher J. Christie, the former U.S. Attorney for the District of New Jersey (now governor of New Jersey). Christie negotiated DPAs in seven cases during his tenure as U.S. Attorney, many of which included the appointment of monitors to observe the corporations' adherence to the agreements. One DPA, involving five manufacturers of orthopedic hips and knees accused of engaging in a kickback scheme with orthopedic surgeons in order to defraud Medicare, resulted in the appointment of five different monitors, one for each company. Christie also negotiated one DPA with Bristol-Myers Squibb that not only appointed a monitor but also required the corporation to endow an ethics chair at Christie's alma mater, Seton Hall University School of Law.

The appointment of monitors to oversee these agreements raises additional questions. Monitors are used in about half of all DPAs, and their use raises issues about how they are selected, whether they are well equipped to set regulatory terms for the companies they oversee, and where they owe their loyalties. Their use has not been without controversy. For example, in one case, Christie appointed former Attorney General John Ashcroft—Christie's former boss—as a corporate monitor. That contract was valued at as much as $52 million and subsequently sparked congressional hearings into the appropriateness of the arrangement.[6]

The practice of regulation by prosecutors thus raises a number of fundamental questions. Perhaps most fundamentally, there is the question of how the government should seek to deter corporate misconduct and the role of the criminal law in that endeavor. Relatedly, there is the question of prosecutorial competence and legitimacy to set regulatory terms. What is the comparative institutional competence of prosecutors to regulate as compared with traditional regulatory agencies like the SEC? Are there differences in the relative competence of state versus federal prosecutors in pursuing this kind of regulation? What factors—accountability, expertise, independence, ethical concerns, efficiency or lack thereof—make prosecutorial participation in the regulation desirable or undesirable? How could these factors be adjusted to improve the quality of that participation? What safeguards can promote good practices in prosecutorial involvement in corporate governance, and what measures can improve coordination and minimize collisions between prosecutors and regulatory agencies? How much power should corporate monitors have, and by what process should they be appointed?

These questions motivate the authors who have contributed to this volume.

Cindy Alexander and Mark Cohen lay the groundwork with a discussion of the causes of corporate crime. Approaching the question from an economic perspective, they focus on the role played by rational, self-interested individuals in causing or preventing corporate crimes. Corporate criminal enforcement must influence the acts and omissions of individuals within the corporation in order to successfully combat corporate misconduct. Because of limitations on prosecutors, they are unlikely ever to learn of the less egregious violations unless corporations put substantial resources toward uncovering and reporting them. For this reason, prosecutors need to incentivize monitoring and cooperation with law enforcement by relaxing or removing penalties on firms that cooperate. And because the collateral consequences of indictment alone can be catastrophic for firms, irrespective of ultimate conviction or acquittal, this bargaining typically requires prosecutors to waive prosecution altogether (as in DPAs). Alexander and Cohen also note that higher levels of enforcement may become inefficient: the goal in corporate enforcement should be to balance the costs imposed on firms through requirements that they undertake monitoring programs against the benefits gained by the incremental reduction in levels of corporate crime.

With Alexander and Cohen's general view of the field as a backdrop, the book then turns to an analysis of prosecutors' current approach. Richard Epstein begins by offering a critique of the power prosecutors wield over corporations. He argues that the existing standard for corporate criminality is too broad and that prosecutors exercise too much power over companies. He goes on to explain how the doctrine of unconstitutional conditions—which he notes applies to precisely the kind of state monopoly power that one sees in the criminal context—should inform the question of what types of terms should be included in DPAs and NPAs. He concludes that while terms directly geared to maintaining compliance are acceptable, he condemns as illegitimate terms that would require corporations to take certain positions in political debates over questions of social policy, to dismiss certain employees who are not themselves suspected of wrongdoing, or to cut off attorney's fees that had previously been promised to employees being investigated.

Jennifer Arlen's chapter shares Alexander and Cohen's view that prosecutors' ability effectively to deter corporate crimes depends on them having the combined power to prosecute firms for their employees' corporate crimes plus the power to offer leniency to firms that monitor effectively, report misconduct, and cooperate. Arlen also shares some of Epstein's concern that prosecutors have gone too far in regulating companies. She notes that those seeking to reduce corporate crime, whether criminal prosecutors or civil regulators, do so in two ways: by securing *ex ante* corporate compliance with monitoring programs to deter and detect employee misconduct, and by gaining *ex post* corporate cooperation in the investigation of infractions and attribution of fault to the responsible employees. Under Arlen's analysis, civil regulatory authorities should exercise the sole authority over mandated corporate governance reforms, including monitoring requirements. Prosecutors, in her view, should not use DPAs or NPAs to prompt structural reforms because it is beyond their expertise to design compliance programs. Instead, prosecutors should use prosecution and the threat of prosecution to secure *ex post* cooperation from firms.

Samuel Buell supports a robust role for prosecutors in regulating corporate behavior, but he believes the balance has tipped too far in favor of prosecution versus regulation. He thus advocates a greater role for agencies in the regulation of corporations. Buell's chapter explains that there are three key actors on the enforcement side of corporate regulation: private actors (potential class action plaintiffs, for instance), criminal prosecutors, and regulatory bodies such as the SEC. Buell argues that criminal sanctions are most effective as the cap of a pyramid of enforcement, where they most often affect corporate behavior through threat rather than through actual use. In this way, the threat of criminal liability can make the lower, more frequently applied sections of the pyramid—such as civil agency enforcement and private civil liability—more effective. However, he finds that actual practice fails to match this efficient ideal; instead, perverse incentives act upon the various enforcement actors to produce a poorly calibrated, inefficient system. The essence of this flaw is overuse of criminal enforcement, which Buell suggests is caused by the weakness of the civil forms of liability. According to Buell, the solution is to augment civil enforcement so that it becomes more attractive to enforcers, making the resort to criminal enforcement less common.

Lisa Kern Griffin, like Buell, pays close attention to the role of private actors in corporate oversight, but her chapter zeroes in on the role of private parties in criminal law enforcement of corporations. She explains the increasingly central role played by private actors in current enforcement strategies, paying particular attention to the compliance industry and corporate monitors. She then analyzes the costs and benefits of this collaboration between public law enforcement officials and private parties and offers suggestions for reform. Because Griffin concludes that there is little evidence that the public/private partnership has produced changes in the internalization of compliance norms, she agrees with Arlen and Buell in urging a greater role for industry-wide regulation by expert agencies.

Mariano-Florentino Cuéllar continues the focus on institutional design by discussing the advantages that prosecutors and others in law enforcement can bring to the enterprise of risk regulation. He argues that criminal and regulatory laws often overlap in scope, and that individuals involved in criminal enforcement tend to develop specific investigative skills that can be helpful in the regulatory context but are often lacking in regulatory agencies. Criminal justice bureaucracies also tend to have greater autonomy at the level of the individual actor and greater independence from organized interest groups and political pressures that may lead to agency capture. For these reasons, Cuéllar concludes that criminal justice authorities indeed have an important role to play in regulation today, including the regulation of corporations. But he cautions that many of the benefits brought by criminal law enforcement come from its interplay with regulatory agencies, so he joins other contributing authors in advocating for a regime where criminal law enforcement officials work with regulators rather than supplanting them.

The next two chapters focus specifically on the capacity of prosecutors to regulate. Brandon Garrett begins this analysis by discussing the current relationship between prosecutors and regulators. He emphasizes that regulators are already playing a significant role in the formulation of DPAs and NPAs. Garrett notes that most corporate prosecutions are begun upon referral from regulators and that regulators often participate in the negotiation of settlements. That said, Garrett also acknowledges that the interaction between prosecutors and agencies is ad hoc and that each actor brings different goals to the process. Garrett suggests some ways to improve the relationship between prosecutors and agencies, including more clearly established norms about when cases should be referred to prosecutors and a potentially greater role for the Financial Fraud Enforcement Task Force in encouraging greater cooperation between regulators and prosecutors.

Rachel Barkow evaluates the capacity of prosecutors as regulators using the same benchmarks that have typically been applied to agencies, namely, democratic accountability, institutional competence, and procedural reliability. From the standpoint of accountability, she finds that prosecutors are at least as accountable to the public as traditional regulators. Institutional competence is a more complicated issue, according to Barkow. DPAs, NPAs, and settlement agreements often decide complex questions of how businesses should operate. These agreements have regulated everything from the commissions companies can charge to codes of conduct for health insurance companies. Barkow notes that one may reasonably doubt whether prosecutors, typically not experts on business in general or on specific industries, can make efficient decisions in the business context. However, given the reality of agency capture, Barkow suggests that it is not always clear that agencies possess greater institutional competence than prosecutors because they might be biased in favor of regulated interests. Barkow thus endorses a model where prosecutors seek input from expert agencies, even if they sometimes override agency positions because of a view that the agency has been captured. Barkow concludes with an analysis of the procedural reliability of prosecutorial regulation and finds that it is in need of improvement.

Sara Sun Beale shifts attention to the relationship among prosecutors, and specifically the overlapping jurisdiction of federal and state prosecutors over corporate misconduct. Beale describes a variety of circumstances under which prosecutors from multiple jurisdictions initiated criminal investigations or brought formal prosecutions concerning the same corporate conduct. Beale analyzes the incentives that determine whether more than one prosecutor will become involved, as well as the complexities that may arise if there is a lack of cooperation in multijurisdictional prosecutions. She then details the current lack of formal mechanisms to harmonize all the prosecutorial actors involved. While noting this lack of formal mechanisms, Beale sets forth the informal measures by which coordination occurs.

Vikramaditya Khanna completes the analysis by examining in greater detail the final player in the criminal regulation of corporations: the corporate monitors. Khanna explains that the use of monitors makes sense when cash fines provide inadequate deterrence. Khanna then considers what rules should govern the selection, compensation, and use of monitors. He encourages the development of a market to improve the selection and compensation of monitors; thus he is in favor of proposed legislation that would create a national list of qualified monitors and the selection of monitors through an open process. Khanna prefers fees to be set by a competitive bidding process or through judicial oversight instead of through a legislatively mandated flat fee schedule. If a market for monitors does not develop, Khanna argues that DPAs and NPAs should make clear that monitors owe fiduciary-like duties to the corporation's shareholders. Because monitors are not themselves stockholders and cannot typically be fired by corporations, they lack the profit motive that acts on most corporate managers. Imposing fiduciary duties on monitors could help remedy this lack of a market-based motivation.

The conclusion draws on the insightful analysis of the contributing authors to present a unified set of potential reforms to the current system of prosecutorial regulation. It also identifies questions that might be addressed in future research. Regulation by prosecutors is an increasingly significant phenomenon, one that is likely to expand during the government response to the current economic crisis. The goal of this book is to describe the practice, analyze it critically, and lay the groundwork for improved public policy and ongoing scholarship on this critical topic.

NOTES

1. Dan Kahan, *Is Chevron Relevant to Federal Criminal Law?*, 110 Harv. L. Rev. 469, 479–81 (1996).

2. Kurt Eichenwald, *Andersen Refused a Probation Deal*, N.Y. Times, Apr. 2, 2002, at A1.

3. David Kocieniewski, *In Testy Exchange in Congress, Christie Defends His Record as a Prosecutor*, N.Y. Times, June 26, 2009, at A19.

4. Brandon L. Garrett, *Structural Reform Prosecution*, 93 Va. L. Rev. 853 (2007).

5. Peter Spivack & Sujit Raman, *Regulating the 'New Regulators': Current Trends in Deferred Prosecution Agreements*, 45 Am. Crim. L. Rev. 159, 167 (2008).

6. Press Release, House Judiciary Committee, Conyers and Sánchez Demand Ashcroft Testimony about $52 Million No-Bid Contract (Jan. 30, 2008), *available at* http://judiciary.house.gov/news/013008.html; Kocieniewski, *supra* note 3.

1

The Causes of Corporate Crime

An Economic Perspective

CINDY R. ALEXANDER AND MARK A. COHEN

This chapter examines the causes of corporate misconduct from an economic perspective, focusing on crime. Our purpose is to provide an understanding of why corporate misconduct occurs and to identify some considerations that are important to enforcement authorities and corporate monitors in determining how best to deter it. These considerations have grown in importance over the past decade, especially with the emergence of governance reform and the related use of DPAs as means for promoting monitoring and related deterrence of crime in business organizations.[1]

The *threat of sanction* is central to the deterrence of corporate crime in this setting. This includes the chance of getting caught and the penalty that the offender expects to pay, if caught. Two features of crimes by corporations are key. First, crimes tend to be committed by multiple individuals, not just by one individual acting alone. Second, individuals are linked within corporations through what some economists have termed a "nexus of contracts."[2] This means that individual choices in the corporation are linked in a predictable manner, depending on the firm's structure and governance. The actions of individuals who would never think of committing a crime can influence the actions of those who are more prone to misconduct. The possibility of deterring crime by penalizing—or holding accountable—an individual who does not directly engage in crime is thus apparent; blaming the top management for inadequate internal controls or a corporate culture that fosters crime can be an effective response to corporate crime in some instances, even when the top management had no direct role in the offense. Similarly, holding shareholders accountable (via the corporate entity) can be an effective means of deterrence in settings where the corporation is generally responsive to the interests of its shareholders, the enforcement authority faces difficulty in identifying the guilty employee (or the guilty employee is judgment proof), and the shareholders are not themselves an injured party in the misconduct.

FIGURE 1.1

Publicly Announced DPAs and NPAs, by Year (estimated)

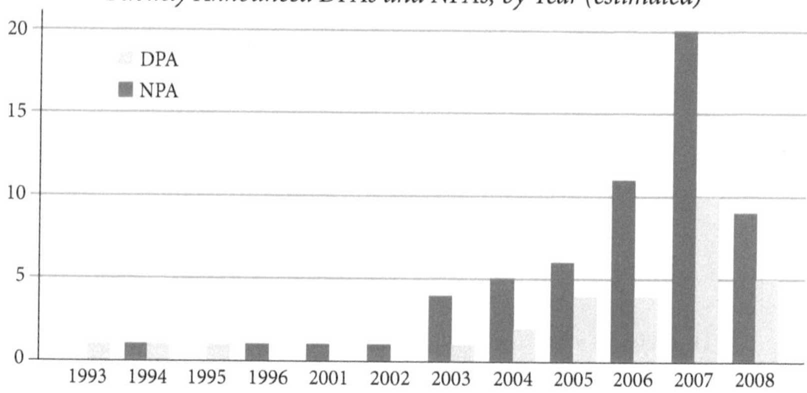

Reforms to governance at the top of the corporation have thus emerged as a potentially effective substitute for higher monetary sanctions in deterring corporate crime. This can be seen in the past decade's reforms under the Sarbanes-Oxley Act of 2002 and in the increased use of prosecution agreements, notably DPAs and NPAs (see Figure 1.1).[3]

The framework of this Chapter applies across the wide array of offenses for which corporations may be held accountable, including violations of health, safety, or environmental regulations; antitrust conspiracies; bribery and corruption on government contracts; and securities fraud. In the United States, those legally responsible for corporate crime can be as varied as the hourly employee who illegally dumps a barrel of hazardous waste, the manager who conspires with competitors to rig bids on a local road-building project, or the senior executive who fails to put effective controls in place to ensure that foreign government officials are not bribed to obtain a contract or that the firm's financial reporting practices meet the needs of investors.

The pattern of increased reliance on prosecution agreements is apparent even when compared with the use of traditional criminal sanctions around the peak period of their use, during 2004–2007. While there has been only a slight decrease in the number of traditional criminal prosecutions resulting in fines of more than $1 million, the number of companies without criminal prosecution but having fines of more than $1 million and a prosecution agreement increased dramatically from as few as seven in 2004 to as many as thirty in 2007. Combined, the number of companies receiving $1 million or more in sanctions doubled, with the number in 2007 being 105 percent higher than in 2004. Our evidence is that more than three-quarters of the prosecution agreements were accompanied by monetary sanctions of more than $1 million in this period. The early experience is that prosecution agreements may be a less costly means of delivering monetary sanctions than traditional channels of criminal enforcement. Since the two can deliver sanctions for similar conduct, they can be thought of as substitute means of promoting deterrence—with prosecutors being able to increase use of the lower-cost substitute while only slightly decreasing the use of the higher-cost substitute and thus producing a greater number of enforcement actions overall. The evidence from the table is consistent with this; prosecutors appear not to have reduced substantially their criminal prosecution rate in exchange for prosecution agreements; instead, they appear to be increasing the overall number of enforcement actions.

Looking forward, the creation of institutions to promote greater diligence within organizations may be seen as a substitute for higher criminal sanctions in promoting general deterrence. That is, efforts to increase the probability of detection and related sanctions—even if undertaken by parties within the corporation—can be an effective substitute for higher criminal penalties or more stringent government monitoring in the prevention of crime. One strategy is to identify more clearly who within the corporation will be held accountable for a crime prior to its occurrence. The effect

TABLE 1.1

Growth in use of prosecution agreements relative to criminal fines against corporations: cases resolved with monetary sanctions above $1 million, by year

	Criminal Fines	*Prosecution Agreements*	*Combined*
2001	18	1	19
2002	16	1	17
2003	13	5	18
2004	14	7	21
2005	15	10	25
2006	9	15	24
2007	13	30	43
Percent change 2004–7	-7%	328%	105%

is to increase the *ex ante* probability of sanction among those individuals (at the expense of reducing the probability of sanction among other individuals), thereby concentrating the incentive to prevent the crime among those individuals. The challenge lies in distinguishing the individuals in the organization who are best equipped to prevent the misconduct (i.e., lowest-cost avoiders), either directly (by not undertaking it in the first place) or indirectly (by taking steps to improve governance or by blowing the whistle against ongoing misconduct).

Although the focus of this chapter is on corporate crime, the underlying behavior we are interested in is organizational "misconduct" that can include administrative or regulatory violations, consumer fraud, securities fraud, or any activity taken by (or on behalf of) an organization that is subject to criminal or other legal sanctions. Whether misconduct is deemed criminal in the U.S. system depends on the independent choices of a judge and prosecutor. The prosecutor's decision to bring criminal charges against an alleged corporate wrongdoer may indeed depend upon many factors—such as the strength of evidence, solvency of the corporation, and prosecutorial priorities. It also depends on the availability of substitute forms of sanction, such as may occur through the use of prosecution agreements. For some offenses, it can thus be difficult to determine at the outset whether a criminal or non-criminal sanction (or both) will apply in the event of detection. Thus, while we are primarily interested in crime, theories of the causes of corporate crime necessarily encompass corporate misconduct more generally.[4]

Section I of this chapter will review the fundamental insights of the economic model of crime and its origins, beginning with a review of the basic economic model and the empirical evidence on its practical relevance. Section II examines implications for the choice of enforcement strategy and design of sanction. Section III briefly recaps the empirical literature on corporate criminal sanctions. Section IV provides a discussion of practical implications for the design of enforcement institutions, followed by a brief conclusion.

I. Why Do Corporations Commit Crimes?

The reasons for corporate crime are numerous and implicate many changing factors. In this section, we examine the causes through the lens of an economic model in which corporate crime is the outcome of decisions by rational utility-maximizing individuals who have the ability to incur criminal liability on behalf of the corporation.[5] Within this rational-choice "deterrence" framework, individuals weigh the costs and benefits of crime-related activity against the expected sanction to maximize their private utility under the constraints of the organization in which they find themselves (or select into). The underlying economic theory of why individuals commit or are deterred from crime is generally attributed to Becker, although the roots can be traced back to classical criminology (e.g., Beccaria and Bentham).[6] This model has both practical and nonnormative applications. Focusing here on a nonnormative analysis allows us to predict when the crime rate is likely to go up or down, and in which companies we are more or less likely to see criminal activity. We begin with the simplest case of the individual acting on behalf of the organization.

Individuals Acting on Behalf of a Corporation

Although corporations can be seen as collections of individuals organized around a series of implicit and explicit contracts, corporate misconduct is often traceable to the choices of specific individuals. Those individuals are then said to have "caused" the criminal activity or been "negligent" in allowing activities that led to corporate criminal violations. Whether explicitly sanctioned or prohibited by their organizations, individuals are legally assumed to be acting on behalf of their employer in these situations. Of course there are various decision makers within any organization, including owners, managers, and employees. While their motivations might be similar—for example, monetary income, leisure time/quality of life, reputation within their community—individuals in corporations will vary in their opportunities, and hence face different private payoffs from committing crimes.

Not all corporate crimes require individual (or corporate) intent; some strict liability offenses carry criminal sanctions, for example, and corporations can face vicarious liability. Nevertheless, it is often possible to consider these strict liability crimes as being the outcome of decisions on the part of individuals. For example, an "accidental" rupture of a chemical tank might be linked to an individual decision maker who chose an inadequate level of prevention. Thus, the individual's action becomes a "causal factor" in the strict liability crime, but not necessarily the only factor. In many cases, a series of inactions (as opposed to identifiable actions) might have contributed to the outcome. For example, top management decisions might have determined the incentives and rewards for plant-level employees' actions that contributed to midlevel managers' budgeting decisions. Midlevel managers might have chosen not only how much to spend on maintenance but also how much of their time to devote to monitoring those employee actions.

Lower-level employees might have decided how to allocate the time spent on maintenance, and so forth. In combination, these decisions can have an impact on the overall probability of a chemical spill—even if it would legally be difficult to directly tie the individual decisions and related behavior to a spill.

Why do some people commit corporate crimes while others do not? In the economic model of crime, rational individuals weigh their expected private gain from committing a crime against their cost. The expected costs of committing a crime include the cost of executing the crime itself and other costs that depend on the probability of detection—such as formal court-ordered sanctions, informal sanctions (loss of future business), and "psychic" costs to the individual (lack of self-respect, loss of standing in the community, etc.). The expected private gain from an individual's participation in corporate crime can include increased income, more leisure time, higher status within the organization, and so forth. Thus, corporate crime is the result of individual decisions made in the face of various opportunities and constraints.

The propensities of individuals to commit crime can be difficult for a corporation to control. Some people have greater moral inhibitions than others; some are extremely averse to going to jail while others are less concerned about the consequences of such punishment. Similarly, individuals will vary according to their job status, economic situation, stature within the community, and so forth. Individuals with little stature in the community may feel they have little to lose if caught committing a crime, whereas those of extremely high stature in the community may feel they have a lot to lose and thus perceive a higher private cost from committing a crime.

The *opportunity* to engage in crime can be easier for the corporation to control. Some corporations may be able to eliminate the opportunity from their business environments altogether. The capacity to influence the risk of crime will vary by firm, industry, and the characteristics of managers. Potentially, every transaction within a firm carries the opportunity to act criminally. For instance, every sale carries with it the opportunity to illegally misrepresent the quality of the product or service to the customer. Every accounting entry may be accurate or fraudulent, day-to-day production may meet or violate emission standards, and so forth.

Opportunities to commit crime vary not just in the ease of committing the crime but also in the *detection risk* they present. For example, it may be easier to violate emissions standards for one day and avoid a random emissions audit than it is to set up a price-fixing conspiracy and risk that one of the potential coconspirators will report the conspiracy to the Department of Justice ("DOJ").

Corporation as the "Decision Maker"

Instead of focusing on individual actions, we can consider crime as the outcome of company-level decisions. A firm that is maximizing expected profits essentially weighs its expected sanction against the expected private gain from the crime. The expected sanction depends, as before, on the probability and severity of corporate punishment, which might exceed any expected monetary sanction imposed by the government to the extent there are reputational losses that hurt the firm's future sales or ability to raise financial capital from external sources. The expected private gain might come about through higher sales (e.g., fraudulent marketing), higher prices (e.g., collusion), or lower costs (e.g., ignoring regulatory requirements for occupational health). Indicators of reputational consequences can include disruption of business dealings, suspension of operations, and costly "reinvestment in reputation" for compliance, such as through turnover or reassignment of key personnel and other remedial actions at the news of crime.[7]

Since firms are likely to weigh the expected costs and benefits, anything that reduces the downside risk of punishment can increase the risk of crime. For example, a firm that is financially distressed and worried about its survival will have less of an incentive than other firms to comply with costly regulations, not only because it is strapped for cash but because the "expected punishment" is now lower to the extent that the firm can declare bankruptcy if government enforcement efforts attempt to bring it into compliance and impose a costly penalty.

Individuals Within Corporations: The Principal-Agency Relationship

Thus far, we have assumed that individuals within a firm decide whether to commit crimes by weighing their own private gains against the costs and that, alternatively, a corporation may "decide" (overtly, negligently, or vicariously) whether or not to commit a crime. An important complexity we now add is that individuals who commit a crime "on behalf" of their employer might not actually be acting in the best interest of the company. This is not surprising, as employers and employees are in a classic principal-agent relationship, in which the interests of the two parties may diverge. Even if top management purposefully engages in criminal activity, this might not be in the best interest of owners/shareholders.[8] The harms that arise from corporate crime can thus be seen as costs arising from the agency relationship between the owners and operators of the company. Furthermore, through their exercise of rights to influence the governance and compensation structure of the organization, shareholders may influence the rewards and punishments accruing to managers and employees, such as monetary compensation, promotions or firings, and nonmonetary benefits of the job. Through these choices, the corporation can influence the probability of internal detection and punishment.

To illustrate, let us consider the incentives of a midlevel manager at a facility that produces a hazardous waste as a by-product of its manufacturing process. Let us assume that the facility is a cost center and that the manager's compensation is based partly on reducing plant-level operating costs. Suppose a less expensive, illegal method of hazardous waste disposal would reduce the manager's costs significantly, thus providing a powerful incentive for the manager to dispose illegally. Suppose that if the manager is caught illegally dumping waste, the firm will be fined by the government, but the manager will not be held personally liable. In the extreme, where the owner has no recourse against the manager and does not observe the manager's actions until they are uncovered by the enforcement authority, the outcome is clear: the manager will commit the crime despite the fact that the company owners do not want the crime committed. This example is obviously a simplification that ignores some of the other constraints on the manager's action, such as moral inhibition, preference for adhering to social norms, and so on. However, the point is that as long as the owner does not perfectly monitor the daily actions of the manager, there is the risk that the expected private gain from illegal activity to the manager may exceed the expected gain from legal activity and that the reverse may hold for the owner. The opposite might also hold, of course, where the owner prefers illegal activity but the manager does not.

Given the preceding scenario, we might expect owners to monitor managers quite closely in order to prevent the misconduct (or to limit the damage from the misconduct). Or the owner could accompany a moderate level of monitoring with a sufficient threat of privately imposed sanction (or denial of reward) to affect the manager's choice and deter the offense. The chosen level of monitoring and enforcement depends, as in the case of crime generally, on the cost and on the payoff from the resulting deterrence. The costs of internal monitoring and enforcement can be substantial and are likely to be higher for larger and more complex firms than for smaller and closely held firms. Depending on the crime, the costs of monitoring within the corporation may in some instances exceed the costs of detection by outside enforcement authorities.

Corporate Governance: Lowering Agency Costs of Crime

To reduce the private costs of monitoring and enforcement—and to make the consequences of misconduct more transparent to managers and other employees—one would expect the owner of the firm in the previous example to put mechanisms in place that encourage the prevention of crime within the corporation. The effect is to expand the scope of corporate governance to include means of detecting and preventing crime even before it is detected by traditional law enforcement such as through internal audits, requiring extra layers of management approval for certain actions, or random inspections by third parties. Companies' use of governance reform as a means of reinvesting in their reputations for compliance dates back to the era before the United States Sentencing Guidelines ("Guidelines") and includes the use of training, audits, and involvement of outside monitors.[9]

Even if owners of firms may have no direct contact with corporate criminal behavior, they have rights to intervene in the internal governance of the corporation in ways that can affect the occurrence of crime. In this sense, corporate owners can be linked as a causal factor in criminal activity. While they may not explicitly choose to commit a crime, their decisions on the size and intensity of internal compliance programs, compensation and performance evaluation processes, strategic plans, and so on may be thought of as choosing a "probability" that crime will be committed by the corporation. The principal-agent relationship thus provides some theoretical justification for "vicarious liability" of corporations for their employees' actions.

The principal-agent framework from the early literature on corporate crime indeed points to the use of governance reform as a deterrence strategy. In Alexander and Cohen, the incentive-aligning feature of managerial stock ownership was seen as promoting deterrence.[10] More recently, enforcement authorities have relied on consent decrees, governance reform, and multi year deferred prosecution agreements as mechanisms for committing the corporation to increased diligence in monitoring and deterring corporate crime. Although the discussion has thus far focused on the owner-manager relationship, there is also a principal-agent relationship between managers and employees with the same fundamental characteristics. Managers might encourage or discourage corporate crimes that are committed by employees on behalf of the firm.

From the perspective of the enforcement authority, the key insight is that corporate crime can occur even over the objections of a company's owners or investors. Evidence that a crime has occurred does not alone reveal that an owner has benefited. It might, however, reveal that insufficient costs were incurred to prevent the crime. This leaves the question of what additional efforts a firm might have taken to prevent the misconduct (or should take to prevent future misconduct). Before turning to the empirical evidence on sanctions, we revisit the notion of an "optimal" legal sanction in the context of this debate.

Practical Application: Enforcement

In the traditional economic model, a prospective offender perceives an expected sanction that, if high enough, will deter the crime. This expected sanction depends on the probability of detection and the size of the sanction. Detection and sanctions are substitutes in the production of deterrence. A higher expected sanction can be obtained by increasing the detection probability, increasing the size of the sanction, or both. Since it is costly to increase the detection rate or increase penalties, the best choice is not perfect deterrence but some lesser optimum level of deterrence.

It is instructive to note that law and economics scholars distinguish between "conditionally" and "unconditionally" deterred offenses. The latter comprise offenses that are absolutely prohibited by society, for example, murder. In contrast, "conditionally" deterred offenses involve situations in which the underlying activity has social value. In such cases, the costs of avoidance may be an important factor to consider in determining whether a given instance of conduct should be deemed a violation subject to prohibition or sanction. Along these lines, many corporate crimes involve a degree of uncertainty. For example, as noted in the previous section, owners of the corporation may not be able to perfectly monitor employee behavior, and many corporate crimes are strict liability—such as the case of oil spills. While most spills involve some level of human involvement and the level of care taken to prevent a spill will affect the likelihood and size of a spill, there are also random factors such as weather or accidents beyond the control of the company that might "cause" it to spill oil. In cases like this, society might want to judge the cost of taking actions to comply with a regulation and/or to avoid an illegal incident against the costs imposed by the "bad outcome." The problem is most apparent in the area of regulatory violations. These violations are generally "conditionally deterred" crimes, since society benefits from the underlying activity that gives rise to the regulatory violation. The concern is that high penalties can lead to "overdeterrence" of activities that society does not wish to prohibit entirely. For example, we do not want to impose such a high penalty on illegal hazardous waste dumping that all firms leave the manufacturing business for fear that one of their employees will violate company policy and dump hazardous waste. While we want firms to invest in training, monitoring, and enforcement activities to reduce the likelihood that an employee will illegally dump, we do not want them to spend more than a socially desirable amount of resources on these prevention safeguards. This problem is especially acute in the case of strict liability crimes for "stochastic externalities" such as oil spills, where the incident itself is not entirely controllable by either the firm or its employees.[11]

Becker characterized this problem as finding the "optimal penalty," which in the simplest case is equal to the net harm to injured parties from the crime, divided by the probability of detection.[12] The probability of detection is evaluated from the offender's perspective at the time of the offense. The idea is to transform the firm's problem into a social problem by requiring the firm to internalize the harm to injured parties, which is the external social cost of the offending firm's action. Becker's basic model has been extended by relaxing some of the more restrictive assumptions, such as risk neutrality, full information, and a static decision framework. In the context of corporate crime, it has been extended to incorporate the principal-agency relationship between owners and managers (or between managers and employees).[13] In this model, there is no theoretical difference between a civil violation and a criminal one. They both involve social harm, and the remedy is to find the appropriate penalty structure that optimally deters socially undesirable behavior. Of course, there are important institutional and legal distinctions between the civil and criminal law, which are to be taken into account when designing an appropriate remedy. For example, the burden of proof might make criminal prosecution more expensive. On the other hand, to the extent that imposing a criminal (as opposed to a civil) sanction on a firm sends a stronger signal to others about the severity of the offense, a criminal sanction could be more cost-effective in terms of deterrence. Among equally harmful offenses, the optimal sanction is higher for offenses that are difficult to detect than for the easy-to-detect offenses, assuming a higher perceived probability of detection in the latter instance. An enforcement authority can thus compensate for a tight budget (and thus lower rate of detection) by aggressively seeking higher sanctions without significant loss of general deterrence in this framework.

One contribution of the economist's optimal-penalty framework is that it highlights the importance of two costly inputs to the production of general deterrence, namely, the effort to detect the offense and the imposition of the sanction. A reduction in one must typically be met with an increase in the other to avoid loss of deterrence. Obstacles to detection can be met with an increase in the sanction. The substitutability between detection and penalties as inputs in producing general deterrence is a fundamental insight of the economic model.

Alternative Sanctions: Markets and Reputation

The potential for corporations to receive sanctions from more than one source introduces added complexity. A corporation could be prosecuted at both the state and federal level in addition to overseas for the same antitrust offense, for example. The advantages of coordination among enforcement authorities are apparent in the optimal-penalty framework. If each of the different enforcement authorities were to impose the penalty it would deem optimal if acting alone, the corporation would receive an excessive total sanction. The costs of overdeterrence would include the duplicative expenditures in levying the penalty and, for conditionally deterred crimes, excessive costs of the corporation's effort to avoid the offense. Coordination among enforcement authorities can thus be an effective means of avoiding overdeterrence.

Markets are another type of institution through which corporations may receive sanctions, such as through the loss of customers or profitable business opportunities. The level of general deterrence and the effort undertaken to avoid misconduct are related to the aggregate total sanction. As in the case of coordinating the penalties of different enforcement authorities, overdeterrence is avoided by adjusting the legal sanction that would occur in the absence of a market sanction downward to reflect the presence of market sanctions for corporate crime.

Efforts to coordinate market sanctions with legal sanctions can encounter complexities beyond what occurs in coordinating multiple legal sanctions, however. One such complexity is that market sanctions can be difficult to distinguish from other losses that a corporation may experience around news of a corporate crime. We regard a loss as part of the market sanction if its presence is a cost of the crime that could have been avoided by not engaging in the crime. To illustrate, consider the types of losses that do not fall into this category. First, the company may experience random losses at the detection of the offense. These are unaffected by the commission of the crime and are not part of the market sanction. Second, the company may experience losses due to the termination of a profitable yet unlawful business enterprise or practice. It might face a decline in its stock price due to news that it is terminating a profitable price-fixing arrangement, for example, or shutting down an otherwise profitable plant to avoid costs of environmental compliance. In these cases, market losses represent the inability of the company to extract further profits from the offense. This is not a cost of the crime but rather the market's response to termination of the benefits of crime. Third, the company may experience a stock price decline equal in size to the expected sanction from the offense. This reflects the presence of legal sanctions but does not reflect a cost of crime beyond the legal sanction.

Finally, news of a corporate crime can cause the company's customers, investors, or other stakeholders to lower their estimation of the quality of the company's management, goods, or services and thereby downgrade the terms under which they are willing to do business with the corporation. The losses arising from this crime-related disappointment of parties on whom the corporation relies for its lawful business activity are what we regard as a reputational sanction. A small body of literature has investigated the potential for reputation loss among those who commit corporate crimes. This literature points to some of the conditions under which a reputational sanction may be sustained, and thus its potential importance as a deterrent against misconduct.

The economic model of reputational sanctions derives from the work of Klein and Leffler and of Shapiro.[14] In the Klein-Leffler/Shapiro context, "reputation" is defined in terms of consumer expectations about product quality, with a "reputational penalty" being borne when these expectations are not met. The corporation's market-based incentive to maintain quality at a high level derives from (1) the reputable firm's ability to earn a positive price-cost margin ("quality-assuring premium"); and (2) private incentives to cease dealing with the firm if an event, such as news of crime, reveals an inability to maintain high quality. The underlying intuition applies to a wide range of settings and is not confined to the buyer-seller environment. Alexander explores the practical application to and limitations of this economic model of reputation in the case of corporate crime;[15] in principle, reputational sanctions can justify reductions in legal sanctions if news of the offense leads to sufficient disappointment on the part of customers or suppliers to impose a cost of crime beyond the costs of legal sanctions and beyond the offender's having to forgo ill-gotten gains after detection; similarly, the absence of a reputational sanction can in some instances justify an increase in the legal sanction.

As a general proposition, the firms that are more likely to suffer significant reputation losses are less in need of either *ex ante* monitoring or *ex post* government sanctions as compared with the firms that lack this added constraint. The practical implication is that for a given harm, sanctions should be higher for firms engaged in misconduct that harms the public in general than for firms engaged in misconduct that harms specific customers, creditors, or others with whom the corporation has ongoing business dealings that may be disrupted by news of crime. As an alternative to raising or lowering the legal sanction, the enforcement authority may adjust its efforts at detection.

To be sure, corporations may reduce their costs of reputation loss through initiatives to improve their internal governance, in a way that is transparent to outsiders at the crime news date. Provisions of DPAs and NPAs that improve monitoring efforts within a company and thus prevent recurrence of crime can have this effect. While such prosecution agreements have grown in prominence over the past decade, the practice of announcing governance reforms at the news of corporate crime is not new. In a study of reputation loss at news of crime prior to the Guidelines, companies were found to announce new training, auditing, and monitoring programs in more than 40 percent of corporate crimes—in addition to other reinvestment in reputation—as potential means of avoiding more costly market and legal sanctions.[16]

II. Empirical Evidence on the Causes of Corporate Crime

Unlike street crime, where there is often an observable victim, many corporate crimes go undetected, and thus empirical studies are generally limited to a selected sample of convicted offenders. Moreover, most studies attempting to explain corporate crime rates have focused on a particular type of crime or regulatory violation such as antitrust or environmental violations or securities frauds (many of which are civil/administrative, rather than criminal offenses). A small body of evidence has nevertheless emerged, initially from efforts to inform the design and implementation of the U.S. Sentencing Guidelines for Organizations. We review here some evidence from that literature on the factors that affect the occurrence of crime—legal penalties, opportunity, principal-agent costs, and market-based sanctions. Evidence on the structure and design of corporate sanctions appears separately in section III.

Size of Penalties

There is little evidence that increasing the magnitude of monetary sanctions has a deterrent effect—most of the evidence on government deterrence relates to increased monitoring and enforcement. In the case of corporate criminal sanctions, Alexander, Arlen, and Cohen found no change in the average number of criminal convictions of publicly traded firms following the introduction of guidelines designed to increase the average corporate criminal penalty.[17] As they note, however, it is possible that any deterrent effect (and hence decrease in offenses) was offset by an increase in the incentive of prosecutors to bring criminal charges against corporations. Thus, even if there were a deterrent effect, it might not be observable in the data.

Opportunity to Commit Crime: Size of Firm

In a study of 156 federal criminal convictions (involving 133 distinct corporations) of publicly traded companies between 1984 and 1994, Alexander and Cohen found firm size (whether measured by sales, number of employees, or book value) to be the most significant variable explaining illegal corporate conviction.[18] This is consistent with the "opportunity" explanation of crime, although it is also consistent with an "agency cost" explanation as larger firms are likely (all else equal) to have larger agency costs. They also found that firms with low growth in sales or employment in previous periods were more likely to be convicted of corporate crime. This result is strongest (and statistically significant) for environmental crimes but not statistically significant for crimes of fraud or crimes in general.

Principal-Agency Explanation: Agency Costs

The emergence of corporate governance and the related appointment of "monitors" to control crime are consistent with the notion that more intensive internal monitoring can promote general deterrence and control crime. There is little evidence on the effect of management's tolerance of misconduct on the occurrence of crime, however. Alexander and Cohen studied a matched sample of criminal and noncriminal corporations of the same size and operating in similar lines of business in the United States.[19] They found that crime frequency is lower among the firms in which directors and officers have a greater ownership stake, particularly as ownership increases from 0 to 20 percent of the stock outstanding. Their interpretation is that holding more equity helps to align manager interests with shareholders; thus the evidence is that higher crime rates are typically against the interests of shareholders. More generally, from the perspective of shareholders, corporate crime is an "agency cost"—a cost of delegating management and operation of the corporation to others over which shareholders have limited control.

This suggests that governance reforms that better align the interests of management and shareholders will tend to reduce the occurrence of crime. By influencing the incentive structures of organizations, outsiders may influence the actions of individuals in the organization and, thus, the occurrence of crime. A study of corporate misconduct by Hill et al. offers further evidence of crime as an unintended consequence—an agency cost—of efforts to promote the interests of shareholders, focusing on the role of management compensation criteria.[20] They studied 174 Fortune 1000 manufacturing companies and matched reported Occupational Safety and Health Administration ("OSHA") and Environmental Protection Agency ("EPA") violations with internal organizational data collected in a 1986 mail survey. They found that the greater importance top management attached to rate of return criteria in evaluations of divisional performance, the greater the incidence of both OSHA and EPA violations.

These studies illuminate the empirical relation between corporate governance and crime. They anticipate the emergence of corporate governance, and governance reform, as a part of the enforcement authority's tool kit for controlling corporate crime through such reforms as the Sarbanes-Oxley Act of 2002 and the accelerated use of prosecution agreements. Evidence on the effectiveness of governance as a tool for controlling crime is only one important part of the picture, however. Evidence on the *efficiency* of governance reform relative to other enforcement strategies (e.g., increased governmental monitoring or increased criminal sanctions) has yet to emerge.

Market Penalties and Reputation

As a general proposition, firms that are more likely to suffer reputation losses are less in need of either *ex ante* monitoring or *ex post* government sanctions. The implication for policymakers is that for a given harm, sanctions should be lower for firms engaged in misconduct that harms customers or creditors than for misconduct that harms the public at large. An argument can be made for less *ex ante* monitoring of such firms.

The empirical evidence that corporations convicted of crimes and their agents sustain losses in the market is extensive, independent of any reputational sanctions. Evidence on market losses around crime is interesting for reasons that go beyond the determination of how best to discourage crime. The request for sentence leniency, for example, may be accompanied by a statement on other losses the offender received. Since only losses anticipated at the time of the offense are germane to the determination of why crime occurs, however, we focus on market-based losses that are likely predictable by the offender at the time of the offense.

There appears to be a market-based sanction for fraud but not for environmental offenses. This reflects empirical evidence on reputational sanctions that has evolved from Karpoff and Lott's study of stock-price consequences of alleged civil corporate fraud.[21] Specifically, Alexander finds that the type of offense affects the size of the reputational or market-based sanction, as losses are larger for offenses in which the injured party has a contractual relationship with the offending firm (average two-day stock price effect of −3.06 percent) than for environmental and other third-party corporate crimes (average two-day price effect of +0.44 percent).[22] Jones and Rubin, as well as Karpoff, Lott, and Wehrly, provide further evidence that firms reasonably expect to incur little or no market-based reputational sanction for environmental and other third-party crimes, using data on stock-price responses to news of environmental offenses.[23]

Turning to potential efforts to reinvest in reputation around crime news, Alexander found that firms announced management or employee turnover in 83 percent of frauds and other contract-related offenses—more than twice the 36 percent rate of employee terminations found in a companion sample of environmental and other third-party corporate crimes.[24] Significant management turnover around news of corporate violations offenses is also found by Desai, Hogan, and Wilkins and by Karpoff, Lee, and Martin in data on financial misreporting.[25] In addition to management and employee turnover, corporate criminals have been found to announce reforms in their training and internal audit procedures, and the appointment of outsiders as monitors, relatively more frequently around related-party offenses, even in the pre-Guidelines era.[26]

Social Norms and Morality

Studies that attempt to understand the effect of norms on corporate misconduct focus on internal organizational characteristics and rely upon surveys of managers within firms in the context of regulatory violations (some of which might be criminal offenses). There is little direct empirical evidence on the reasons that individuals commit offenses on behalf of their organizations. For example, Fisse and Braithwaite interviewed corporate managers and concluded that the negative effects of publicity weighed heavily on managers' self-esteem and social relationships, and were more of a deterrent than formal sanctions.[27] Simpson interviewed top and midlevel managers and found a greater deterrent effect of informal sanctions and norms compared with formal criminal justice interventions.[28] Clinard interviewed retired middle managers of Fortune 500 companies concerning why some corporations were more ethical than others.[29] More than 50 percent stated top management behavior was the main reason for ethical behavior (or lack thereof), whereas only 3 percent believed it was related to the presence or absence of financial difficulties.[30] Finally, Braithwaite and Makkai studied nursing home managers in Australia and concluded that formal legal sanctions had little deterrent value, although a higher probability of detection did have such an effect.[31] Moreover, they found managers were more likely to comply when they held strong moral beliefs in the regulatory standard.

III. Empirical Evidence on U.S. Sentencing Guidelines and Sanctions

This section reviews the empirical evidence on corporate criminal sanctions around the introduction of U.S. federal sentencing guidelines for corporations. Much of this literature is now fifteen to twenty years old and reflects the emergence of economic and legal scholarly interest during the 1988–90 time frame when the U.S. Sentencing Commission was formulating its first set of guidelines to sanction organizations convicted of criminal offenses.[32] While the Sentencing Commission does publish data annually on both individuals and corporations sentenced in the federal system, data are not disclosed in a format amenable to rigorous research to address many of the questions of interest to scholars.[33] Names of individuals and corporations are not disclosed, there is no way to match companies with individuals who were sentenced for the same underlying offense, and many variables that researchers might want to include are either not collected or not reported (e.g., measures of harm, firm size, management structure). As a result, most studies are based on data prior to the 1990s and were developed as part of the background study material in drafting the Guidelines. The earliest data were collected confidentially by the Sentencing Commission, although summary results were published.[34] However, because of Sentencing Commission confidentiality policies redacting the offender name, subsequent studies relied upon external public sources such as the news media, trade publications, and document filings with the SEC to identify corporate offenders.[35] As such, subsequent analyses tend to focus on public companies, for which news reports are more likely to appear. Even then, however, these studies cannot fully link up their data with official sentencing data due to the refusal of the Sentencing Commission to identify the names of convicted organizations. We note also that some empirical studies of "corporate crime" are actually about wrongdoing punished through administrative or civil court actions.[36] While we exclude these studies when reviewing the literature on criminal sanctions, they can be useful when analyzing causes (or market consequences) of corporate criminal behavior. As noted earlier, in many cases there is little practical distinction between offenses that are charged civilly and those that are sanctioned through criminal proceedings.

Government Enforcement and Corporate Crime

One problem in assessing the extent to which increased monitoring and enforcement reduce crime is that we generally have information on observed crimes and not the base number of crimes, as victims do not always know they have been harmed. As a result, if we observe an increase in the number of convictions, we do not know if this is due to an increase in the number of crimes or an increase in detection. Despite this concern, a few studies have been able to demonstrate a deterrent effect of government enforcement. Block, Nold, and Sidak found increased antitrust enforcement (whether civil or criminal), and the prospect of private legal actions had the deterrent effect of reducing markups in the bread industry.[37] Simpson and Koper found that recidivism among criminal antitrust offenders was related to the severity of the sanction, suggesting that corporate crime might be the outcome of rational cost-benefit calculations.[38] Similarly, in studies of regulatory enforcement (not necessarily leading to criminal liability), Cohen found that the size of oil spills was related to government enforcement intensity,[39] and Magat and Viscusi found a similar result for water pollution levels of pulp and paper mills.[40]

Evidence on Corporate Criminal Sanctions in the Pre-Guideline Era

While the data are now quite old, some of the most comprehensive studies of sentencing practice occurred during deliberations regarding the 1991 Guidelines. Now that judges have more discretion following the 2005 decision by the Supreme Court of the United States that changed the Guidelines from mandatory to advisory, pre-Guideline sentencing patterns take on more salience.[41] The most recent data on corporate criminal sanctions prior to enactment of the Sentencing Guidelines in 1991 were taken from the late 1980s following passage of the Criminal Fine Enforcement Act of 1984 that raised statutory maximum penalties. Cohen estimated the ratio of corporate criminal fine to monetary harm to be 0.18 (median = 0.45), while the mean total sanction (including civil penalties and restitution) was 0.93 (median = 1.0).[42] Thus, it appears that in the pre-Guideline era, fines were less than harm, but once all monetary sanctions were accounted for, they just equaled harm.[43] These monetary sanctions, however, exclude nonmonetary sanctions such as debarment from government contracting or lost reputation with customers, suppliers, and other related parties that might manifest itself in lower sales and/or market value.[44] However, it was also shown that judges do not fully trade off fines and other monetary sanctions on a dollar-for-dollar basis. It was estimated that a 10 percent increase in noncriminal monetary sanctions reduced the criminal fine by about 1.8 percent.[45]

Alexander and Cohen found that the average duration of crime in their sample of publicly traded firms convicted of crimes was almost four years before it was detected.[46] When compared with all publicly traded firms in the United States, the rate of conviction represents about 0.8 percent of all firm-years in the data. This is of a similar magnitude as the estimated 0.5 percent of adults in the United States convicted annually of felony offenses.[47]

The data on individuals convicted of corporate crimes are not as complete as those for organizations because it is impossible to identify which individual criminal offenses in the Sentencing Commission database were perpetrated in the context of an organization. Based on non-antitrust offenses in 1989–90, Cohen estimated that at least 65 percent of corporate convictions also involve individual codefendants convicted of the same underlying crime.[48] For those individuals sentenced, Cohen reported that 71 percent (39 of 55) were incarcerated, with an average sentence length of 16.8 months.[49]

One of the practical implications of the theoretical model of optimal penalties is that the government can trade off individual versus corporate liability and sanctions without loss in general deterrence. Thus, we would expect a negative relationship between individual and corporate liability. Consistent with this, Cohen found that among firms that could afford to compensate for the harm caused by their offenses, 58 percent had individuals convicted along with the corporation—compared with 74 percent of companies that could not afford to compensate for the harm.[50] A more detailed study over the same time period, but limited to environmental crimes, found that individuals were more likely to be convicted along with their corporation when the company was closely held (i.e., when the owners were essentially managers).[51] Interestingly, Cohen also found firms that "cooperated" with prosecutors in the criminal investigation had higher individual conviction rates.[52]

Two other interesting empirical observations came out of the Cohen study. First, similar to individual street crime, firms are offered a significant reduction in monetary sanctions for pleading guilty as opposed to being convicted at trial. For example, controlling for offense type and harm, a firm predicted to pay $86,000 in criminal fines when pleading guilty would expect to pay $1.8 million when convicted at trial.[53] Second, despite evidence in tort litigation of a "deep pocket" effect, Cohen found no such evidence for corporate criminal sanctions.[54] Controlling for crime characteristics and monetary harm, larger firms and publicly traded firms were not penalized for their size.

Evidence on Corporate Criminal Sanctions in the Post-Guideline Era

The Sentencing Commission passed its first guidelines for individual criminal offenders effective November 1, 1989, with guidelines for organizations following two years later. While the primary goal of the law establishing the Sentencing Commission was to reduce judicial disparity, there was also a clear indication from Congress that white-collar offenders were not dealt with harshly enough. Thus, the Sentencing Commission Guidelines for individuals were designed both to increase the likelihood that a white-collar offender would be imprisoned and to increase the average length of incarceration.

Similarly, Congress took several steps in the 1980s to increase criminal penalties for corporate offenders, who, prior to 1984, were subject to the same statutory maximum fines as individuals. Following this call for higher corporate penalties, and the empirical evidence that criminal fines were often a small fraction of the harm,[55] the Sentencing Commission concluded that criminal fines in the past had been too low and issued 1991 Guidelines that were estimated to increase corporate sanctions two to four times greater than their pre-Guideline level.[56] Alexander, Arlen, and Cohen examined criminal sanctions for publicly traded firms pre- and post-Guidelines and found a significant increase in criminal fines.[57] For example, the median fine increased from $632,000 to $3.0 million, and the total sanction increased from $1.6 to $4.4 million. Interestingly, they found post-1991 criminal sanctions were also higher for offenses that were not yet subject to the Guideline fines. Judges presumably took their guidance from the Guideline-related signal that society now desires a higher penalty than in the past.

IV. Looking Forward: Greater Accountability and Diligence

Among the results of the scandals of the past decade, we are seeing increased attention to the institutions of enforcement and their capacity to deter organizational misconduct. In this section, we consider the lessons from our experience in applying the economic model of corporate crime for the choices that public and private officials now face in meeting the challenges of future enforcement.

As we have seen, enforcement authorities can achieve greater deterrence of corporate crime by confronting prospective offenders with an increased detection probability and an increased penalty in the event of detection. This is customarily achieved after scandal by increasing enforcement budgets and by authorizing higher maximum penalties. The ability to do these things publicly might explain their popularity, as the enforcement authority's effectiveness in deterring misconduct depends on its ability to convince prospective offenders that they are indeed likely to be caught and face sanctions if they engage in the offense. According to the economic perspective we offer here, the effect of greater funding is to establish a credible signal that more investigations will be opened and that, if opened, an investigation is more likely to uncover facts necessary to impose a sanction. That is, increased funding leads potential offenders to anticipate a greater probability of detection. Similarly, the effect of authorizing a higher maximum sanction is to establish a public signal that offenders will likely pay a higher penalty in the event of detection. These traditional means of responding to scandal make good sense in the context of our economic model if we take the news of each scandal as evidence of "too many" scandals from a social benefit-cost perspective. As mentioned earlier, while raising the probability of detection or increasing the sanction for misconduct should lead to less misconduct, one also needs to take into account the cost of government enforcement efforts and the risk of overdeterrence, which have received less attention in the literature to date.

What else can be done? *Adjustments to the corporate governance practices of public companies* were among the changes required by Congress and regulators, after the financial reporting scandals of the past decade. The economic framework we review here points to corporate governance as a tool for increasing the accountability of influential individuals within the organization in a way that intensifies their incentives to avoid organizational misconduct. Our 1999 paper explored this by considering stock ownership of insiders as a governance mechanism that makes top management more sensitive to the interests of shareholders in preventing misconduct. Alexander documents pre-Guidelines efforts by corporations themselves to strengthen governance after news of misconduct.[58] Since then, a growing literature has emerged to document the propensity of corporations to hold individuals accountable, either through changes in governance instituted in response to the scandals of the past decade or by imposing penalties or other sanctions on individuals in organizations.

Finally, *changes in regulatory and legal rules to heighten the accountability of individuals* within corporations can have an effect similar to that of increasing the probability of detection and sanction for the individual. Perhaps the clearest example from the past decade is the requirement under the Sarbanes-Oxley Act that senior executives attest to the quality of financial reporting practices of their organizations, under Sections 302 and 404 of the act. While these reforms remain controversial, their capacity to deter misconduct is apparent from the perspective of our economic model. From that perspective, the requirement of greater accountability has the effect of increasing the probability of detection, sanction, and magnitude of sanction for executives who are being held accountable. This results in a potentially powerful change in private costs (or downside risk) of either participating in misconduct, condoning misconduct, or remaining passive in prevention or in uncovering misconduct within the corporation, hence providing a powerful incentive to put internal mechanisms in place to reduce the risk of organizational misconduct.

The economic model also points to a possible unintended consequence of deterrence-related governance reforms. Specifically, efforts to focus accountability and responsibility for crime prevention on certain actors within corporations can have the perverse effect of weakening the incentives of other individuals within the corporation to prevent crime. The net effect on deterrence of the implied trade-off between greater accountability for some, and lesser accountability for others, has yet to be explored in the literature to our knowledge and remains an appropriate topic for future research.

V. Concluding Remarks

Both theoretical and empirical research have explored the origins of corporate crime and traced it to the rational decisions of individuals within an organization, among other factors. Although these decisions may explicitly involve choices to commit a crime, they may also be choices that are not illegal by themselves but instead affect the probability that a firm will commit an illegal act and the magnitude of the harm. As this economic perspective makes clear, the mechanisms that affect criminal behavior are complex and tend to involve more than one decision maker.

Although the literature is still very sparse, the existing theory and evidence point to a relation between corporate crime and factors that include (1) prior financial performance of the firm; (2) perceived gain to individuals who decide to commit (or prevent) a crime; (3) perceived risk of detection and severity of punishment if a crime is detected; (4) moral climate, tone at the top, or "culture" of the company; (5) industry- and firm-specific factors that affect the opportunity to commit crime; and (6) the internal governance, including degree of internal controls, within a company. Despite this general knowledge, little is known about the exact relationship between these factors and the crime rate, or the interaction between factors.

NOTES

1. Our economic perspective is essentially that of Becker, as well as Polinsky and Shavell, focusing on the public and private enforcement authority's use of sanctions to influence the incentives and thus the choices of the individuals within corporations. *See generally* Gary S. Becker, *Crime and Punishment: An Economic Approach*, 76 J. Pol. Econ. 169 (1968); A. Mitchell Polinsky & Steven Shavell, *Should Employees Be Subject to Fines and Imprisonment Given the Existence of Corporate Liability?*, 13 Int'l Rev. Law & Econ. 239 (1993).

2. *See generally* Armen A. Alchian & Harold Demsetz, *Production, Information Costs, and Economic Organization*, 62 Am. Econ. Rev. 777 (1972); Michael C. Jensen & William H. Meckling, *Theory of the Firm: Managerial Behavior, Agency Costs and Ownership Structure*, 3 J. Fin. Econ. 305 (1976).

3. The authors collected the data in this figure by reviewing publicly available data from a variety of sources. The source of data for traditional criminal sanctions is the U.S. Sentencing Commission. *See* U.S. Sentencing Commission, Organizations Convicted in Federal Criminal Courts 2001–2007, *available at* http://www.icpsr.umich.edu/icpsrweb/ICPSR/studies?author=United+States+Sentencing+Commission&keyword=organizations. For nontraditional sanctions and related instances of agreements accompanied by monetary sanctions of more than $1 million, the authors performed keyword searches of the DOJ website and the Factiva and Lexis/Nexis databases for press announcements and references to DPAs and NPAs. Before netting out the DPAs and NPAs associated with smaller monetary sanctions, the authors compared their case counts with the counts reported in published studies in comparable years and found the counts to be comparable. *See, e.g.*, Peter Spivack & Sujit Raman, *Regulating the 'New Regulators': Current Trends in Deferred Prosecution Agreements*, 45 Am. Crim. L. Rev. 159, 167 (2008).

4. In some cases, empirical studies highlighted in this chapter focus on the broader concept of corporate misconduct, while in other instances studies identify only corporations convicted under criminal statutes. We are careful to delineate the nature of the sample when discussing these empirical results.

5. *See* Cindy R. Alexander, *Corporate Crime, Markets and Enforcement: A Review*, *in* New Perspectives on Economic Crime 20 (Hans Sjögren & Göran Skogh eds., 2004).

6. *See* Becker, *supra* note 1, at 170, 176, 185, 193–95; *see generally* Cesare Beccaria, On Crimes and Punishments (Henry Paolucci trans., 1963); Jeremy Bentham, An Introduction to the Principles of Morals and Legislation (1789).

7. *See* Cindy R. Alexander, *On the Nature of the Reputational Penalty for Corporate Crime: Evidence*, 42 J.L. & Econ. 489, 501–04 (1999).

8. *See generally* Cindy R. Alexander & Mark A. Cohen, *Why Do Corporations Become Criminals? Ownership, Hidden Actions, and Crime as an Agency Cost*, 5 J. Corp. Fin. 1 (1999).

9. *See* Alexander, *supra* note 7, at 502–03.

10. *See* Alexander & Cohen, *supra* note 8, at 30.

11. *See, e.g.*, Mark A. Cohen, *Optimal Enforcement Strategy to Prevent Oil Spills: An Application of a Principal-Agent Model with Moral Hazard*, 30 J.L. & Econ. 23, 23–25 (1987).

12. *See* Becker, *supra* note 1, at 180–85.

13. *See* Alexander, *supra* note 5, at 22–24; Mark A. Cohen, *Environmental Crime and Punishment: Legal/Economic Theory and Empirical Evidence on Enforcement of Federal Environmental Statutes*, 82 J. Crim. L. & Criminology 1054, 1063–66 (1992).

14. *See* Benjamin Klein & Keith B. Leffler, *The Role of Market Forces in Assuring Contractual Performance*, 89 J. Pol. Econ. 615 (1981); Carl Shapiro, *Premiums for High Quality Products as Returns to Reputations*, 98 Q. J. Econ. 659 (1983).

15. *See* Alexander, *supra* note 7, at 493–94.

16. *See id.* at 514.

17. *See generally* Cindy R. Alexander, Jennifer Arlen & Mark A. Cohen, *The Effect of Federal Sentencing Guidelines on Penalties for Public Corporations*, 12 Fed. Sent'g Rep. 20 (1999).

18. Cindy R. Alexander & Mark A. Cohen, *New Evidence on the Origins of Corporate Crime*, 17 Managerial & Decision Econ. 421, 430–32 (1996).

19. Alexander & Cohen, *supra* note 8, at 22.

20. *See* Charles W. L. Hill, Patricia C. Kelley, Bradley R. Agle, Michael A. Hitt & Robert E. Hoskisson, *An Empirical Examination of the Causes of Corporate Wrongdoing in the United States*, 45 Hum. Rel. 1055 (1993).

21. *See generally* Jonathan M. Karpoff & John R. Lott, Jr., *The Reputational Penalty Firms Bear from Committing Criminal Fraud*, 36 J.L. & Econ. 757 (1993).

22. Alexander, *supra* note 7, at 507.

23. *See generally* Kari Jones & Paul H. Rubin, *Effects of Harmful Environmental Events on the Reputations of Firms*, *in* 6 Advances in Financial Economics 161 (2001); Jonathan M. Karpoff, John R. Lott, Jr. & Eric W. Wehrly, *The Reputational Penalties for Environmental Violations: Empirical Evidence*, 48 J.L. & Econ. 653 (2005).

24. Alexander, *supra* note 7, at 514.

25. *See* Hemang Desai, Chris E. Hogan & Michael S. Wilkins, *The Reputational Penalty for Aggressive Accounting: Earnings Restatements and Management Turnover*, 81 Acct. Rev. 83 (2006); Jonathan M. Karpoff, D. Scott Lee & Gerald S. Martin, *The Consequences to Managers for Financial Misrepresentation*, 88 J. Fin. Econ. 193 (2008).

26. *See* Alexander, *supra* note 7, at 502.

27. *See* Brent Fisse & John Braithwaite, The Impact of Publicity on Corporate Offenders 227–45 (1983).

28. *See* Sally S. Simpson, *Corporate Crime Deterrence and Corporate Control Policies: Views from the Inside*, *in* White Collar Crime Reconsidered 289, 302–03 (Kip Schlegel and David Weisburd eds., 1992).

29. *See* Marshall B. Clinard, Corporate Ethics and Crime: The Role of Middle Management (1983).

30. *See id.* at 54.

31. *See* Toni Makkai & John Braithwaite, *The Dialectics of Corporate Deterrence*, 31 J. Res. Crim. & Delinq. 347, 347–48 (1994); John Braithwaite & Toni Makkai, *Testing an Expected Utility Model of Corporate Deterrence*, 25 Law & Soc'y Rev. 7, 7–10 (1991).

32. *See* U.S. Sentencing Guidelines Manual Ch.8 (1991).

33. Cindy R. Alexander, Jennifer Arlen & Mark A. Cohen, *Evaluating Trends in Corporate Sentencing: How Reliable Are the U.S. Sentencing Commission's Data?*, 13 Fed. Sent'g Rep. 108 (2000).

34. Mark A. Cohen, *Corporate Crime and Punishment: An Update on Sentencing Practice in the Federal Courts, 1988–1990*, 71 B.U. L. Rev. 247, 249–50 (1991); Mark A. Cohen & David T. Scheffman, *The Antitrust Sentencing Guideline: Is the Punishment Worth the Costs?*, 27 Am. Crim. L. Rev. 331, 346–47 (1989).

35. *See, e.g.*, Alexander, Arlen & Cohen, *supra* note 17, at 21.

36. *See* Alexander, *supra* note 7, at 510–12.

37. Michael K. Block, Frederick C. Nold & Joseph G. Sidak, *The Deterrent Effect of Antitrust Enforcement*, 89 J. Pol. Econ. 429, 429 (1981).

38. Sally S. Simpson & Christopher S. Koper, *Deterring Corporate Crime*, 30 Criminology 347, 347 *(1992)*.

39. *See* Cohen, *supra* note 11, at 37.

40. Wesley A. Magat & W. Kip Viscusi, *Effectiveness of the EPA's Regulatory Enforcement: The Case of Industrial Effluent Standards*, 33 J.L. & Econ. 331, 358–60 (1990).

41. *See* United States v. Booker, 543 U.S. 220 (2005).

42. *See* Cohen, *supra* note 34, at 257–59.

43. Cohen excluded antitrust offenses from the analysis because the Sentencing Commission already had established Guidelines for antitrust, effective in 1989. *See id.* at 250–51. Cohen and Scheffman analyzed pre-Guidelines antitrust fines and found mean fines of $200,000 (median = $75,000); the mean total penalty was $340,000 (median = $125,000). *See* Cohen & Scheffman, *supra* note 34, at 338–39, 363. While they did not have "harm" estimates, these penalties represent about 15 to 16 percent of the volume of commerce involved in the conspiracy.

44. *See* Alexander, *supra* note 7, at 503–05.

45. *See* Cohen, *supra* note 34, at 261.

46. *See* Alexander & Cohen, *supra* note 18, at 426.

47. There were an estimated 1.14 million felony convictions in state and federal courts in 2004, compared with 220 million adults age eighteen and older in the United States as estimated by the Census Department in 2004. *Compare* U.S. Bureau of Justice Statistics, *available at* http://www.ojp.usdoj.gov/bjs/sent.htm#publications, *with* U.S. Census Bureau—Population Estimates, *available at* http://www.census.gov/popest/national/asrh/NC-EST2007-sa.html.

48. *See* Cohen, *supra* note 34, at 268.

49. *See id.*

50. Mark A. Cohen, *Theories of Punishment and Empirical Trends in Corporate Criminal Sanctions*, 17 Managerial & Decision Econ. 399, 406–08 (1996).

51. *See* Cohen, *supra* note 13, at 1094–95.

52. *See* Cohen, *supra* note 50, at 408.

53. *See id.* at 409.

54. *See id.*

55. Mark A. Cohen, *Corporate Crime and Punishment: A Study of Social Harm and Sentencing Practice in the Federal Courts, 1984–1987*, 26 Am. Crim. L. Rev. 605, 605 (1989).

56. U.S. Sentencing Commission, Supplementary Report on Sentencing Guidelines for Organizations 22–23 (1991).

57. *See* Alexander, Arlen & Cohen, *supra* note 17, at 23.

58. *See* Alexander, *supra* note 7, at 493, 502–03.

2

Deferred Prosecution Agreements on Trial

Lessons from the Law of Unconstitutional Conditions

RICHARD A. EPSTEIN

Deferred prosecution agreements are arrangements between prosecutors and potential criminal defendants to impose a provisional cessation of ongoing litigation. Under a DPA, the case is not plea-bargained to a final settlement. Instead, as its name suggests, the DPA only defers the prosecution so long as the defendant complies with the terms of the agreement. Only upon full compliance with its terms will the DPA finally terminate the prosecution. If, however, the defendant does not comply with the terms of the agreement, the prosecutor may institute formal charges wholly without regard to the statute of limitations defense that was waived in the original agreement. In effect, the DPA sets out an elaborate settlement protocol, which, of necessity, includes administrative provisions to determine whether the DPA has itself been breached. The ongoing administration of these agreements is often the source of much delicate negotiation, given that the existence, extent, and reasons for any breach may raise potential bones of contention. DPAs are not self-enforcing contracts.

The origin of these scripted DPAs stems from one simple truth: all litigation involves the use of coercion—on both sides. The state prosecutor, for example, is not seeking to buy goods or services from the defendant. Given the duties of the office, he or she wishes to marshal the full power of the state to force the defendant to pay a fine, to go to jail, or to forfeit a license. Yet the situation is not one-sided, for just as the state has the power to initiate prosecution, the accused has legal tools to shield himself from federal force. Litigation is a struggle to seize control over the coercive power of the state. Like the Marquis of Queensbury rules, codes of criminal procedure impose limits on how each side may resort to the use of state force. For example, the prosecutor is required to turn over exculpating evidence to the accused, and the accused to comply with subpoenas.

All litigation can thus be modeled as a bilateral monopoly game—each player has only one party with whom it can make a deal—in which the outcome of any deal depends upon the skills that each side brings to the table. In this environment, settlements continue to yield gains to both parties by saving on administrative costs and by reducing uncertainty. But there is no unique point for settlement, given that a range of sanctions may prove acceptable to both sides. From a private point of view, each side works to get the best deal within the range. From the social point of view, the key question is whether the settlement simply reflects these bargaining dynamics, or whether it represents a fair estimation of the seriousness of the offense, taking into account the underlying strength of the evidence.

Against this background, DPAs in criminal cases have been the source of much uneasiness. Critics who denounce DPAs as "coercive" well understand that the criminal justice system will grind to a halt if the settlement of criminal cases is barred, so that all cases must be litigated to final judgment. But these critics are deeply concerned with the huge leverage that the current law lets government lawyers exert against criminal defendants, both individuals and corporations.

The entire issue has cooled down considerably since the publication of the Filip Memo under the guidance of former Deputy Attorney General Mark Filip, to whom much praise is due.[1] Three years ago, this issue was on the front burner. Now, thankfully, the exercise can be directed toward a theoretical inquiry about the dangers that always lurk in DPAs.

This essay seeks to explain the appropriate limit of DPAs in light of what I regard as the serious dangers in using any principle of corporate criminal liability. Section I explains what I call the "grand inversion," which arises when the state's decision to prosecute imposes greater burdens on individual defendants than conviction of the underlying offense. Section II then critiques the role that the Holder, Thompson, and McNulty memos played in exploiting this grand inversion against corporations, which is augmented by the expansive doctrine of corporate criminal vicarious liability. The government prosecution against the now defunct Arthur Andersen & Co. helps illustrate the dangers that existed under the old order. Section III gets to the heart of the essay by using the doctrine of unconstitutional conditions to explore the appropriate use and limits of DPAs. Section IV then uses this framework to sort out benign from malignant terms for inclusion in DPAs, in light of today's expansive rules on corporate criminal liability. Section V concludes with some recommendations for change.

I. The Grand Inversion

The ordinary rules of criminal prosecution are characterized by the following stark dichotomy. The entrenched rules on prosecutorial discretion give government prosecutors extensive discretion to decide whom to investigate, whom to charge, when to charge them, and what to charge them with. The protections afforded by the criminal law typically kick in after a decision to prosecute is made, by requiring disclosure to the accused of exculpatory information before trial, limiting the admissibility of evidence at trial, structuring jury charges, establishing the need for proof of all elements of the case beyond a reasonable doubt, and guarding against double jeopardy.

This orderly, if imperfect, progression of the criminal process makes sense within the confines of the criminal law system. The government gets less of a return from an indictment than from a conviction, and accordingly has an easier time at the first stage than at the second. But in today's hyperactive regulatory state, the consequences of prosecution extend outside the boundaries of the criminal justice system.

The increased scope of government action generates a sharp increase in the number and kinds of licenses and permits that both individuals and firms must obtain, and retain, in order to remain in business. These licenses are administered by independent administrative boards whose activities are not formally tied to federal and state prosecutors. Many licensing systems require these boards to pull or suspend licenses from any person or firm that has been indicted, even before proof of guilt.[2] Not all businesses are equally vulnerable to these actions. Unlike insurance, security, banking, and finance corporations, many less visible corporations may be able to survive a criminal prosecution because they are less subject to direct prosecution. But even the least visible corporations may take a sharp reputational hit from a high-profile criminal prosecution that could shake the confidence of their business partners.

It is often the case that triggering corporate offenses carry only modest criminal fines or short jail sentences. Yet many license suspensions do not turn on the anticipated severity of the offense or the anticipated size of the sanction. Nor are reputational hits precisely calibrated to the seriousness of the wrong. Since it is quite rational for outsiders to steer clear of firms singled out for any kind of prosecution, most government decisions to prosecute thus impose collateral sanctions more severe than those attached to a conviction for the underlying offense. The combined operation of criminal and regulatory sanctions, augmented by reputational harms, is thus the theoretical source of the grand inversion. Indictment poses a greater threat than conviction, even though it offers a defendant weaker protections than a convicted criminal.

The results of a possible trial shape all that goes before, as prosecutors and defendants bargain over settlement in the shadow of this grand inversion.[3] The smart prosecutor knows that this inversion generates powerful leverage over individuals and firms that are desperate to avoid a prosecution lest they suffer financial or business ruin. The terms of settlement thus include more onerous terms than could be obtained through conviction—indeed, sometimes they include concessions that could *never* be obtained through conviction—which allows the prosecutor to set himself up as a de facto regulator of a particular firm.[4] For example, the deferred prosecution of Bristol-Myers Squibb for a violation of the securities law resulted in the endowment of an ethics program at Seton Hall Law School (from which the prosecutor, Christopher Christie, graduated).[5] Wal-Mart's settlement of potential criminal prosecution for a stampede at one of its stores included not only compensation for the victim but also hefty grants of $1.5 million to Nassau County's Youth Board and $300,000 to United Way's Youth Build Program.[6]

These results, unique to DPAs, should not happen in settlement negotiations, where the parties typically split the difference. By that standard a DPA should result in a compromise that gives the prosecutor *less* than he could have obtained through conviction, while imposing on the accused sanctions *greater* than those that flow from conviction of a lesser offense, or, in the limit, an acquittal. However, after factoring in collateral consequences, the costs of a DPA could exceed the costs of conviction. Hence, the rise of the grand inversion. The collateral consequences increase the upper end of the settlement range by exposing firms to millions or billions in potential economic loss from any criminal indictment, without regard to the magnitude of the underlying offense.

These dynamics are at play in individual prosecutions, but they make DPAs more potent and more troublesome in the corporate context. Settlements with guilty individuals do not necessarily affect third parties. In contrast, corporate sanctions may cost thousands of innocent employees their jobs and wipe out the equity position of thousands of innocent shareholders. The officers and directors who negotiate on behalf of the corporation face overwhelming incentives to avoid prosecution. It is quite rational for them to cast individual employees overboard in order to keep the firm afloat.

The overlap between criminal punishment and regulatory sanctions also creates obvious opportunities for prosecutors and licensing agencies to coordinate efforts prior to initiating settlement discussions with the targeted firm. Professor Samuel Buell, an experienced former prosecutor, wrote me the following: "I don't think prosecutors prefer to have no control over licensing authorities. I think they like to fold the delicensing problem into settlement discussions, and often involve licensing authorities in the discussion in order to facilitate resolution."[7] The linkage between prosecution and regulation could not be more explicit.

It is hard to figure out whether this prosecutorial strategy offers the prosecutor the maximum leverage. The prosecutor who does not bring the regulators in can say the following: unless you make a deal with me, you are at the mercy of a regulator who may have no choice but to pull the license. But the prosecutor who *does* bring the regulators in can present a united front that might wring larger concessions from would-be criminal defendants. As an outsider to the practice, my sense of the bargaining dynamics runs as follows: the reason for the absence of uniform behavior depends upon the prosecutor's strategic assessment. He or she will work with outside agencies if the costs of coordination are smaller than the perceived gains from a more substantial set of sanctions. Put otherwise, the lack of any uniform practice on coordination reflects the determination of prosecutors to choose that strategy which, on a case-by-case basis, yields the highest return.

II. The Use of Deferred Prosecution Agreements: Herein of Corporate Criminal Liability

A. The General Framework

Given the potency of DPAs, it is not surprising that government departments regularize their use. Of particular salience is the use of DPAs against corporations. At one time, three memos controlled the field. The then Deputy Attorney General Eric Holder's 1999 memo, entitled "Bringing Criminal Charges Against Corporations," first tightened the screws in this area.[8] The partisan pressure on corporations intensified four years later when the then Deputy Attorney General Larry Thompson issued his still tougher memo, "Federal Prosecution of Business Organizations," in January 2003.[9] That memo was in turn followed by the McNulty Memo of December 2006, which softened the tone of the Thompson Memo but did not reverse its course.[10] The final break came with the August 2008 publication of the Filip Memo.[11]

The most aggressive view on corporate criminal liability was set out in the 2003 Thompson Memo. Its basic tone is set in Section I.A, which reads: "Corporations should not be treated leniently because of their artificial nature nor should they be subject to harsher treatment."[12] In essence, the level of punishment given to corporations should be identical to that which is given to individuals, neither more nor less. A second proposition follows hard on the heels of the first: "Vigorous enforcement of the criminal laws against corporate wrongdoers, where appropriate, results in great benefits for law enforcement and the public at large, particularly in the area of white collar crime."[13] Similar themes were also voiced in both the Holder Memo and the McNulty Memo.

The reason for this tough approach rests on the unexamined assertion that we can be confident that "vigorous enforcement" of the law against "corporate wrongdoers" (a phrase that begs all the conceptual questions) allows the government to be "a force for positive change of corporate culture, [to] alter corporate behavior, and [to] prevent, discover, and punish white collar crime."[14] Matters should only be so simple.

B. Vicarious Corporate Responsibility

The potency of DPAs in the pre-Filip era was heightened by the expansive rules of vicarious criminal liability for individuals and corporations in both civil and criminal contexts. To be sure, the use of vicarious liability in *private* tort and contract settings makes good social sense. Its use in criminal cases, however, gives rise to serious concerns.

Start with liability under private law. The private rules of vicarious liability have as their objective the compensation of victims and the deterrence of wrongdoers.[15] In order for these rules to work at all, vicarious liability must be strict in its application: as long as an employee commits an act within the scope of his or her employment, the liability attaches to the employer, that is, the firm, even if the employer did all that it could to forbid the action that brought about the plaintiff's harm.

That principle can, and today does, apply with equal force to individual and corporate defendants. Any other system creates too much uncertainty for both individual and corporate actors, under both contract and tort law. In typical contracting situations, *ex ante*, it is very much in the interest of the employer to be bound by actions of employees within the course of their employment. It is the best way to attract and hold customers and suppliers. Otherwise, commerce would come to a standstill if each business transaction required express ratification from senior officials. Businesses of all stripes want to avoid mindless hurdles, in order to encourage outsiders to do business with them. No firm could long prosper if it could constantly disavow its own deals, by claiming that its agents acted outside the scope of their responsibility.

In stranger situations, such as explosion cases or traffic accidents, the rationale for vicarious liability is different but every bit as potent. Here the objective of the law is to protect innocent individuals from harms committed by others. Accordingly, the role of vicarious liability prevents a firm from escaping liability by laying all the blame on the misconduct of its employees. The rule also cuts through uncertainty when no one can pinpoint which employee has failed to perform some routine task of installation or inspection. All roads lead to Rome under vicarious liability cases. The plaintiff does *not* have to identify which employee is culpable given that the employer is responsible for all employees indifferently. Finally, the strict rule avoids strategic behavior by firm managers, who now have no incentive to place the most dangerous activities of the firm in the hands of the least solvent workers. Since the firm is responsible either way, it will tend to choose and train its workers to minimize the risk.

As articulated, the rule of vicarious liability works hand in glove with the principle of limited corporate liability, whereby the liability of investors in the firm is capped by the capital they have invested in or committed to the firm. That doctrine encourages investors to make contributions that they would otherwise be reluctant to make, and thus increases the chance of recovery by delineating clear rules that indicate which assets can be reached to settle judgments and which cannot. Better to have a suit against a limited liability corporation stocked with cash than a suit against a bankrupt individual with unlimited liability. Not unsurprisingly, personal liability for senior corporate personnel, so critical in the criminal context, rarely if ever enters the picture. No plaintiff has an incentive to join them as codefendants.

This principle of strict vicarious liability, however, does not mesh well in the criminal law, where mens rea is the keynote for liability.[16] The requirement of mens rea should apply both to the immediate actor and to those persons who are held secondarily liable. There is no good theoretical reason why the mental conditions for criminal liability should be weakened for parties who are one or more steps removed from the commission of the harm. In practice, this requirement means that one person should be held criminally responsible for the actions of another only if the first person, as principal, authorizes or condones the second person, his agent, to commit the wrongful act. The tort standard of "arising out of and in the course of employment" does not suffice to establish criminal vicarious liability precisely because there is no need to impose criminal sanctions against corporations already on the hook for extensive civil liability. On first principles, the law should reject corporate criminal liability on the widely acknowledged ground that corporations do not have the state of mind to authorize actions, to turn a blind eye to their occurrence, or to display callous indifference to their effects.

Conversely, the same line of arguments also explains why senior corporate officials, who face virtually no tort exposure, should be criminally responsible for their own actions insofar as they, like any person in a noncorporate context, authorize or condone criminal actions. The great advantage of scrubbing corporate criminal liability is that it insulates innocent employees and shareholders from the harsh financial consequences of wrongs that they did not commit and could not prevent. Corporate liability should be limited to the tort side, where it is needed to provide the compensation to individual parties. This is not the office of the criminal law.

In an ideal world, corporate criminal responsibility would give way to the exclusive use of civil sanctions. The current state of the criminal law does not take this position but rather starts from the assumption that a very extensive form of vicarious liability should apply to corporations. The Thompson Memo did not mince words when it described the current legal position as follows:

> Corporations are "legal persons," capable of suing and being sued, and capable of committing crimes. Under the doctrine of *respondeat superior*, a corporation may be held criminally liable for the illegal acts of its directors, officers, employees, and agents. To hold a corporation liable for these actions, the government must establish that the corporate agent's actions (i) were within the scope of his duties and (ii) were intended, at least in part, to benefit the corporation.[17]

Far from refusing to apply corporate criminal liability in any case, the Thompson Memo actively embraced its expansive use. The memorandum's pointed use of the phrase "employees and agents" explicitly disavowed any compromise position that would limit corporate criminal responsibility only to cases where top firm officials authorized or condoned the underlying actions. Formally at least, the tortlike rule of strict vicarious liability gives the corporate entity *zero* protection against a criminal indictment.

In practice the situation is more complex because the government guidelines do not rely on the criminal rules of vicarious liability in making their internal decision on indictment. For that purpose, DOJ rules require prosecutors in their "sound discretion" to take into account the position of various stakeholders, including shareholders, employees, pension holders, and the public at large.[18] But a consideration of multiple factors could result in unleashing the full force of the government against a firm nonetheless. This uncertain state of affairs has been justified on the ground that it imposes desirable reputational sanctions on the corporation or other entity. Professor Buell has defended this thesis as follows: "Such reputational sanctions can flow through to affiliated individuals in ways that can alter behavior, cause re-evaluation and reform of institutional arrangements, and reduce wrongdoing in organizational settings."[19] And so they do. But at what price? Imposing civil liability on particular corporations is likely to induce the same response, without forcing ruination on innocent employees and shareholders of the indicted firm. Potency is not enough; specificity and overkill matter as well. Ultimately, the social desirability of these prosecutions depends on whether the power to prosecute is used for constructive ends. Increased deterrence and punishment is never the social objective. *Optimal* deterrence is. By that standard, the most salient objection to corporate criminal prosecution is that it leads to systematic *overdeterrence* whose massive social dislocations could be avoided by a more focused use of the criminal law.

C. The Andersen Prosecution

The relative infrequency of actual criminal prosecutions is a hopeful sign because it suggests that prosecutors have some reluctance about pushing the envelope on criminal vicarious liability to its logical extreme. And for good reason, as the much-moot corporate criminal prosecution against the now defunct Arthur Andersen & Co. reveals.[20] No one could claim that this prosecution used criminal vicarious liability to attack the petty misbehavior of corporate underlings. The prosecution honed in on Andersen's handling of the explosive Enron, which generated about $50 million in annual fees to Andersen as its second-largest client.[21] In the midst of Enron's grave financial difficulties the Andersen lawyer assigned to the account, Nancy Temple, and the partner in charge of the account, David Duncan, sought to reinvigorate Andersen's standard but dormant document destruction policy. Keep one set of all key documents in the account on file, and then destroy all other intermediate steps including emails, letters, notes, drafts, and the like.

As a general matter, this policy has a lot to commend itself, for greater candor derives from the ability not to be embarrassed by gaffes that were corrected before the work was done. Following this advice does not generate a risk of criminal liability, at least if it had been routinely done long before signs of imminent danger. The supposed smoking gun in this Andersen prosecution was an email sent by Temple to a Houston partner stating that it "might be useful" to remind Andersen's team working on the Enron matters to "follow the document policy."[22] Duncan then took proactive steps to implement this policy, with which other partners cooperated, eventually destroying huge quantities of written and electronically stored documents. Prompt orders were issued to stop the shredding only after the SEC issued a subpoena for documents in connection with the Enron meltdown. There was no evidence that any of the actions taken were done to shield Andersen or its partners from criminal liability. The self-interested motivations of Andersen personnel were directed toward protecting Andersen's reputation as an auditor.

Those are certainly actions of high-level officials within the firm, but only by a small subset of the senior management. Perhaps there was a serious culture problem within Andersen that made it difficult to decide which of its partners to prosecute and which not. But exactly how does this matter? It only shows that getting the right individuals—Temple, Duncan?—in the government's crosshairs is not easy. It does not explain why the government prosecutor should be able to escape ambiguities by indicting the corporation, or seeking a DPA under the threat of indictment. It does not matter that the Guidelines require prosecutors to look at the scope and severity of the misbehavior, or the efforts to cooperate afterward. Even if that is done, the broad definitions of criminal liability shield those judgments from any form of independent review.

In my view, the proper course of action is to junk corporate criminal liability, which means that any obstruction of justice case would be focused primarily on Temple and Duncan. That case is not easy to make out, even against individuals, for the government cannot win if it only shows that Duncan had ordered the destruction of these documents on Temple's advice. To complete the elements of the offense, their actions must have been done "corruptly" with the intention, not just the effect, of impeding or undermining the investigation[23]—an element on which the government's case eventually foundered.[24] But let the corporation be punished for this action, and an indictment seeking a $500,000 fine could—and did—trigger the demise of a $9 billion firm with hundreds of partners, 28,000 employees, and others, such as retirees, who were dependent on the continued life of the firm. The question of collateral consequences should have counseled against using, and therefore against threatening, the nuclear option. Unfortunately, it did not.

The entire episode should raise doubts about the claim in the Thompson Memo of the "great benefits" from corporate criminal prosecutions. The wrongdoing in question was confined to a single account, headed by a single partner, who had no role in the management structure. Once the matter came to the attention of the senior officials, they promised complete cooperation and offered total capitulation. There were no prior acts of document destruction that could have beefed up an obstruction of justice charge. The chief officers of Andersen were prepared to comply with each and every condition laid down for compliance and restitution of the firm, including the removal of Duncan from the partnership. And the collateral consequences of the indictment, none of which depended on a conviction, were vastly in excess of the puny fine sought for the violation.

Once Andersen went down for the count on its record, the rest of the world got the message. Set against this background, it is hard to credit the initial claim in the Thompson Memo that its chief concern was with the "authenticity" of the corporate cooperation, or that the tough enforcement policy is a "force for positive change of corporate culture."[25] The question today is to explain the preconditions that let these events get so far out of control.

III. Unconstitutional Conditions and the Power to Bargain

As we saw in the example of Andersen, the state's use of its monopoly power is not without risk. It is therefore imperative to think about what types of provisions are appropriate for DPAs and which are not. On that topic, a point of departure is found in the law surrounding the elusive doctrine of unconstitutional conditions. The key social inquiry asks whether the current framework for DPAs is consistent with optimal deterrence. In order to see why it may not be, I start by comparing bargaining in competitive and monopoly markets.

The strongest argument in favor of accepting unbounded DPAs is that the mutual gain for the parties (who could otherwise not agree) normally results in a social improvement. That argument works well in ordinary competitive markets but is less potent when the government possesses monopoly power, as prosecutors surely do. In competitive markets, the parties reach agreement over price and terms precisely because each side to a potential sales transaction is free to search the other side of the market for the best deal, and to walk away from any offer that it does not like. This unconditional power to accept or refuse any given offer necessarily carries with it the power to take an intermediate position, including a decision to accept the offer subject to stated conditions that each party can impose at will, or to accept an offer from one party while rejecting an identical offer from a second party. Hence, a legal regime that places no restriction on how contracts are formed in competitive environments will in general lead to the optimal allocation of resources.

The monopoly position of the government, however, renders this optimistic conclusion theoretically untenable in the context of DPAs. Quite simply, state monopoly power skews the bargaining process, as the doctrine of unconstitutional conditions reveals, across a broad range of noncriminal contexts. The definition of government power is the exclusive use of physical force within the jurisdiction. That power cannot be eroded by new entry, and no party in the crosshairs of the prosecutor can just walk away. Given the absence of a right to exit, the fact that any DPA generates mutual gains for the parties in the short run does not mean that the agreement has maximized social welfare, as would be the case for parties acting in competitive markets.

Given that risk, the doctrine of unconstitutional conditions arose as an all-purpose counterweight to the state's use of monopoly power in a bewildering variety of noncriminal settings. This doctrine implies that we should reject the "greater/lesser" argument that universally controls bargaining behavior in competitive markets.[26] That argument runs as follows. If a party has the greater right to enter no bargain at all, it necessarily has the lesser right to impose whatever terms and conditions it sees fit. But government monopoly power is an issue when government officials prosecute and when they regulate. Sometimes the greater power does not encompass the lesser power.

As an example, it is commonly said that the government owns the roads and the beaches. It hardly follows that the government can tell all prospective drivers that they will be allowed to travel on public roads only if they agree to waive all their First Amendment rights to protest the military actions overseas or waive their Fourth Amendment protections against unreasonable searches and seizures in unrelated criminal cases. Nor can the government decide to exclude men and admit only women, or the reverse. "Over-the-top" is the intuitive reaction to these efforts. In these cases withholding the benefit earns the title of "coercive" because the government requires the illegitimate sacrifice of vested constitutional rights. Thus coercion, broadly understood, does not require a threat of physical injury or incarceration.

By the same token, however, state ownership of the highways cannot be so feeble as to leave the state powerless to make any rules or regulations for their use. Intuitively, state power looks far more legitimate when the state requires drivers to receive licenses by passing certain proficiency tests in driving, or to demand that they cooperate with police officers during an arrest, or agree to litigate any accident disputes within the state. To capture the difference, it is commonly said that this last set of restrictions is "germane" to the state's legitimate functions as an owner of the highway. That elusive verbal formulation, however, conceals many practical difficulties.

The question then arises, whether more than intuition and neat phrases can separate germane from nongermane restrictions. I believe that we can do better on this front by returning to the insistent question of what conditions are likely to maximize social welfare. In this context, it is not wise to think of a highway as state-owned property subject to the normal rules of exclusion that apply to private property. The need for an open access regime has made roads and waterways common property under customary law from the earliest times. In light of that ingrained practice, it is better to think of highways as common facilities that the state operates for the benefit of its citizens. In this special rule it must articulate and apply rules of the road in ways best calculated to maximize the expected value of highway use to all comers—which is the exact same obligation that is imposed on common carriers such as stagecoaches and inns that enjoyed monopoly status in the formative period of the common law.

At this point we can give a test for what conditions are permissible and what are not by looking at the asserted condition in its larger institutional context. Germane, or appropriate, conditions are those that, when uniformly applied, tend to *increase* the overall value of the use of the highway for all participants, in this instance by increasing driving safety for all.

The First and Fourth Amendment cases alluded to earlier, however, do not come within a country mile of meeting the social welfare constraint. Instead they look like dangerous versions of a monopoly leverage ploy, whereby parties surrender rights that look to be of little value to them individually, but which in the aggregate are critical to uphold the basic structural features of a constitutional order that offers consistent and reliable protection to individual rights against government aggrandizement. Each individual knows that the loss of access to the highways imposes an immediate concrete burden, but the waiving of constitutional protections is likely to cost far less, at least until the need to exercise these rights arises. So it is rational for all people to waive individually a value that the Constitution preserves collectively to "the people." Stopping this deal does not impair operation of the roads, and it decidedly improves the operation of the criminal system. Therefore, stopping this form of free contract improves overall social welfare.

This basic argument also explains why people fear selective prosecution even as they understand the need for prosecutorial discretion. The unconstitutional conditions parallel is that the state may not use its selection power to impose higher tolls on Republicans than on Democrats, or the reverse, even if, when the dust settles, the disadvantaged class of users is better off paying the differential toll relative to forgoing access. This discretionary exercise of power poses a deadly threat to a sound political order.

Holding monopoly power imposes on the state fiduciary obligations, which means that it must use its power over the roads to maintain the kinds of competitive conditions that normally maximize human welfare. In other words, the proprietary/regulatory distinction turns out in practice to have less significance than is commonly supposed. The state, in its capacity as the owner of the roads, has a fiduciary duty to maximize the welfare of its citizens. But that is the same objective as its general obligation as a regulator. So if competition is the ideal solution for the state in its capacity as a regulator, it is also the ideal solution for the state acting in its proprietary capacity. In other words, the state should use its monopoly platform as owner of the highway to promote competition among its users.

The trick with the unconstitutional conditions doctrine is that it is not directed toward stopping win/lose transactions, as is done with the simple just compensation requirement of the Takings Clause. Rather, its function is to maximize the surplus from positive sum games, which is best done by avoiding the factional intrigue that could result in its dissipation. This risk explains why favoritism has to be ruled out even in the context of positive sum games.

IV. Shaping Deferred Prosecution Agreements

A. Benign Conditions

This analysis of the unconstitutional conditions doctrine gives instructive guidance to the question of what kinds of conditions should be routinely allowed in DPAs. We want those conditions that improve the bargaining process, and hope to prevent those that move it away from the social goal, which is to make the punishment match the severity of the wrong. In view of these objectives, nothing in principle does, or should, ban or call into question DPAs in either the individual or the corporate case simply because they postpone a prosecution in exchange for a promise not to plead the statute of limitations.

In many contexts, DPAs, like the settlement of ordinary private suits, have all the earmarks of mutually beneficial exchanges, with no adverse third-party effects. On the one side, the defendant avoids the public embarrassment of a suit that might otherwise disappear. On the other side, the defendant avoids the collateral but deadly consequences that may be triggered once the suit is filed—default under a collateral loan agreement or avoid the need to make additional disclosures to the SEC or investors, or to amend its financial statements. Giving further time for quiet settlement and resolution is often better than the unilateral consequences of bringing suit, especially since further investigation may persuade the prosecutor to back off the case altogether.

Similarly, it seems appropriate to ask corporations to take steps to ensure that they remain in compliance with the law, as long as the conditions imposed are tied closely to this goal. Care should also be taken to ensure that these conditions do not hamper the ability of the firm to compete. There is little reason to think that prosecutors are engaging in an illicit extension of their power when they require audits, reports, and other forms of monitoring of firm behavior as a condition for avoiding a criminal indictment. Likewise, there does not seem any difficulty in requiring the payment of fines or restitution to individuals who have been injured by the improper corporate behavior. The money sanctions do not have any collateral consequences above and beyond the loss of funds needed for the operation of the business. These arrangements are often part of final settlements, and it is hard to rule them out of bounds because they are done through the DPA.

B. Some Malign Conditions

Juxtaposed with these benign conditions are those that should not pass muster precisely because they go outside the scope of proper punishment of the corporation (to the extent that this idea is conceptually coherent) for its past sins, all of which have unfortunate social ramifications. Here are four particular illustrations of the underlying problem.

1. First Amendment Issues

The hypothetical of whether anyone can be made to waive his or her First Amendment rights for the use of state roads has had a real analogue in New York's prosecution against various brokerage houses—Marsh & McClennan, Aon, and Willis. The NY AG's Office insisted that one condition in settlements against these houses was a promise that the brokerage houses would support legislation that made the use of certain insurance contracts (so-called contingent commission contracts) illegal.[27]

These variable payment arrangements were attacked in investigations for antitrust bid-rigging, and for incomplete disclosure to the insured customers of the brokerage houses. Both sets of claims fall easily within traditional criminal law, but the individual cases were all litigated on the footing that these contingent commissions were legal at the time in the absence of any violations of the applicable disclosure and collusion laws. There was not any evidence that contingent commissions, unlike other fee arrangements, were widely susceptible to bid-rigging or nondisclosure. Why, then, ask for a broader ban as part of the criminal settlement?

The problem with the condition is that it was used to reshape the public debate over important issues by forcing a criminal defendant to take sides on an issue that does not represent his or her views. It could be said that this condition is hardly dangerous because it is so difficult to indicate the form that the firm's support of public initiatives should take, or the resources that should be devoted to the mission. But even if that element is left vague, the condition remains unacceptable because it prevents a firm from participating in the public debate *against* the position it has pledged to support under the decree. The removal of one knowledgeable party from that larger debate has the potential to distort the operation of the political market. Should any firm found to violate the minimum wage laws be required under a DPA to advocate its increase? Do we really want forced speech here any more than we want forced declaration of loyalty to the United States?[28]

If not, what institutional response is appropriate for prosecutors who are tempted by proposals of this sort? The open-ended structure of the current guidelines does not in so many words preclude imposing conditions as part of some overall settlement package. Yet any DPA guidelines could just prohibit prosecutors from imposing any term relating to political participation—period. The odds of finding some unique circumstances that call for this restriction are too remote to warrant consideration, and should one arise, other regulatory schemes outside the criminal system are available, so that that there is no reason to run the major risk of abuse. Unilateral disarmament should clear that air not only in corporate DPAs but in individual ones as well, at both the federal and state levels.

2. *Dismissal of Corporate Officials*

It is also troublesome when, as a condition of settlement, a criminal prosecutor demands that various employees (from the chairman of the board on down) be required to resign from the firm. That condition is of course legitimate with respect to officers and employees of the firm who have already been convicted of criminal actions or even noncriminal violation of their regulatory duties. Here, the conditions imposed by the prosecutor simply echo substantive law when, for example, they bar individuals who have committed securities fraud from participating in the securities business. Most director and employer contracts doubtless have provisions that track the substantive law on these matters.

Beyond this case, however, matters become more difficult. Suppose that a prosecutor demands the dismissal of senior employees who are subject to indictment but who have yet to be convicted of any offense. At this point, one might say that the general presumption of innocence continues to apply, so that it is wrong to prejudge the defendant as a criminal before any proceedings determinative of guilt are resolved. But the burdens of proof complicate the issue. It is possible that a key employee will escape conviction because a case against him or her has not been proved beyond a reasonable doubt, even for someone who nonetheless is more than likely to have committed the offense in question. Hopefully, this matter would sort itself out by the simple expedient that the officer under indictment receives (perhaps paid) leave until the matter is resolved—something that a prudent corporation is likely to do in any event.

On balance, pushing for the removal of key employees should count as an acceptable condition of a corporate compliance program in most, but perhaps not all, cases. One critical caveat in this context is that it would be wholly improper for any prosecutor to trump up an indictment for the sole collateral purpose of forcing that individual out of the firm. But apart from that rare situation, these are conditions related so closely to the rehabilitation of the firm that they do not raise serious questions of prosecutorial abuse.

The use of a DPA, however, seems far more dubious when the prosecutor concedes that no criminal misconduct has occurred by individuals whom he or she wishes to remove from office, say, on grounds of perceived incompetence. I think that these conditions intrude far too much into the prerogative of the board of directors, which should decide, for example, whether the chief executive officer's ("CEO's") lapses in judgment or performance warrant a dismissal from the job or a realignment of duties within the firm. The risk of prosecutorial misconduct is sufficiently great that any revision of government guidelines should rule out forced personnel changes of nonindicted persons from the list of concessions that the prosecutor could exact as part of a DPA.

The risk here is that even if the prosecutor does not press for this result in negotiations, a desperate board seeking to avoid an indictment could offer up the CEO's scalp as a way to appease the prosecutors. Even an explicit statement that personnel changes will not factor into the prosecutorial decision cannot solve this problem, so long as the DOJ culture radiates the impression that it will. The smart board will fire the CEO first and negotiate with the prosecutor thereafter. But some clear declaration of principle might well influence at least some cases at the margin. And there is no doubt that it could constrain the way in which settlement negotiations are undertaken in still other cases. The adjustment is not purely cosmetic simply because it is at best partially effective.

3. *Waiver of Attorney-Client and Work Product Privileges*

It seems unwise—indeed unconstitutional—for the government ever to insist on any waiver of the privileges that normally attach to the provision of legal advice. The targets of these actions are frequently third persons that are not subject to direct criminal prosecution. In addition, any work product privilege belongs to the attorney and not to the client,[29] so that it is doubly unwise to seek its elimination. There seems little doubt that the imposition of this condition is an effective limitation on the right to assistance of counsel and raises the real question of whether it is consistent with the fundamental principles of procedural due process.

The earlier government memos gave little defense of these positions, so it is most welcome that the consistent criticism on this matter has resulted in the recent announcement by former Deputy Attorney General Mark Filip that the DOJ has backed off of asking corporations not to assist individual defendants.[30] But what is needed is some social explanation why DPAs should go beyond the exceptions already built into this privilege, such as the crime-fraud exception that applies in all cases, and that surely applies in this one.[31] The fierce resistance from the organized bar has induced the DOJ to pull back on this front. But an explicit acknowledgment that the DOJ oversteps the line in this context would be most welcome, especially with the change in administration and the return of Eric Holder, the crafter of the original memorandum.

4. *Cutting Off Attorney's Fees*

Without doubt the most controversial aspect of DPAs concerns an insistence by prosecutors that the corporation can only avoid prosecution by agreeing to cut off codefendants from the financial oxygen needed to mount a defense against a government prosecutor who is already primed for action. This issue arose in the KPMG LLP case, where the potential prosecution of the firm was for its abusive tax shelter practice, which allowed high-income taxpayers to escape federal taxes by a set of elaborate transactions.[32]

When the matter came before Judge Kaplan in connection with the government prosecution of individual defendants in the KPMG tax shelter case, he found a due process violation when the government's threats against KPMG led the firm to stop funding the individuals' defense efforts.[33] His language was blunt: "[The prosecutor's] deliberate interference with the defendants' rights was outrageous and shocking in the constitutional sense because it was fundamentally at odds with two of our most basic constitutional values—the right to counsel and the right to fair criminal proceedings."[34] His opinion did not treat this issue as closely when he dismissed the prosecution, even after he recognized that this was an "extreme and drastic" action that should only be invoked if it were impossible to rectify the matter by lesser means.[35]

In thinking about the soundness of Judge Kaplan's decision, the innocence or guilt of the particular parties is of no consequence. The sole question is whether the public could have confidence in convictions obtained by these strong-arm tactics. To pursue an antitrust analogy, suppose the dominant firm in a particular industry sought to establish by contract with its buyers that it could use as many lawyers as it pleased, but the buyers and their employees could not hire lawyers to assist in litigation arising out of their business relationships. That clause would be swiftly invalidated. The ability to present a case in court concerns not just the fate of the two litigants but also the soundness of a public confidence in our legal system.

The government has more power by far than any dominant firm, making it all the more urgent that collateral restraints on abusive power be strictly enforced. Judge Kaplan rightly held that the demands of the government in the KPMG case, no matter how veiled or muted, were an interference with an advantageous relationship between firm and employee, which triggered due process violations. For these purposes, it does not matter whether the interference involves the blocking of a strict contractual right of indemnification or disrupting a customary, if nonbinding, practice of paying these arrangements. The differences between these two might be decisive if the only question was whether the employee had a private right of action against the firm. But it has long been established under tort law that the use or threat of force that disrupts an "advantageous relationship" is also actionable unless it has been justified, which in this case it cannot be.[36]

Historically, there were hot behind-the-scenes disputes as to exactly how often the government would impose conditions of this sort. Some prosecutors insist that this condition was imposed only in "rare" or "extraordinary" cases. Others disagree and could point to KPMG, where the tactic was used against sixteen former employees. In principle, however, the right response does not depend on the frequency of the practice, once its risk is accepted.

The danger of withholding financial support from employees charged with criminal conduct is far greater than a prohibition against firing particular individuals from the firm. Conducting an individual defense has nothing to do with the ongoing operations of the firm, which is only asked to foot a bill. The firm is not being told how to run its internal operations, so the empirical evidence on the frequency of the practice should not matter. If blocking financial assistance were commonplace, a flat prohibition on its use could have avoided serious abuse. If the practice had been only rare, the government gave up little by abjuring the practice except in the rarest circumstances.

In this regard, the DOJ under Mark Filip came to the right conclusion when it ruled this tactic out-of-bounds in all but the rarest cases of obstruction of justice.[37] This categorical rule avoids the ad hoc uncertainty about whether any corporate undertaking to fund defense costs is strong enough to resist prosecutor requests for its termination.

V. Some Welcome Changes

It may be presumptuous for an outsider to pass judgment on norms that govern a field in which he has no litigation experience. But what is at stake here is not so much how one plays the game, which does require an experienced hand. The large question here is structural—how should these rules be formulated in the first place?

As a long and vocal critic of the Holder/Thompson/McNulty memos,[38] I thought then, and think now, that the inbred and insular attitudes within the DOJ lead to the loss of all common sense as to how to proceed. In this regard, it is welcome to see the real, open, and candid changes in the Bush DOJ under the guidance of Mark Filip. In principle, it is welcome that the government's internal evaluations of corporate criminal responsibility do not rest on the thin requirements that are said to make out forms of corporate criminality. The more comprehensive overview is surely more desirable. But even here, I am still troubled by the fact that, once the DOJ has concluded that a corporation's conduct does merit criminal responsibility, it will not be prepared to prove all the considerations that led it to ask for the indictment in the first place. In this regard, it is disappointing that the Filip Memo follows the earlier DOJ position in their willingness to rely in litigation on broad corporate conceptions of criminal responsibility.[39] Even if the prosecutors have given the most agonizing and thorough private review of a potential indictment of a corporation, they should not be able to rely in court on the tortlike rules of vicarious liability.

When the dust settles, Congress and state legislatures should go one step beyond sound rules of prosecutorial discretion; they should scrap the doctrine of corporate criminality altogether. So long as corporate criminality is available, prosecutors can use the threat of indictment as a club to beat down legitimate corporations. Since it is not appropriate to ask individual prosecutors to disclaim a practice that others use, the most that can be expected is an earnest effort of prosecutors to limit prosecutions to cases where high-level corporate officials either authorize or condone criminal conduct of subordinate employees, preferably in a pattern of conduct, not just a single instance.

The DOJ under Mark Filip was right to review the types of substantive conditions it was willing to include in DPAs. Any conditions that relate to matters of compliance, audit, and monitoring generally pose few structural concerns, and certainly none that trigger constitutional objections on grounds of procedural due process. But just the opposite should be said about other conditions on settlement that have structural consequences beyond the resolution of particular criminal charges.

As noted earlier, any settlement conditions that require corporations to take public positions on matters of social policy or legal reform should be dismissed out of hand, given their manifest conflict with the First Amendment. Demands to force the dismissal of innocent employees should be rejected for their intrusive nature in the life of the corporation. The treatment of employees whose guilt is uncertain raises harder questions, on which the Filip Memo equivocates: "While corporations need to be fair to their employees, they must also be unequivocally committed, at all levels of the corporation, to the highest standards of legal and ethical behavior. Effective internal discipline can be a powerful deterrent against improper behavior by a corporation's employees."[40] The position leaves open the possibility that corporations will be penalized if they do not dismiss or discipline employees who have not met these "highest standards," as determined in a harsh light after the fact. The point continues to be problematic. Finally, any revived efforts to undermine the attorney-client privilege or, most critically, to deprive key employees the funds to mount a legal defense should be regarded categorically as off-limits, as is provided under the Filip Memo.[41]

In a real sense, however, the hard question is one of culture. To what extent do the problems of the Holder/Thompson/McNulty memos survive in a DOJ culture that endorses a leave-no-stone-unturned attitude toward the prosecution of corporations? Judge Kaplan in the 2007 KPMG case performed a great public service by exposing an endemic weakness in government culture by roundly condemning the prosecutor's decision to deny individual employees financial assistance from KPMG. I only wish that the transformation in legal practice under Mark Filip had explicitly acknowledged that DOJ conduct crossed this line. And one can only hope that, with the zeal with which the Obama administration seems to attack such matters as executive compensation, the administration will revive earlier tactics in service of a supposedly noble cause.

In the age of big government the risks of excessive criminal sanctions are legion. That makes it all the more important that effective limitations on the use of DPAs be available to check the excessive zeal of government prosecutors to whom the law deals such a powerful hand. The problem of the grand inversion is inherent in the operation of any prosecutorial office. It is gratifying that some steps have been taken to curb its excesses, but the Filip Memo still leaves a lot of room for prosecutorial discretion. On matters of this sort there is still more work to be done.

NOTES

1. *See* Memorandum from Mark Filip, Deputy Attorney General, U.S. Dep't of Justice, to Heads of Department Components and United States Attorneys, *Principles of Federal Prosecution of Business Organizations* (Aug. 28, 2008), http://www.usdoj.gov/dag/readingroom/dag-memo-08282008.pdf.

2. *See, e.g.*, 15 U.S.C.A. § 7215 (allowing for the suspension or forfeiture of a public accounting firm's registration for a failure to cooperate with an investigation of the Public Company Accounting Oversight Board). For a discussion of the constitutionality of vesting these extensive powers in a Board subject to oversight of the SEC, see *Free Enter. Fund v. Pub. Co. Accounting Oversight Bd.*, 537 F.3d 667 (D.C. Cir. 2008).

3. *See* Robert H. Mnookin & Lewis Kornhauser, *Bargaining in the Shadow of the Law: The Case of Divorce*, 88 Yale L.J. 950 (1979) (discussing how outcome that law will impose if no agreement is reached gives each parent bargaining chips).

4. For a detailed account, see *infra* Rachel E. Barkow, *The Prosecutor as Regulatory Agency*.

5. U.S. Dep't of Justice, U.S. Attorney, District of New Jersey, Bristol-Myers Squibb—Deferred Prosecution Agreement (June 13, 2005), http://www.usdoj.gov/usao/nj/press/files/pdffiles/deferredpros.pdf ("20. BMS shall endow a chair at Seton Hall University School of Law dedicated to the teaching of business ethics and corporate governance. . . .").

6. *Settlement in Fatal Wal-Mart Stampede*, ABC News, May 6, 2009, http://abclocal.go.com/wabc/story?section=news/local&id=6798753.

7. Email from Samuel Buell to author (May 18, 2009) (on file with author).

8. *See* Memorandum from Eric Holder, Deputy Attorney General, U.S. Dep't of Justice, to Heads of Department Components and United States Attorneys, *Bringing Criminal Charges Against Corporations* (June 16, 1999), http://www.usdoj.gov/criminal/fraud/docs/reports/1999/chargingcorps.html.

9. *See* Memorandum from Larry D. Thompson, Deputy Attorney General, U.S. Dep't of Justice, to Heads of Department Components and United States Attorneys, *Principles of Federal Prosecution of Business Organizations* (Jan. 20, 2003), http://www.usdoj.gov/dag/cftf/corporate_guidelines.htm.

10. *See* Memorandum from Paul J. McNulty, Deputy Attorney General, U.S. Dep't of Justice, to Heads of Department Components and United States Attorneys, *Principles of Federal Prosecution of Business Organizations* (Dec. 12, 2006), http://www.usdoj.gov/dag/speeches/2006/mcnulty_memo.pdf.

11. *See* Filip, *supra* note 1.

12. Thompson, *supra* note 9, at I.A.

13. *Id.*

14. *Id.*

15. *See generally* Alan O. Sykes, *The Boundaries of Vicarious Liability: An Economic Analysis of the Scope of Employment Rule and Related Legal Doctrines*, 101 Harv. L. Rev. 563 (1988).

16. *See* Albert W. Alschuler, *Two Ways to Think about the Punishment of Corporations*, 46 Am. Crim. L. Rev. 1359 (2009).

17. Thompson, *supra* note 9, at I.B (citing, e.g., United States v. Automated Med. Labs., Inc., 770 F.2d 399 (4th Cir. 1985); United States v. Cincotta, 689 F.2d 238 (1st Cir. 1982)). These cases were also relied on in the Filip Memo. *See* Filip, *supra* note 1, at 9–28.200.

18. *See* Filip, *supra* note 1.

19. Samuel W. Buell, *The Blaming Function of Entity Criminal Liability*, 81 Ind. L.J. 473, 478 (2006).

20. *See* Buell, *supra* note 19, at 479–90.

21. *Id.* at 480.

22. *Id.* at 481.

23. *See* 18 U.S.C. § 1512(b)(2) ("Whoever knowingly uses intimidation, threatens, or corruptly persuades another person, or attempts to do so, or engages in misleading conduct toward another person, with intent to— . . . (2) cause or induce any person to—(A) withhold testimony, or withhold a record, document, or other object, from an official proceeding; (B) alter, destroy, mutilate, or conceal an object with intent to impair the object's integrity or availability for use in an official proceeding").

24. *See* Arthur Andersen LLP v. United States, 544 U.S. 696, 703–04 (2005) (holding that even "'persuad[ing]' a person 'with intent to . . . cause' that person to 'withhold' testimony or documents from a government proceeding or government official is not inherently malign") (internal citations omitted).

25. Thompson, *supra* note 9, at I.A.

26. For an extensive discussion of my views, see Richard A. Epstein, Bargaining with the State (1993).

27. For discussion, see Richard A. Epstein, *Contingent Commissions in Insurance: A Legal and Economic Analysis*, 3 Competition Policy Int'l 281 (2007), *available at* http://www.globalcompetitionpolicy.org/index.php?id=439&action=907.

28. *See* West Virginia State Bd. of Educ. v. Barnette, 319 U.S. 624 (1943) (upholding an injunction to restrain enforcement of a regulation requiring children in public schools to salute the American flag).

29. *See* Hickman v. Taylor, 329 U.S. 495 (1947) (recognizing work product privilege in lawyers).

30. *See* Mark R. Filip, Deputy Att'y Gen., U.S. Dep't of Justice, Remarks Prepared for Delivery at Press Conference Announcing Revisions to Corporate Charging Guidelines (Aug. 28, 2008), *available at* http://www.justice.gov/archive/dag/speeches/2008/dag-speech-0808286.html ("The new policy forbids prosecutors from asking for such information, with only two exceptions, both of which are well-recognized in existing law.").

31. *See* Clark v. United States, 289 U.S. 1, 15 (1933) ("A client who consults an attorney for advice that will serve him in the commission of a fraud will have no help from the law. He must let the truth be told.").

32. *See* Buell, *supra* note 19, at 488.

33. United States v. Stein, 495 F. Supp. 2d 390 (S.D.N.Y. 2007).

34. *Id.* at 414.

35. *Id.* at 419.

36. Restatement (Second) of Torts § 766B (1979); *see* Richard A. Epstein, Cases and Materials on Torts 594–96 (Aspen Publishers) (1999).

37. *See* Filip Press Conference, *supra* note 30 ("The new policy instructs prosecutors not to consider whether a corporation has advanced attorneys' fees to its employees, officers, or directors when evaluating cooperativeness.").

38. *See, e.g.*, Richard A. Epstein, *The Deferred Prosecution Racket*, Wall St. J., Nov. 28, 2006, at A14.

39. *See* Filip, *supra* note 1.

40. *See id.*

41. *See id.*

3

Removing Prosecutors from the Boardroom

Limiting Prosecutorial Discretion to Impose Structural Reforms

JENNIFER ARLEN

Prosecutors in the United States are no longer content to sanction corporations for their employees' crimes. They also now regularly intervene in corporations' internal affairs by pressuring firms to adopt structural reforms ostensibly designed to reduce the likelihood of future wrongdoing. Moreover, prosecutors do not restrict their structural reform mandates to corporations convicted of federal crimes. They also use DPAs and NPAs to pressure firms that are merely *potentially* subject to conviction to agree to structural reforms in order to avoid indictment or conviction. Through these DPAs and NPAs, prosecutors have required firms to adopt prosecutor-approved compliance programs, alter the structure of the board of directors, accept and pay for an outside monitor, and, in some cases, change their business practices.

Prosecutors' use of DPAs and NPAs to intervene in the internal affairs of nonprosecuted corporations represents a change in strategy. The DOJ developed its nonprosecution policy to help federal authorities detect and sanction individuals responsible for corporate crime. To accomplish this goal, the DOJ abandoned its adherence to traditional vicarious criminal liability and adopted a policy governing corporate indictment and conviction designed to encourage corporations (and their directors)[1] to report detected wrongdoing, identify individual wrongdoers, and cooperate with federal prosecutions of individual wrongdoers. To encourage reporting and cooperation, the DOJ offers to exempt from prosecution firms that report wrongdoing and cooperate with prosecutors, while threatening firms that do not do so with enormous criminal sanctions.[2]

Traditionally, prosecutors took a relatively hands-off approach to firms eligible for nonprosecution. The boards of directors of these firms were free to decide how best to deter and detect wrongdoing in the future. This is no longer the case. Today, prosecutors regularly inject themselves into the internal affairs of firms eligible for nonprosecution by requiring them to accept prosecutor-approved compliance programs, corporate monitors, and other corporate governance reforms in return for prosecutors' agreement not to indict or prosecute them. In so doing, prosecutors substitute their own judgment about what internal corporate governance reforms are needed for the judgment of both the firm's board of directors and civil federal regulators.

Federal prosecutors' propensity to require publicly held firms to agree to structural reforms as a condition of nonprosecution raises two important questions. The first is: Should federal authorities ever impose structural reforms on publicly held firms? The second is: When direct federal oversight is needed, should this oversight be exercised by prosecutors, or should it instead be the exclusive purview of federal civil regulatory authorities whenever possible? This chapter is concerned with the latter question.

This chapter contends that prosecutors should not impose structural reforms on nonindicted corporations. Instead, civil regulatory authorities should exercise sole authority over mandated corporate governance reforms, in those situations where it is appropriate for federal authorities to require firms to accept structural reforms (including outside monitors). Prosecutors generally should not use DPAs and NPAs to induce firms to adopt structural reforms, such as compliance programs, because compliance program design involves difficult judgments about when and where to centralize decision making and to collect and channel information. Industries and firms vary enormously as to whether, and in what areas, the compliance benefits of decision-making centralization and oversight exceed the costs. Prosecutors rarely have sufficient experience working in any business, much less adequate industry-specific expertise, to make these decisions reliably. By contrast, civil federal regulatory authorities are more likely to have this expertise, at least with respect to the industries they regulate. In addition, prosecutors are subject to little, if any, external oversight when they intervene in internal corporate affairs. Moreover, prosecutors' offices do not have a formal process for assembling and evaluating data on different compliance programs and monitoring plans to assess their effectiveness. By contrast, regulatory agencies are subject to greater oversight; moreover, they have the information-gathering abilities needed to assess compliance decisions. Agencies' ability to gather information and collect public comments reduces the risk that federal authorities will mandate expensive, but ultimately ineffective, measures. Finally, regulatory agencies are in a position to conduct more widespread, industry-specific, and formal assessments of compliance to determine if any firm-specific mandated reforms should be adopted on a more widespread basis. Delegating authority over governance reforms and corporate monitoring to civil authorities would enable the federal government to use corporate liability to induce firms to adopt effective compliance programs while reducing the risk that federal authorities will intervene in corporate affairs without sufficient expertise or incentives to do so effectively.

This chapter proceeds as follows. Section I describes the unusual structure of U.S. practice governing corporate liability and presents reasons to question the wisdom of granting prosecutors authority to regulate corporate governance. Section II presents the traditional U.S. approach to corporate criminal liability and explains why the DOJ had to abandon it in order to adequately deter crime. Section III describes how corporate criminal liability evolved to embrace a proactive policy of using nonprosecution to induce corporations to deter crime. Section IV shows that the central goals of these reforms can be achieved, at lower cost, if prosecutors refrain from using NPAs and DPAs to interfere in firms' internal operations. Whenever possible, they should leave full authority over a firm's internal affairs to its board of directors or, where intervention is necessary, civil regulatory authorities.

I. U.S. Prosecutors' Unusual Power to Induce Structural Reforms

U.S. prosecutors have considerable ability to pressure firms whose employees apparently have committed a crime to adopt structural reforms ostensibly designed to reduce the likelihood of future wrongdoing. This unusual power is the result of four unique features of U.S. law that combine to give prosecutors both the leverage needed to induce corporations to comply with their wishes and the incentive to use that influence. Yet whereas prosecutors once used this influence to induce corporate boards to report wrongdoing and cooperate, prosecutors now use their authority to intervene directly in internal corporate affairs, by both mandating structural reforms and requiring corporate monitoring. This expansion of prosecutorial power raises concerns.

A. Corporate Criminal Enforcement in the United States

Federal prosecutors are able to induce corporations subject to investigation to comply with their wishes because U.S. corporate criminal liability is unusually expansive and costly.

The United States has a wide range of criminal laws governing corporate activities, including laws imposing criminal liability for not acting to deter crimes by others. Moreover, the scope of U.S. corporate criminal liability is especially broad. Corporations are potentially criminally liable for all crimes committed by employees acting in the scope of employment, with some intent to benefit the firm.[3] A firm can be criminally liable even if the wrongful employee was relatively low level. Indeed, the firm can be held criminally liable even if senior managers told employees not to commit any crimes and adopted measures intended to deter them.[4] Accordingly, a corporation has few (if any) defenses once a prosecutor can show that any of its employees committed a crime in the course of employment.[5]

In addition, corporations convicted of a federal crime are subject to unusually high monetary and nonmonetary penalties. Criminal fines and other associated sanctions can reach into the hundreds of millions of dollars. Enormous government civil penalties often are imposed as well.[6] Beyond this, U.S. Sentencing Guidelines grant prosecutors broad authority to impose nonmonetary sanctions on corporations. These sanctions range from ones that can be quite damaging but are minimally intrusive—such as a mandate that the corporation publicize the fact that it committed a crime—to those that intrude on internal corporate operations, such as federally mandated compliance programs. Finally, many firms convicted of a federal crime are potentially subject to ruinous collateral sanctions, such as an inability to do business with the federal government. For some firms, such as accounting firms, the collateral consequences of a conviction may be fatal.

These distinct features of U.S. corporate criminal law combine to enable prosecutors to impose substantial and intrusive sanctions on firms convicted of a federal crime. The next two features enable and encourage prosecutors to extend their influence to firms that are merely *potentially* subject to criminal conviction. First, U.S. law is unusual in its commitment to the view that the government can best deter corporate crime by both imposing criminal liability on individual wrongdoers and using the *threat* of corporate criminal liability to induce corporations to help federal authorities detect crimes and prosecute individual wrongdoers. This instrumental approach to corporate criminal liability has led to the fourth and most distinctive feature of U.S. corporate criminal liability: the formalized divide between the rules governing when corporations *can* be held criminally liable and the formal standards governing when federal prosecutors actually *do* subject corporations (especially publicly held firms) to criminal liability for employee wrongdoing. This divide does not arise from a law enacted by Congress. Instead, it results from a formalized exercise of discretion by the DOJ.

Beginning in 1999, the deputy attorney general issued guidelines directing federal prosecutors to refrain from indicting corporations for their employees' crimes when the corporation engaged in specified acts of good conduct, such as maintaining an effective program to induce compliance with criminal laws, promptly reporting detected wrongdoing, and fully cooperating with federal authorities in order to bring individual wrongdoers to justice.[7] These guidelines transformed the broad de jure rule of strict corporate criminal liability into a de facto rule under which a corporation could avoid criminal prosecution by adhering to specific enforcement duties.

Initially prosecutors employed this formalized discretion to induce firms both to detect and report wrongdoing and to cooperate with federal investigations, in order to help the government to identify and convict the individuals responsible for crimes. Firms that satisfied their duties often avoided both conviction and indictment, paying only monetary civil penalties. Over time, however, prosecutors changed their approach and started intervening more directly in the internal affairs of corporations potentially subject to indictment. Specifically, prosecutors started using their power to impose ruinous criminal liability on corporations, in concert with their authority not to prosecute, to pressure firms to agree to adopt structural reforms in return for not being prosecuted (or even indicted), in addition to paying monetary penalties.[8]

Some of these structural-reform-imposing DPAs and NPAs do little more than require firms to adopt compliance programs that the firms would have adopted anyway. But others go far beyond this, requiring firms to adopt corporate governance reforms and intrusive compliance programs that they would not have adopted on their own.[9] Indeed, some DPAs and NPAs require firms to eliminate certain business areas.[10] Others require firms to accept (and pay for) an outside monitor who may be granted substantial authority to monitor and interfere in the firm's internal operations.[11] These mandates can persist for many years.

B. Some Reasons for Concern

These structural reform DPAs and NPAs represent a change in prosecutors' practice. Previously, prosecutors tended to use the threat of financial sanctions and ability to offer leniency to provide corporations with *incentives* to prevent crime, report it, and help prosecutors sanction individual wrongdoers. Prosecutors generally allowed unconvicted publicly held firms to decide how best to deter crime. By contrast, prosecutors imposing structural reform DPAs and NPAs assert authority to design and oversee the internal operations of firms that have not been convicted of a crime, both directly through mandated structural reforms and indirectly through the use of monitors who report to prosecutors. Prosecutors' assertion of broad, largely unfettered discretion to impose substantial structural governance changes and to use monitors to oversee internal operations appears to be largely unique to the corporate crime area. It raises many concerns.[12]

The most basic concern is that prosecutors may abuse this discretion because they are not subject to any significant outside oversight. This concern was heightened by the Bristol-Myers Squibb DPA that required the firm to spend $5 million to endow a business ethics chair at Seton Hall Law School—the alma mater of Christopher Christie, the U.S. Attorney supervising the case.[13] While the DOJ has taken steps to address known abuses such as this,[14] prosecutors' ability to impose a wide range of nonmonetary sanctions opens the door to other similar abuses because such sanctions can be hard for courts to scrutinize.

But there also is a more serious concern: that prosecutors, even when acting in good faith, may impose reforms on corporations that are both excessively costly and ineffective. Prosecutors, in mandating internal governance reforms and asserting authority to impose corporate monitors, are stepping outside their areas of greatest expertise—the detection, investigation, and prosecution of crimes—and venturing into internal corporate governance reform, a subject in which few of them have any deep experience.

Prosecutors who take the task of structural reform seriously[15] necessarily inject themselves directly into corporate governance when they either dictate the structure of corporate compliance or require a firm to accept an effective corporate monitor. Compliance program design and oversight is a complicated task because it involves trade-offs between structures that help deter crimes and those that promote effective business. Crime often can be most effectively deterred and detected when corporate decision making is top-down, information about corporate affairs is collected in a central location, and senior management is subject to genuine scrutiny. Yet this structure may not be best for business. Businesses often are best able to generate new initiatives and respond quickly to changes in the market when they grant discretion to relatively lower level managers and employees. Similarly, efforts to centralize information require firms to pay more attention to record keeping, which may slow and bureaucratize decision making. While effective in many situations, such efforts may be excessively expensive and time-consuming in others. Other prosecutor-mandated decisions—such as requirements that the CEO not also be the chairman of the board of directors—involve equally fundamental decisions affecting how the firm should be governed. Monitors have an even greater potential to alter internal corporate structure, particularly when they are granted and assert broad authority to oversee, and make recommendations about, corporate practices. Thus, prosecutors cannot require structural reforms without altering a firm's internal operations in ways that may make it a less effective business.

This raises two important issues. The first is whether federal authorities should ever impose structural reforms, particularly on publicly held firms, as opposed to using the threat of corporate financial sanctions to induce directors to take the actions they believe will most cost-effectively deter crime.[16] The second is whether prosecutors are the best authority to impose structural reforms, or whether this authority should be exercised by civil regulatory authorities, whenever possible. This chapter focuses on this second issue.

The resolution of this issue depends on whether federal prosecutors can properly serve the central goals of corporate criminal liability while granting civil regulators sole authority over whether to impose structural reforms, wherever possible. To answer this question, we first need to understand the central goals of corporate criminal liability. To do this, we must understand why federal criminal enforcement authorities abandoned the traditional system and adopted formal guidelines governing nonprosecution.

II. The Traditional Approach and Its Limitations

The DOJ did not always encourage prosecutors to refrain from indicting firms whose employees clearly had committed criminal violations—quite the contrary. At one point, prosecutors targeted corporations. Yet this more aggressive approach to corporate prosecution was not effective at inducing firms to take the most basic actions needed to deter corporate crime.

A. The Traditional Approach

Prior to the 1990s, corporations whose employees committed crimes were considered criminals, properly subject to corporate criminal liability for crimes committed by employees in the scope of employment through the doctrine of *respondeat superior*. *Respondeat superior* not only governed when prosecutors *could* indict a firm, it often determined when prosecutors *would* indict. Indeed, many prosecutors focused their enforcement efforts on obtaining corporate convictions, often without convicting the individuals who caused the crime.[17]

Although corporate criminal liability was very broad, corporate criminal sanctions were relatively weak. Prior to the mid-1980s, convicted corporations were subject to the same fines as individuals. These fines, which were established with individuals in mind, were quite low relative to both the harm caused by corporate crime and most firms' ability to pay. Indeed, 60 percent of federal corporate convictions resulted in the firm being fined $10,000; the average fine was only $45,790.[18]

Criminal penalties not only were lower than they are today, they also were less intrusive. Convicted corporations generally faced only financial penalties. Prosecutors generally did not impose even relatively mild nonmonetary penalties, such as probation, and rarely used criminal liability to affect internal corporate governance, for example, by dictating the structure of corporate compliance efforts. Finally, unindicted corporations were not subject to substantial penalties, and prosecutors did not require corporations to adopt substantial internal reforms in return for agreeing not to prosecute.[19]

B. Deterrence Function of Corporate Criminal Liability and the Need for Reform

In the 1990s, federal authorities abandoned the traditional approach to corporate criminal liability because it could not achieve its primary goal—deterring corporate crime—particularly as applied to crimes arising from publicly held corporations. To deter corporate crime, the government must ensure that the individuals tempted to commit crimes expect to be punished. Traditional corporate criminal liability did not achieve this goal because it both targeted liability on the wrong place—on corporations rather than individuals—and deterred corporations from helping the government detect and prosecute crime.

1. *Importance of Individual Liability for Publicly Held Firms' Crimes*

The traditional focus on corporate liability was well suited to the crimes that prosecutors tended to focus on at the time: crimes by closely held firms.[20] Closely held firm crimes often are committed by, or with the indirect encouragement of, the firms' owners/managers. Strict *respondeat superior* corporate criminal liability thus can serve as an effective deterrent by ensuring that owners pay for the firm's crime even when prosecutors cannot establish their complicity directly.

Strict corporate vicarious criminal liability is not effective when applied to crimes committed by publicly held firms, however. A publicly held firm's crimes generally are committed by managers or other employees, not by shareholders. Moreover, the individual wrongdoers usually commit such crimes for their own personal benefit—often job retention or promotion—and not to benefit equity. The wrongdoers often have relatively low equity stakes. Moreover, they often are willing to commit crimes even when the crime hurts shareholders.[21]

The recognition that publicly held firm corporate crime is committed by managers and other employees at their own direction to serve their own interests leads naturally to two conclusions. First, criminal law cannot deter such crimes unless it targets liability at individual wrongdoers and ensures that crime does not pay. Second, criminal law generally should not seek to punish publicly held firm shareholders for corporate crimes. Instead, corporate criminal liability should be used to ensure that corporations—thus, indirectly, directors—have strong incentives to deter crime.[22]

2. Goals of Corporate Criminal Liability

Federal authorities cannot effectively deter corporate crime unless corporate criminal liability provides firms with an incentive to aid the government's enforcement efforts because, absent such assistance, federal authorities often will be unable either to detect corporate crimes or to identify and sanction those responsible with sufficient regularity. Given the complex, far-reaching, and often decentralized nature of the modern publicly held firm, corporate crimes usually are hard to detect. They can remain hidden for years, even forever.[23] Moreover, even when the government does detect wrongdoing, it may be unable to identify and punish the individuals responsible because corporate crimes often involve actions by many people, and often the person who committed the physical act that constitutes the crime is not the person who made the decision to commit it. As a result, many perpetrators of corporate crime could reap large rewards safe in the knowledge that the government would not be able to convict them. Accordingly, to deter crime effectively, the government needs corporations' assistance.[24]

Corporations can be powerful allies in the war against corporate crime, if they so choose. First, they can reduce employees' incentives to commit crime—for example, by structuring their compensation and promotion policies to ensure that employees faced with poor short-run results do not feel compelled to seek illegal profits in order to save their jobs.[25] Firms also can deter crime by creating a corporate culture that promotes legal compliance.[26]

In addition, corporations can deter crime by helping the government detect and prosecute wrongdoing. They can do this in three ways: by adopting compliance programs to monitor internal activities, reporting suspected wrongdoing, and cooperating with federal authorities' investigations (hereinafter, "policing").[27] Corporate monitoring is important because corporations can detect internal wrongs more easily than can the government. Firms know their own operations and how particular activities should be done. Thus, they can better spot suspicious activities. Corporate cooperation also is important because corporations generally are in a better position to identify which individuals ultimately are responsible for the crime.[28]

Corporate liability is needed because corporations will not spend money to deter crime unless the government provides them with strong financial incentives to do so.[29] Corporations will not undertake these actions unless threatened with liability because they otherwise would not have sufficient incentive to deter their employees' crimes. Market forces alone are not sufficient because, absent liability, corporations and their managers rarely are injured by these crimes.[30] Indeed, market forces may deter firms from detecting, reporting, or aiding in the prosecution of crimes that would undermine the firm's reputation with customers, suppliers, creditors, or shareholders, in order to avoid the resulting reputational market penalty.[31]

Corporate criminal liability is one of the tools the government can use to induce corporations to engage in prevention and policing. The government can use a combination of criminal and civil corporate liability to induce firms both to prevent wrongs and to aid the government's enforcement efforts by monitoring, reporting, and cooperating. Unfortunately, the traditional approach to corporate liability, which combined strict *respondeat superior* liability with low criminal sanctions, did not achieve either goal.

3. Problems with the Traditional Approach

The traditional strict *respondeat superior* corporate criminal liability failed to achieve its central goal—deterrence—because it discouraged firms from engaging in policing activities: monitoring, reporting, and cooperating. A corporation will spend money on policing—notwithstanding the threat of any financial penalties (government-imposed, private damage actions, and/or reputational)—if criminal liability is structured to ensure that firms that do not monitor, report, or cooperate fare worse than those that do. Traditional strict *respondeat superior* corporate criminal liability created the opposite incentive structure. It discouraged firms from policing because under this rule a corporation that worked to bring individual wrongdoers to justice also increased its own expected criminal liability for its employees' crimes. A firm that adopted an effective compliance program to detect wrongdoing thereby increased the risk that the evidence it created would be used to convict it if a crime occurred. A firm that reported wrongdoing could not do so without increasing its own risk of being found criminally liable. By contrast, a company that turned a blind eye to the risk of crime, or even evidence of crime, might avoid sanction altogether. In addition, if the wrong was detected, the firm would not be subject to any formal increased sanction for not reporting or cooperating.[32]

Thus, far from encouraging monitoring, reporting, and cooperating, traditional corporate liability actually discouraged it. Moreover, this rule created the greatest incentives not to police in the very situation where policing was most needed: when the government could not detect the crime without the corporation's assistance. Accordingly, it should come as no surprise that, under the traditional regime, publicly held corporations did not generally rush to adopt effective compliance programs or to report crimes and cooperate with federal authorities.[33]

The traditional approach also failed to provide corporations with adequate incentives to prevent crimes directly—such as by changing compensation and promotion policies—because traditional corporate criminal sanctions were too low to provide firms an adequate incentive to refrain from profitable business practices that increased the risk of crime.[34] Moreover, given the lack of corporate monitoring and cooperation, publicly held firms faced a relatively low risk that wrongs would be detected or successfully prosecuted.

III. Evolution of Federal Corporate Criminal Liability

Beginning in the mid-1980s, federal authorities adopted a series of reforms designed, in significant part, to improve the deterrence function of corporate criminal liability. These reforms (1) increased corporate criminal sanctions; (2) increased prosecutorial authority to impose non-fine criminal sanctions, including government-imposed compliance programs, on firms *convicted* of a crime; (3) transformed the traditional de jure regime of strict corporate criminal liability into a de facto regime in which corporations face criminal liability only if they neglect all their policing duties; and (4) encouraged prosecutors to target their enforcement efforts at convicting wrongful individuals. This initial slate of reforms dramatically transformed corporate liability yet left prosecutors in their traditional role: free to use the threat of financial sanctions and their discretion to award leniency to deter wrongdoing. Then prosecutors took these reforms a step further, using DPAs and NPAs to impose structural reforms on nonindicted corporations.

A. Increased Monetary Sanctions

In the mid-1980s, Congress took the first step toward reform when it adopted statutes specifically governing the fines to be imposed on corporations. These statutes dramatically increased the sanctions imposed on corporations convicted of federal crimes. To further enhance corporate sentences, Congress later empowered the U.S. Sentencing Commission to promulgate sentencing guidelines governing the sentencing of organizations. In 1991, the commission adopted the U.S. Sentencing Commission Guidelines for Organizations, with the explicit intent of increasing criminal fines imposed on corporations. The Guidelines also substantially increased the use of criminal non-fine monetary sanctions, such as criminal restitution and remediation.[35]

These measures achieved their goal. Average criminal fines imposed on publicly held corporations after the Guidelines were ten times higher than previously. Whereas in the four years prior to the Guidelines, the average fine imposed on a convicted publicly held firm was $1.9 million, in the five years after the Guidelines, a publicly held firm convicted of a federal crime was subject to an average fine of $19 million in cases constrained by the Guidelines (in 1996 dollars).[36] Median fines increased from $633,000 to $3.1 million in cases where the judge was legally bound to follow the Guidelines. Average total sanctions imposed on convicted publicly held firms—including criminal fines, non-fine criminal monetary sanctions, government civil penalties, and private civil sanctions—increased from $13.3 million[37] to more than $49 million (1996 dollars).[38]

B. Expanded Nonmonetary Sanctions: Compliance as a Punishment

The Guidelines also expanded the non-fine interventions imposed on corporations convicted of a federal crime by both requiring courts to impose probation in more circumstances than previously and expanding the range of sanctions that would be imposed pursuant to a probation order.[39]

In its narrowest form, probation simply prohibits the firm from committing another criminal violation, of any sort, for a particular period of time. Yet even this form of probation has potentially serious consequences because it substantially increases the cost to the firm of any future violation. Any future crime would subject the firm to criminal penalties directly as well as to additional penalties for the original crime (since the subsequent crime would violate the probation order). Beyond this, the Guidelines also encourage prosecutors to use probation as a vehicle for imposing additional nonmonetary sanctions on a firm, such as requiring the firm to implement a monitoring program, submit to inspections, publicize its conviction, or undertake community service. Indeed, the Guidelines mandate the imposition of court-mandated compliance programs in certain circumstances. The Guidelines also permit courts to take a variety of actions to reduce the probability of future wrongdoing, including prohibiting the corporation from engaging in specific business practices.[40]

C. Broad Individual Liability: Duty-Based Corporate Criminal Liability

During the 1990s, federal authorities also changed their approach to the proper roles of both individual and corporate criminal liability for corporate crimes. Prosecutors came to recognize that individual liability should be the cornerstone of the government's effort to deter crime and focused more attention on obtaining individual convictions. Eventually, they became more willing to send executives of publicly held firms to jail for white-collar crimes.

This move toward enhanced individual liability was accompanied by a transformation of corporate criminal liability. During the 1990s, the United States moved away from strict *respondeat superior* liability toward a more "duty-based" corporate criminal liability regime in which corporations could reduce, or eliminate, criminal liability by engaging in effective policing, such as adopting effective compliance programs, self-reporting, and cooperating with federal authorities. The transformation in the structure of corporate criminal liability took place in stages.

The 1991 Organizational Sentencing Guidelines took the first step away from strict *respondeat superior* liability by mandating a lower minimum and maximum fine for any convicted corporation with an effective compliance program. The Guidelines require additional mitigation if the firm reported the wrong within a reasonable time and/or cooperated fully with federal authorities. The Guidelines also provide that corporations taking these steps could avoid being subject to criminal probation, with the attendant threat of ongoing government involvement in the corporations' affairs.[41]

The Guidelines are an improvement over the prior system, but they do not offer sufficient reward for reporting and cooperation to induce firms to adopt effective policing. The central problem is simple: the Guidelines *reduce* the criminal sanction imposed on firms that monitor, self-report, and cooperate but nevertheless leave them subject to criminal liability. This discourages firms from reporting suspected wrongdoing and cooperating because many would suffer enormous negative consequences from any federal conviction, as a result of collateral penalties, civil damages actions, and, in some situations, enhanced reputational penalties.[42]

Recognizing this problem, the DOJ intervened to alter the de facto application of corporate criminal liability by offering to insulate firms that engage in effective policing from the threat of criminal liability. In order to ensure that firms retain incentives to prevent wrongs even when they expect to avoid criminal sanctions, federal authorities continued to impose civil penalties on firms potentially subject to criminal liability.[43]

Specifically, starting in 1999, the then Deputy Attorney General Eric Holder issued federal prosecutors a set of guidelines detailing factors for them to consider in deciding whether to prosecute a corporation whose employees committed a crime.[44] Of particular importance, the Holder Memo stated that, in deciding whether to exempt a corporation from prosecution, prosecutors should consider the effectiveness of the firm's compliance program, whether it promptly reported, and its level of cooperation with the government. The Holder Memo indicated that prosecutors should not prosecute firms that had satisfied all their enforcement obligations. Prosecutors were left with considerable discretion about how to handle firms that satisfied some, but not all, of their enforcement duties. Firms exempt from criminal prosecution based on good corporate policing nevertheless could be, and often were, subject to financial penalties.

In 2003, the Holder Memo was superseded by the Thompson Memo. The Thompson Memo encouraged prosecutors to focus on the "authenticity" of cooperation as a precondition for non-indictment and added "pretrial diversion" (e.g., deferred prosecution) to the other options available to prosecutors seeking to reward good corporate conduct.[45] Following the adoption of the Thompson Memo, prosecutors increasingly employed DPAs and NPAs, under which they agreed not to prosecute only if firms satisfied certain conditions.

D. Structural Reforms Mandated through DPAs and NPAs

Initially, prosecutors usually used DPAs and NPAs to give them leverage over corporations, in order to ensure that corporations paid any monetary penalties imposed (including by state authorities) and continued to cooperate with the federal prosecution of any individual wrongdoers. Yet, over time, leading prosecutors' offices changed their approach. They started using these agreements to impose on nonconvicted firms the type of internal governance reforms that the Guidelines had encouraged them to impose on convicted firms, such as requiring firms to adopted prosecutor-sanctioned compliance programs. Moreover, prosecutors started requiring firms to hire corporate monitors with broad authority to oversee firms' operations, and sometimes with authority to intervene in internal operations. Through these measures, prosecutors no longer sought simply to *induce* firms to engage in effective prevention and policing. They now sought to dictate to firms both how they should deter wrongdoing and to directly supervise their efforts to comply. In so doing, prosecutors in effect stepped out of their traditional role and into a role usually assumed by civil regulatory authorities.

IV. Deterring Crime without Governance by Prosecutors

Prosecutors' use of DPAs and NPAs to impose structural reforms and monitors on publicly held firms represents a fundamental shift in the goals that motivated both the Organizational Sentencing Guidelines and the Holder Memo. The reforms of the 1980s and 1990s were intended to deter corporate crime by both targeting federal prosecutions at wrongful executives and providing corporations with strong financial incentives to adopt effective prevention and policing measures. The premise was that corporations—at least those entitled not to be convicted—could best determine for themselves what measures would best enable them to fulfill their compliance duties. Federal regulators could provide any additional needed oversight or regulation. Structural reform DPAs and NPAs represent a determination that the federal authorities in charge of criminal enforcement not only should act to detect and sanction wrongs—and induce corporations to cooperate—but also should intervene directly in the affairs of unconvicted (and usually unindicted) corporations to help ensure compliance.

Many reasons exist to question the wisdom of this approach as applied to publicly held firms. Of particular importance, this approach allows prosecutors to assume authority to make decisions affecting the very structure of how a corporation is run—authority usually enjoyed by its board of directors—notwithstanding the fact that prosecutors rarely have either any experience working for or running a business or a deep understanding of the industry being regulated. They also have only a limited understanding of the internal workings of the specific corporations that the compliance programs would apply to. Moreover, prosecutors' offices rarely employ any institutional mechanisms for auditing or collecting information on the effectiveness of any reforms imposed, in order to evaluate whether the measures are cost-effective. Finally, they are subject to little if any genuine oversight and have no formal mechanisms for public feedback.

The limitations of prosecutorial imposition of structural reforms raise the question of whether it is possible to achieve the deterrence goals of corporate liability without granting prosecutors the authority to impose internal structural reforms on publicly held firms—particularly those that have not been indicted. It is. The answer lies in recognizing that, although there arguably are situations where nonconvicted publicly held corporations will not attend properly to compliance unless federal authorities intervene more directly in their internal affairs, those situations are likely to be rare. Moreover, there is no reason why this intervention needs to be done by prosecutors, when there exists a civil regulator with authority to intervene.

Deterring Crime without Prosecutor Supervision of Compliance

As previously explained, a central goal of corporate liability is to induce corporations to help deter crime by monitoring for wrongdoing, and, if any wrongs are detected, by reporting wrongdoing to federal authorities and cooperating with investigations to help identify and sanction all culpable individuals. Corporate liability is needed to induce firms to undertake these policing expenditures because, without the threat of liability for failure to do so, they often will find that the cost of policing exceeds the benefits. Corporate criminal liability can be used to induce corporations to monitor, report, and cooperate if it is structured in such a way that a firm that assists the government in the detection of crime faces a lower *expected* sanction than a firm that does not—where the expected sanction is the actual sanction adjusted by the probability of detection.[46] Given that policing inevitably increases the probability that a firm is sanctioned, the only way that the government can induce corporations to police is to ensure that the sanction imposed on them when they do is *much* lower than the sanction imposed on them when they do not.[47]

Federal authorities generally can accomplish this goal through a two-step mitigation regime. Firms should face default civil liability whenever an employee commits a crime in the scope of employment. The firm should face an additional penalty if it did not have an effective compliance program and a second penalty if it failed to report and cooperate.

The best way to ensure that firms have adequate incentives to satisfy each aspect of policing is to ensure that they can be confident of benefiting from one aspect of policing (e.g., cooperation), even if they are not sure that they will satisfy their duties with respect to the other aspect (e.g., compliance).[48] To induce reporting and cooperation, the government must give publicly held firms credit for reporting and cooperating even if the firm's compliance program was ineffective. In turn, a firm must expect to get credit for adopting an effective compliance program even if the board thinks the firm might later fail to promptly report or cooperate (e.g., because of resistance by executives).[49]

This analysis has important implications for the debate over prosecutorial authority over corporate compliance. It demonstrates that federal authorities must evaluate the effectiveness of a corporate compliance program, imposing higher sanctions on firms that fail to adopt effective compliance programs than on firms that adopt and supervise effective compliance programs. This ability to review compliance programs, and to penalize those that are inadequate, inevitably grants federal authorities de facto ability to induce firms to adopt compliance programs likely to satisfy federal authorities.

Yet it also reveals that there is no particular reason why federal *prosecutors* should be in charge of assessing compliance program effectiveness. As previously explained, federal authorities cannot induce effective policing unless they separately reward effective monitoring and effective reporting and cooperation. Federal authorities could effectively do this by encouraging prosecutors to base their charging decisions on whether the firm self-reported and cooperated. Prosecutors can tell corporations that any publicly held firm that self-reports detected wrongdoing and fully cooperates is exempt from prosecution. Civil regulatory authorities could then determine the magnitude of the civil sanction based on whether the firm had an effective compliance program, imposing a higher sanction on firms that did not than on those that did.[50]

Moreover, and more important, the preceding analysis reveals that federal prosecutors can achieve the goals of corporate criminal liability without using DPAs and NPAs to impose structural reforms on publicly held firms as a precondition of non-indictment. First, when liability is structured properly, federal authorities rarely should need to require publicly held firms to adopt firm-specific structural reforms because the threat of liability for ineffective compliance should induce firms to take compliance seriously. Second, in those relatively rare circumstances where federal authorities may need to mandate firm-specific structural reforms,[51] there is no particular reason why these mandates should be imposed by federal prosecutors. Indeed, analysis of the relative institutional expertise and structures of prosecutors and regulatory agencies reveals that federally mandated structural reforms are most likely to be effective if the task of designing and imposing structural reforms is left entirely to federal civil regulators, at least in the areas over which they have jurisdiction and competence.

Federal prosecutors step outside their proper role and institutional expertise when they require publicly held corporations to accept structural reforms as a precondition of not being prosecuted. It is true that federal criminal law does impose specific duties on firms in some circumstances. When it does, prosecutors are within their rightful authority to require that firms adhere to these duties as a condition of probation or nonprosecution. Similarly, prosecutors operate within the traditional confines of the criminal law when they decide to subject firms to a higher penalty if the firm actively encouraged a crime or failed to take active steps to deter it. But most DPAs and NPAs that mandate structural reforms do not restrict themselves to measures previously required by Congress or a federal regulatory agency. Instead, they require firms to adopt internal reforms that are not required by either a statute or an agency ruling as a precondition for not being indicted. In so doing, prosecutors are crossing the line from criminal enforcement to direct regulation, a line that they generally should not, and need not, cross. The task of imposing structural reforms should, wherever possible, remain the purview of civil regulatory authorities.

Federal civil regulators should be granted sole authority over whether to impose structural reforms because they are more likely to have the expertise needed to determine when and which structural reforms are needed. Federal authorities seeking to design an effective compliance program and monitor corporate behavior must attend carefully to the most likely sources of criminal activity within an industry and a specific firm. They also must evaluate the best way to deter such activity without hobbling the firm excessively. To do this effectively, authorities must have expertise that reaches beyond the criminal arena. They must understand business operations, both in general and in the industry in question. Civil regulators often come from industry and thus often have firsthand knowledge of both the factors in a given industry that are likely to induce people to violate the law and the compliance measures that are best able to detect such wrongs. Moreover, civil regulators also often have better information about what structural reforms are needed because they tend to be engaged in long-term formal and informal dialogues with regulated firms and thus have better information about the costs of various compliance measures.

Prosecutors, by contrast, generally have little direct experience working in the industry in question. Indeed, many have little experience working for any business. Moreover, many prosecutors evaluating compliance programs have little long-term experience regulating firms in the industry in question. Accordingly, they often lack the expertise needed to assess the best way to achieve effective compliance. As a result, prosecutorial assertion of authority tends to lead toward the adoption of standardized boilerplate compliance measures, which are expensive and may not be tailored to the special risks or concerns of individual firms or particular industries. These mandated reforms not only are expensive, they also may inhale resources the firm otherwise could have used to adopt more effective measures better tailored to its situation.

In addition, prosecutors appear to be more likely than are civil regulators to impose unnecessarily costly or ineffective structural reforms because few (if any) formal mechanisms exist to ensure that prosecutors imposing DPAs and NPAs learn from either their own mistakes or those of other prosecutors. Many DPAs and NPAs enable prosecutors to exert supervisory authority over a firm for an extended period of time. Yet prosecutors' exercise of this authority is subject to little, if any, oversight. Moreover, prosecutors rarely receive the kind of detailed ongoing information about either the firm or the industry to enable them to reevaluate their decisions. Nor do prosecutors' offices have the ability to conduct the type of industry-wide cost-benefit assessments of program effectiveness needed to mandate reforms that are effective on average. Without the incentive or the ability to conduct ongoing studies of their own decisions to determine which ones work, there is little reason to expect that the benefits of prosecutor-mandated programs are worth the cost.

By contrast, federal regulatory agencies often gain firm-specific information and industry-specific information over time. They also have the institutional ability to conduct ongoing empirical assessments of the effectiveness of their own measures,[52] as well as industry-wide assessments of how best to induce compliance. Civil authorities also are subject to considerably more oversight, since they are required to act in the open, and risk potential challenge on cost-benefit grounds. Finally, civil authorities are better able to adopt procedures to enable corporations to obtain *ex ante* input on the effectiveness of compliance measures.

Thus, federal civil regulators with authority over the firm generally are in the best position to determine both whether to impose any structural reform on a firm and, if so, which reforms should be imposed. They also can better assess whether the reforms should be firm-specific or industry-wide. Thus, federal prosecutors should retain their policy of not indicting firms that self-report and cooperate but should refrain from using this authority to gain leverage to force firms to adopt structural reforms, so long as there exists a competent civil regulatory agency with the ability to impose structural reforms as part of its own enforcement process.[53]

V. Conclusion

Deterring corporate crime is an important goal of federal law. Yet federal law can achieve this goal only if it is properly structured. In particular, firms need strong *ex ante* incentives to adopt effective compliance programs. They also need strong *ex post* incentives to report detected wrongdoing and cooperate in the conviction of responsible individuals. Until recently, federal criminal authorities attempted to achieve these goals through the use of financial incentives, in the form of the threat of criminal and civil sanctions for corporate crime and the offer of leniency for good corporate citizens. They did not seek to regulate the internal corporate governance of individual firms. During this decade, however, federal prosecutors have asserted broad authority to interfere in the internal affairs of firms potentially subject to prosecution by using the threat of indictment to induce firms to agree to structural reforms and corporate monitors, in return for an agreement not to prosecute.

While well-intentioned, federal prosecutors generally should be precluded from exercising this quasi-regulatory authority whenever there is a civil enforcement authority well-positioned to oversee compliance. This complete grant of authority to civil enforcement authorities to regulate corporate compliance (where possible) is superior to the current approach because civil authorities are better positioned to design compliance programs because they generally have a deeper understanding of the regulated industry and also have formal mechanisms to permit internal assessment of their own policies. This approach will remove prosecutors from where they do not belong, thereby better enabling those authorities with the requisite expertise to regulate corporate compliance where necessary.

NOTES

1. The DOJ leniency policy for corporations provides directors with an incentive to cooperate and report so long as directors expect shareholders to lay the blame for corporate criminal liability at the directors' feet if the corporation winds up being indicted because the directors either failed to report detected wrongdoing or failed to cooperate fully. Directors will be particularly inclined to satisfy their duty to report and cooperate to the extent that shareholders are able to replace them easily.

2. Memorandum from Eric Holder, Deputy Attorney General, U.S. Dep't of Justice, to Heads of Department Components and United States Attorneys, *Bringing Criminal Charges Against Corporations* (June 16, 1999), http://www.usdoj.gov/criminal/fraud/docs/reports/1999/chargingcorps.html; *see also* U.S. Dep't of Justice, U.S. Attorneys' Manual, § 9-28.900 (Principles of Federal Prosecution of Business Organizations), *available at* http://www.usdoj.gov/opa/documents/corp-charging-guidelines.pdf; Jennifer Arlen & Reinier Kraakman, *Controlling Corporate Misconduct: An Analysis of Corporate Liability Regimes*, 72 N.Y.U. L. Rev. 687, 753 (1997) (explaining the essential deterrence function of civil liability when corporations can avoid criminal liability if they satisfy their policing duties). DOJ policy also takes into account the effectiveness of a firm's compliance program in determining whether to indict. *See* Holder Memo, *supra* note 2. Nevertheless, prosecutors appear to focus on corporate reporting and cooperation in deciding whether to indict because these activities directly affect their ability to identify and punish the individuals responsible for the wrong.

3. *See* New York Cent. & Hudson River R.R. Co. v. United States, 212 U.S. 481, 493 (1909). The benefit requirement does little to restrict the scope of liability because it is satisfied if the employee incidentally intended to benefit the firm, even if his primary goal was to benefit himself. Thus, corporations can be criminally liable for officers' materially misleading statements to securities markets even though such securities frauds hurt shareholders both by dissuading them from acting (to sell stock or remove management) and by subjecting the firm to a reputational sanction when the truth is revealed. *See* Jennifer H. Arlen & William J. Carney, *Vicarious Liability for Fraud on Securities Markets: Theory and Evidence*, 1992 U. Ill. L. Rev. 691, 729–30 (1992).

4. *E.g.*, United States v. Twentieth Century Fox Film Corp., 882 F.2d 656, 660–61 (2d Cir. 1989); United States v. Hilton Hotels Corp., 467 F.2d 1000, 1004 (9th Cir. 1973).

5. By contrast, other countries generally restrict corporate criminal liability to crimes by senior managers or allow a formal good faith defense. *See generally* Sara Sun Beale & Adam G. Safwat, *What Developments in Western Europe Tell Us About American Critiques of Corporate Criminal Liability*, 8 Buff. Crim. L. Rev. 89, 155 (2005); Angelo Castaldo & Giorgio Nizi, *Entity Liability and Deterrence: Recent Reforms in Italy*, 3 Erasmus L. & Econ. Rev. 1, 6 (2007); Kensuke Ito, *Criminal Protection of the Environment and the General Part of Criminal Law in Japan*, 65 Int'l Rev. Penal L. 1043 (1994); Gudrun Stangl, *Austria: Corporate Criminal Liability*, 24 Int'l Fin. L. Rev. 75–76 (2005); Jennifer G. Hill, *Corporate Criminal Liability in Australia: An Evolving Corporate Governance Technique?*, 2003 J. Bus. L. 1 (2003).

6. *See generally* Cindy R. Alexander, Jennifer Arlen & Mark A. Cohen, *Regulating Corporate Criminal Sanctions: Federal Guidelines and the Sentencing of Public Firms*, 42 J. Law & Econ. 393 (1999).

7. Holder Memo, *supra* note 2.

8. While prosecutors employed DPAs as far back as 1994, Mary Jo White, *Corporate Criminal Liability: What Has Gone Wrong?*, 2 37th Ann. Inst. Sec. Reg. 815, 818 (PLI Corp. Law & Practice, Course Handbook Series No. B-1517) (2005), their use increased significantly after the Thompson Memo in 2003. *See, e.g.*, Lisa Kern Griffin, *Compelled Cooperation and the New Corporate Criminal Procedure*, 82 N.Y.U. L. Rev. 311, 323 (2007); Peter Spivack & Sujit Raman, *Regulating the 'New Regulators': Current Trends in Deferred Prosecution Agreements*, 45 Am. Crim. L. Rev. 159, 163, 166–67 (2008). Also, earlier DPAs and NPAs generally did not have some of the common and controversial features of modern DPAs, such as waiver of attorney-client privilege, mandated structural reforms, and the appointment of an independent compliance monitor. *See* Griffin, *supra* note 8, at 323; *see also* Miriam H. Baer, *Governing Corporate Governance*, 50 B. C. L. Rev. 949, 969–70 (2009).

9. *See, e.g.*, Brandon L. Garrett, *Structural Reform Prosecution*, 93 Va. L. Rev. 853, 898–99 (2007); Spivack & Raman, *supra* note 8, at 184–87.

10. For example, KPMG International agreed to eliminate its private tax practice. Garrett, *supra* note 9, at 855.

11. *See, e.g.*, Vikramaditya Khanna & Timothy L. Dickinson, *The Corporate Monitor: The New Corporate Czar*, 105 Mich. L. Rev. 1713, 1724 (2007).

12. Although firms often complain that prosecutors enjoy nearly unfettered discretion to decide whether to indict or prosecute, any problems associated with this discretion are not unique to corporate criminal law and thus are best addressed through general solutions that are not limited to executives and corporations. *See* Sara Sun Beale, *Is Corporate Criminal Liability Unique?*, 44 Am. Crim. L. Rev. 1503, 1523–29 (2007).

13. Interview with Mary Jo White, 19 Corp. Crime Rep. 48 (Dec. 12, 2005). Prosecutors' insistence in another case that a corporation refuse to honor its contractual obligations to pay for its employees' attorneys' fees arguably represents another prosecutorial abuse of power. *See* United States v. Stein, 435 F. Supp. 2d 330, 362–65 (S.D.N.Y. 2006).

14. Memorandum from Mark Filip, Deputy Attorney General, U.S. Dep't of Justice, to Holders of the U.S. Attorneys' Manual, *USAM 9-16.325: Plea Agreements, Deferred Prosecution Agreements, Non-prosecution Agreements and "Extraordinary Restitution"* (May 14, 2008); *see* Memorandum from Craig S. Moreland, Acting Deputy Attorney General, U.S. Dep't of Justice, to Heads of Department Components and U.S. Attorneys, *Selection and Use of Monitors in Deferred Prosecution Agreements and Non-prosecution Agreements with Corporations* (Mar. 7, 2009), http://www.justice.gov/criminal/fraud/docs/dag-030708.pdf.

15. The present objections do not apply to structural reforms that are merely window dressing, as when DPAs and NPAs are limited to provisions that a firm planned to adopt in any event and prosecutors exercise no postagreement oversight. Of course, such agreements raise other problems, since prosecutors' appearance of action may dissuade others, such as shareholders, from intervening more effectively.

16. By contrast, Delaware has taken a largely hands-off approach to compliance programs. Delaware imposes a duty on directors to attend to compliance but vests them with full authority to determine how best to satisfy that duty, subject to a threat of liability only if they act in bad faith by utterly failing to satisfy their compliance duties. Stone *ex rel.* AmSouth Bancorporation v. Ritter, 911 A.2d 362, 370 (Del. 2006) (en banc); *see also In re* Caremark Int'l Inc. Derivative Litig., 698 A.2d 959, 970 (Del. Ch. 1996). Delaware does

not hold directors liable for gross negligence for failure to monitor in order to give directors leeway to exercise their good faith discretion. Delaware also focuses on maximizing firm value and does not require directors to guarantee compliance with federal law at any cost. *See* Jennifer Arlen, *The Story of Allis-Chalmers, Caremark, and Stone: Directors' Evolving Duty to Monitor*, *in* Corporate Law Stories 323 (J. Mark Ramseyer ed., 2009).

17. Mark Cohen, *Corporate Crime and Punishment: An Update on Sentencing Practice in the Federal Courts, 1988–1990*, 71 B.U.L. Rev. 247, 268 (1991) (between 1988 and 1990, individual codefendants were *not* convicted in 35 percent of the federal cases in which an organization was sentenced for a non-antitrust crime); *see* Leonard Orland, *The Transformation of Corporate Criminal Law*, 1592 1 Brooklyn J. Corp., Fin. & Comm. L. 197, 201 (PLI Corp. Law & Practice, Course Handbook Series No. 1592) (2007) (observing that corporate executives were rarely convicted prior to 1960). Publicly held firms convicted prior to the Holder Memo include General Electric, Twentieth Century Fox, Disney, Emerson Electric, Waste Management, Boeing, Texaco, Baxter International, Borden, Shell Pipeline, Exxon, AT&T Microelectronic, Mitsubishi, Nynex, Chevron, Archer Daniels, Rocketdyne, Warner Lambert, Hyundai Motors of America, Samsung America, Daiwa Bank, and Bristol-Myers Squibb.

18. Cohen, *supra* note 17, at 254–56.

19. *See* Garrett, *supra* note 9, at 855.

20. Cohen, *supra* note 17, at 251–52 (noting that the vast majority of federal convictions involved closely held firms).

21. *E.g.*, Cindy R. Alexander & Mark A. Cohen, *New Evidence on the Origins of Corporate Crime*, 17 Managerial Dec. Econ. 421, 432 (1996); *see* Arlen & Carney, *supra* note 3, at 692–93.

22. *See supra* note 1.

23. *See* Alexander Dyck, Adair Morse & Luigi Zingales, *Who Blows the Whistle on Corporate Fraud?* (forthcoming), *available at* http://papers.ssrn.com/sol3/papers.cfm?abstract_id=891482 (fewer than 7 percent of corporate frauds committed between 1996 and 2004 were detected by the SEC; only 13 percent were detected by nonfinancial market regulators).

24. *See* Jennifer Arlen, *The Potentially Perverse Effects of Corporate Criminal Liability*, 23 J. Legal Stud. 833, 847 (1994); Arlen & Kraakman, *supra* note 2, at 690–91.

25. Studies show that employees (including officers) are more likely to commit certain crimes when their firms focus on short-term financial returns when evaluating the performance of a division or individual. *E.g.*, Charles W. L. Hill et al., *An Empirical Examination of the Causes of Corporate Wrongdoing in the United States*, 45 Hum. Rel. 1055, 1069–70 (1992) (finding that EPA and OSHA violations are more likely when top managers focus on rate of return criteria in evaluating division performance); *see* Mark A. Cohen & Sally S. Simpson, *The Origins of Corporate Criminality: Rational Individual and Organizational Actors*, *in* Debating Corporate Crime: An Interdisciplinary Examination of the Causes and Control of Corporate Misconduct 33 (William S. Lofquist, Mark A. Cohen & Gary A. Rabe eds., 1997). For additional analysis of this issue, see N. Craig Smith, Sally S. Simpson & Chun-Yao Huang, *Why Managers Fail to Do the Right Thing: An Empirical Study of Unethical and Illegal Conduct*, 17 Bus. Ethics Quar. 633 (2007).

26. *See, e.g.*, Tom R. Tyler & Steven L. Blader, *Can Business Effectively Regulate Employee Conduct? The Antecedents of Rule Following in Work Settings*, 48 Acad. Mgmt. J. 1143, 1153

(2005); John M. Conley & William M. O'Barr, *Crimes and Custom in Corporate Society: A Cultural Perspective on Corporate Misconduct*, 60 Law & Contemp. Probs. 5, 19 (1997).

27. *See* Arlen, *supra* note 24, at 839–40; Arlen & Kraakman, *supra* note 2, at 691.

28. *See, e.g.*, Arlen & Kraakman, *supra* note 2, at 691–93, 699; Samuel W. Buell, *Criminal Procedure Within the Firm*, 59 Stan. L. Rev. 1613, 1626 (2007).

29. The central difference between corporate "policing" and corporate "prevention" (as defined earlier) is that the latter deters crimes directly, whereas policing deters crime by increasing the likelihood that the government can detect and sanction wrongdoing. Arlen & Kraakman, *supra* note 2, at 701–12.

30. Indeed, firms may benefit from a lax attitude toward crime because they benefit either directly from the crime itself (if not sanctioned) or indirectly from the extra productivity generated by promotion and compensation policies known to increase the risk of crime. *See supra* note 25.

31. A corporation potentially can reduce the reputational penalty of any crimes it reports if it can act to reassure the markets that the criminal activity will not reoccur, for example, by replacing the CEO and other senior managers with an outsider. These actions do not eliminate the penalty, however, and indeed may impose their own costs on the firm.

32. Under *respondeat superior* liability, the firm does not have a net incentive to police if the deterrence effect of policing on employees' willingness to commit crimes is less than the cost to the firm of its increased liability resulting from its liability for the crimes that it detects and reports that otherwise would have remained unsanctioned. Arlen, *supra* note 24, at 836; *see* Arlen & Kraakman, *supra* note 2, at 712–17.

33. Consistent with this, Delaware law held that directors are not obligated to adopt a compliance program absent notice of potential wrongdoing. Graham v. Allis-Chalmers Mfg. Co., 188 A.2d 125, 130 (Del. 1963). Delaware changed its approach after federal authorities abandoned strict corporate criminal liability in practice. *See* Arlen, *supra* note 16.

34. *See supra* text accompanying notes 18–19 (discussing sentencing prior to the Guidelines).

35. *See* U.S. Sentencing Commission, Guidelines Manual Ch. 8 §§ 8B1, 8D1 [hereinafter Guidelines].

36. Alexander, Arlen & Cohen, *supra* note 6, at 410. In 2005, the Guidelines became advisory, and not mandatory. *See* United States v. Booker, 543 U.S. 220, 223–24 (2005).

37. This estimate excludes the $10.3 billion total sanction imposed for the Exxon *Valdez*. *Id.*

38. *See* Alexander, Arlen & Cohen, *supra* note 6, at 240.

39. Guidelines, *supra* note 35, at § 8D.

40. *Id.*

41. Under the Guidelines, a firm potentially becomes eligible for a reduced sanction if the offense occurred while the firm had an effective program in place to prevent and detect violations and it reported all detected violations within a reasonable time after becoming aware of them. Guidelines, *supra* note 35, at § 8C2.5(f). It can earn additional mitigation by reporting wrongdoing, fully cooperating in its investigation, and accepting responsibility for wrongs that have already occurred. Guidelines, *supra* note 35, at § 8C2.5(g).

42. In many industries, firms convicted of a crime face substantial collateral consequences that are completely independent of the level of fine involved. For example,

they may be barred by federal or state regulators from engaging in certain activities. In addition, corporations in the business of selling their reputation can expect to suffer a huge reputational penalty if convicted of a crime.

43. *See* Arlen & Kraakman, *supra* note 2, at 690.

44. Holder Memo, *supra* note 2. Prior to the Holder Memo, various federal enforcement agencies adopted a similar approach to particular crimes, such as government procurement fraud, antitrust, and environmental laws. U.S. Environmental Protection Agency, Final Statement, Incentives for Self-Policing: Discovery, Disclosure, Correction and Prevention of Violations, 60 Fed. Reg. 66,706 (Dec. 22, 1995); Antitrust Division, U.S. Dep't of Justice, Corporate Leniency Policy (Aug. 10, 1993), 328 Trade Reg. Rep 20,649–21 ¶ 13,113 (Aug. 16, 1994).

45. *See* Memorandum from Larry D. Thompson, Deputy Attorney General, U.S. Dep't of Justice, to Heads of Department Components and United States Attorneys, *Principles of Federal Prosecution of Business Organizations* (Jan. 20, 2003), http://www.usdoj.gov/dag/cftf/corporate_guidelines.htm.

46. To be precise, the government must set sanctions so that the firm's expected costs if it engages in policing—*Policing Costs* + (*Probability Sanction if police*)(*Sanction if police*)—are less than its costs if does not, as given by (*Probability sanction no policing*)(*Sanction no policing*). Thus, the firm must face a lower *expected* sanction if it polices than if it does not, even though the probability of sanctioning is higher if it polices.

47. Arlen & Kraakman, *supra* note 2, 706–12.

48. *Id.* at 728–29.

49. *Id.* at 729.

50. Federal agencies must ensure that firms that police nevertheless expect to pay for the harm caused by their employees' crimes, for example, through civil sanctions. This "residual" liability is needed to ensure that firms have an incentive to prevent crime even when they expect to avoid criminal liability and to receive credit for effective monitoring. Liability is superior to direct regulation because it gives each firm an incentive to make the right choice given the particular circumstances facing that firm. *See id.* at 701–05. Federal agencies can grant full mitigation, however, if the firm will bear the cost of the crime through either reputational sanctions or private actions for damages.

51. The situations where such mandates may be required or useful are beyond the scope of this chapter but include those where managerial agency costs are so severe that federal authorities cannot induce needed reforms through sanctions imposed on the firm. Recent reforms giving shareholders greater access to the ballot may reduce the need for such interventions, however.

52. *See, e.g.*, Baer, *supra* note 8, at 1004.

53. Of course, federal agencies cannot necessarily be relied upon to use their expertise in the public interest, since they are subject to capture. This concern is evident in debates about the recent role of the SEC. This suggests a potential role for prosecutors if federal agencies appear to be captured. Yet this raises the issue of whether this role is best assumed by federal or state prosecutors. *See infra* Rachel Barkow, *The Prosecutor as Regulatory Agency*.

4

Potentially Perverse Effects of Corporate Civil Liability

SAMUEL W. BUELL

Careful analysis of incentives dominates the mature academic field of enterprise liability. Vicarious liability rests on the idea that firms can control the conduct of their agents. Assigning liability to firms promises to reduce legal violations by encouraging firms (really managers) to influence agent behavior.[1] Remaining arguments in the field center on how optimally to calibrate incentives when attaching liability to firms. For example, in an important work from which I have lifted my chapter title, Jennifer Arlen demonstrated that imposing strict liability on firms for agent misconduct, without crediting firms with a liability reduction for self-policing efforts, would encourage firms to avoid learning of legal violations by their agents.[2] Such an incentive would be perverse for a system aimed at effective outsourcing of some of the public enforcement function to firms—a necessary strategy in the modern environment of huge, complex, and opaque organizations.

As this volume perhaps makes clear, the abundant literature on enterprise liability has been missing an important part of the picture. The problem of adjusting incentives extends beyond the triangular relationship among liability rules, the firm, and the firm's agents. The enforcer of the liability rule is also a major, perhaps dominant, actor in determining the success of a liability scheme. The problem of the enforcer's incentives, like the problem of firm and agent incentives, grows more complex if multiple forms of enterprise liability—private civil, civil regulatory, and criminal—are layered over one another. A prime example is the law of securities fraud, under which class action plaintiffs, SEC enforcement lawyers, and DOJ prosecutors all enjoy potent authority to initiate big-ticket litigation.

As with incentives on firms to control their agents, miscalibrating incentives affecting enforcers may impede efforts to achieve the desired reduction of legal violations at acceptable cost. Consider the criminal enforcer whose conduct is the subject of this volume. Most students of corporate liability agree that criminal prosecution of firms is the most severe form of enterprise liability and that the criminal remedy should be reserved for a small number of the "worst" cases in which it is most needed. (Some argue, of course, that criminal liability for firms should be abolished, a debate I will not enter here.) This stance ordinarily leads to discussion of two forms of control: replacing the *respondeat superior* regimes that dominate corporate criminal liability with more discerning vicarious liability rules that would select for the gravity of cases;[3] and altering prosecution guidelines and other forms of control that determine how prosecutors select corporate cases for charging.[4]

This perspective on criminal enterprise liability omits something potentially crucial. The prosecutor's decision whether and how to charge a corporate case criminally depends in important part on the operation of civil liability regimes that run alongside the criminal enforcement apparatus.[5] Ian Ayres and John Braithwaite famously argued that an effective scheme for regulating organizations should be pyramidal, with escalating layers of increasingly sharp measures of control, starting at the bottom with self-regulation and capping off at the top with harsh forms of punishment.[6] In such a pyramidal scheme, each more serious form of control ought to be used more sparingly than the less intrusive measure below it. The most powerful sanctions should be used least. But some form of very damaging sanction is essential because, without a sharp point on the pyramid, lower tiers of control lose influence.

Something like the converse also holds true. Lower levels of regulation must be sufficiently effective to prevent too many cases being pushed too quickly to the top of the pyramid. Holding with the metaphor, a system for regulating organizations that too soon and too often bypasses civil tiers to reach for the criminal capstone will become an inverted pyramid that will be unstable and lack a graduated scheme of incentives. Assuming for purposes of argument that the imposition of corporate criminal liability is as potentially costly as its critics argue, a regulatory scheme that tends to start with that form of liability will fail beneficially to balance regulatory effectiveness against cost.

How might a system of enterprise liability end up as an inverted pyramid? If civil forms of control appear to lack sufficient bite, regulators seeking to control conduct within organizations will tend to reach for criminal remedies. This effect will be most pronounced with respect to the level just below criminal liability: liability in civil regulatory actions. Especially if civil regulatory liability does not introduce sufficiently more meaningful sanctions than private civil liability (the next tier in turn below), there is risk that public enforcers will conclude that only criminal liability can achieve marginally greater effectiveness than private lawsuits, self-regulation, and other forms of control.

There is reason to think this dynamic operates to some degree in the relationship between criminal cases brought by the DOJ and civil regulatory actions brought by the SEC. Contrast the usual remedies obtained by the DOJ in a contemporary corporate prosecution with those the SEC usually obtains. A DOJ action typically will settle with a DPA. Under a DPA the offending firm, in addition to paying a monetary penalty, will admit criminal wrongdoing, accept institutional fault for having encouraged or allowed the violations, and agree to undertake a package of novel reforms and controls that is designed to reduce risk of future violations and is accompanied by severe consequences for failure to follow through.[7] Notice that there is nothing traditionally criminal in this arrangement—no guilty plea or jury verdict, no sentencing, no punishment other than a fine.

An (often parallel) SEC action will usually settle with a consent decree under which the offending firm will neither admit nor deny wrongdoing, will agree to be enjoined for some period from further violations, will pay a large monetary penalty, and sometimes (though often not) agree to some institutional changes.[8] Other than the injunction, violations of which are rarely if ever charged, little in this arrangement distinguishes it from private civil liability as a means of sanctioning firms. The replacement of a private citizen as plaintiff with the federal securities cop adds some gravity to the proceedings, but the routine practice of concluding cases without any finding or admission of wrongdoing by the firm may substantially blunt that effect. The SEC very rarely tries a case against a firm, and the "neither admit nor deny" settlement is a fixture in SEC practice.

In the current arrangement, the public enforcer asking herself how to achieve regulatory objectives in a major matter of financial misconduct within a large corporation or partnership is apt to say something like this: "In civil proceedings, the firm is likely to end up writing two checks, one to the class action plaintiffs and one to the SEC. These payments will hurt but they probably have been planned for and, the stock price having taken the expected hit from revelation of sanctionable wrongdoing, funds are being set aside for this if they had not been reserved already. Beyond the checks, the firm will have to admit nothing and will not be required to do much, if anything, to change itself, nor does it face a substantial risk of a later charge for violating an injunction. Does any of this accomplish enough, especially if this instance of wrongdoing occurred even though this firm or peer firms were subject to these forms of liability in the past? Only a potential criminal action that produces a clear normative signal about wrongdoing, a lasting admission from the firm, and a set of serious, enforceable reform measures promises to achieve what is supposed to be the objective here: the use of enterprise liability to reduce risk of harmful wrongdoing in corporations in the future."

The situation, at least in securities fraud liability for firms, is one of civil regulatory liability marginally distinguishing itself from private liability and criminal liability striving to rework itself into a form of civil regulatory liability. Maybe this is not cause for worry. If one thinks criminal liability should be avoided when possible and civil regulatory liability ought to do materially more to control firms than private civil liability, then the DOJ's hybrid civil-criminal system of DPA settlements might fit comfortably in the regulatory space one wants occupied. But worries about too much criminal enforcement against firms have only grown stronger through a period of institutionalization of the criminal settlement. Still, we hear the claim that criminal liability is potentially disastrous for firms—that it is a legal weapon of mass destruction that can unleash reputational and other forces that cannot be controlled and that it affords too much leverage to DOJ actors who may wield this power without clear vision of proper regulatory objectives.

The response to these concerns should be plain. Enhance civil regulatory liability so that it, not criminal proceedings or the settlement thereof, lays claim to the regulatory tier between private civil liability and full-blown criminal prosecution. Failing to do so perpetuates a perverse dynamic whereby civil liability practices encourage resort to criminal redress. A different system of civil regulatory liability could alter the incentives operating on public enforcers. The result could be reduced use of the criminal action that everybody seems to agree is overdeployed and should be reserved, at most, for the infrequent, egregious, example-making case.

In the remainder of this chapter, I will address how to reform the civil regulatory action with this objective in mind, what is necessary to bring about such reforms, and problems that might arise from the adoption of such reforms. I will focus on the SEC enforcement action, where substantial changes appear most readily available under existing law. My arguments ought to be amenable to extension to other realms of enterprise regulation.

I. The Civil-Criminal Gap

In current practice, three features primarily distinguish a criminal enterprise case from a civil regulatory action: it stigmatizes more, it decides more, and it requires more of the firm.

The stigmatic effect—what economic analysis designates the reputational sanction—comes largely from the category of the proceeding itself. While the matter is extremely hard to measure or quantify, the mere ascription of the label "criminal" to a firm, even at a preliminary investigative stage, can be punitive. This must be true because routinely in the corporate context rational, well-informed managers strive mightily to avoid even criminal allegations against their firms, and they move rapidly, often at major expense, to forestall or resolve potential criminal proceedings short of charging and trial. The potential stigmatic effect of a criminal proceeding will vary, of course, with the reputational stake of the firm (a pharmaceutical manufacturer will fear a criminal charge more than a garbage hauler) and the relevance of the particular matter to reputation (an oil company's spoiling of an ecosystem may not have much effect on people's desire to buy its fuel).[9] But the prospect of criminal charges always gets a firm's attention and frequently is perceived as threatening the firm's survival.

The communicative impact of a criminal case will be greater, of course, if the legal proceedings say more, and say more decisively, about the nature of the firm's wrongdoing. Criminal proceedings against a firm can be resolved in three ways (excepting the rare acquittal) but almost always end in only one of them. A trial might take place that results in a jury verdict. This resolution speaks particularly loudly because it represents the judgment of a disinterested group that considered a full portfolio of evidence and was instructed to base its judgment on near certainty. Of course, virtually no corporate criminal cases go to trial. Alternatively, a firm might plead guilty to a criminal charge. This speaks loudly as well. Admission of wrongdoing by a corporation is always unusual and noteworthy. The solemnity of a criminal plea before a judge lends particular weight to a corporate admission.

More commonly, a firm will enter into a criminal settlement with the government short of charging, or at least short of a guilty plea or trial. The idea of a "criminal settlement" is arguably an oxymoron. Ordinarily criminal cases are not "settled"; the defendant pleads guilty, usually with a plea agreement, or persists in a not-guilty plea and the case goes to trial. DPAs, pretrial diversion, and other nontraditional forms of resolution are modern innovations. Corporate criminal practice has adopted this approach as a means of resolving cases while avoiding pleas and trials, in part because of the potentially overpotent communicative effects of pleas and verdicts. A DPA is crafted to retain some of the message effects of a criminal proceeding by requiring the firm to admit a criminal violation and the facts making out that violation. In current practice, DPAs do "decide" the criminal case even if they do not result in adjudication.

Criminal cases against firms also tend to require more of firms. If a firm pleads guilty or is convicted at trial, it is subject to sentencing by a judge. The U.S. Sentencing Guidelines, while no longer binding, are the most influential authority in corporate sentencing. The Guidelines authorize courts not just to levy monetary sanctions on firms but also to impose probationary conditions requiring them "to remedy the harm caused by the offense and to eliminate or reduce the risk that the instant offense will cause future harm."[10] The Guidelines' principal innovation in corporate sentencing is to tether the determination of financial penalties to the quality of a firm's compliance efforts.[11] In theory at least, firms that make more extensive compliance efforts will be punished less should those efforts fail than they would be had they made no such efforts. In other words, in addition to empowering courts to order firms to change their practices *ex post*, the Guidelines encourage *ex ante* changes in the internal practices of firms.

Current DPA practice goes beyond the Guidelines in requiring changes in firm practices and governance. A typical DPA will require a firm to agree to alter or halt specific business lines or practices, to adopt or strengthen mechanisms for detecting and responding to agent wrongdoing, to accept intervention of an outside monitor with broad power to measure and report on the firm's compliance, and to afford managers and employees additional resources for reporting violations and learning how to avoid them.[12]

The reformative provisions of a DPA are connected directly to the aspect of the DPA that is decisive about the firm's wrongdoing. The firm is required fully to admit wrongdoing in the settlement, including through a detailed factual admission. Though the firm has not pled guilty or been found guilty, it can no longer contest the merits of the case because it has conceded them. The firm must follow through on its commitments under the DPA or it faces near-certain and swift criminal liability.

Setting aside questions of the success of DPA practice, the aim is clear: to use the special bite of the criminal remedy against firms not just to punish them monetarily, in the form of a fine that might not be distinguishable from a large damages award in a civil class action, but to change firms to make future harm and wrongdoing by the firm's agents less likely.

Compare the civil regulatory action, using the context of securities fraud. The SEC also settles almost all its enforcement actions. These civil settlements stigmatize less, decide less, and require less of the firm. Not only does an SEC settlement not match the criminal action's tendency to ascribe the label of wrongdoer to a firm, it ascribes nothing. Standard practice in SEC enforcement is to permit settling firms to "neither admit nor deny" allegations in the

SEC's legal filings.[13] In other words, an SEC enforcement action typically proceeds this way: the government says Firm A lied to the market about its financial results; Firm A denies having lied; some months later, the SEC says Firm A has agreed to pay a fine and be enjoined from future lies in order to resolve the charges against it; Firm A says it neither admits nor denies it lied and is happy to have put this liability matter behind it. Except that the complainant (the SEC) can re-trumpet its allegations in public documents, this practice does not seem distinguishable from a typical corporate settlement of a large lawsuit.

Undeniably, SEC enforcement actions have some stigmatic impact. The evidence shows that firms suffer hits to their share price, sometimes substantial, upon first revelation of an SEC investigation.[14] It is less clear whether that impact stems from the SEC's involvement in the matter or simply from the market learning that a firm's financial practices might be unreliable.[15] A later settlement with the SEC does not seem to impose large additional reputational sanction on a firm, suggesting that the regulatory action itself may be of lesser informational significance to the market.[16]

But the enforcement action itself says little. In the criminal action, a firm is both accused of and admits wrongdoing, usually in the form of a detailed description of the conduct and actors who violated the law and the relationship of those actions to the firm's management and practices. In the SEC action, the firm is alleged to have engaged in a less serious form of wrongdoing. Less culpability is required to establish civil liability, the burden of proof is much lower, and so on. The firm does not admit even bare-bones liability, much less facts of the wrongdoing. If one purpose of public enforcement of the law is to communicate messages, the SEC process greatly underexploits the message potential of law enforcement. This is a major thrust of U.S. District Judge Jed S. Rakoff's noted recent decision to reject the SEC's settlement of a high-profile matter of fraud relating to the 2008 financial crisis.[17]

SEC enforcement also has underexploited the forward-looking potential of public law enforcement. Criminal DPAs now routinely require firms to reorganize business operations, adopt compliance measures, submit to enhanced monitoring for legal violations, and create systems to encourage and protect whistle-blowers. Recently SEC settlements have begun to incorporate some of these measures.[18] But these settlements rarely grant broad powers to independent monitors to ensure compliance (at most they require hiring a consultant and following its advice), and they lack sufficient incentives for firms to follow through.[19]

Legally, the forward-looking element of an SEC settlement is an injunctive order that tells a firm what securities laws have always told it: do not violate the law. The injunction represents, at most, a probation under which the firm faces swifter, more certain, and larger penalties for a future violation than it did prior to its first violation. But these orders almost never produce later charges of injunction violation against firms. I failed to discover evidence of a single instance in which the SEC has sought redress for a firm's inadequate compliance with so-called undertakings in an injunctive settlement (judicial or administrative) requiring reform measures by the firm.

The lack of enforcement for compliance produces a double deficit. It deprives the enforcement system of a potentially powerful incentive on firms to comply with reform commitments, in the form of a tangible, observable risk of legal consequences for noncompliance. And it misses a potentially efficient legal device for regulating firms. A shortcut proceeding for an injunction violation is likely to be far quicker, less costly, and more difficult for a defendant to resist than the SEC's filing of an original lawsuit.

The point about admissions in settlements connects tightly to the point about settlements having reform requirements that carry real teeth. The criminal DPA highly motivates firms to follow through on their obligations because the admission of facts and liability generally required in a DPA means that, if DOJ seeks relief for noncompliance with the settlement, it does so with a very big stick. Admission in hand, DOJ could proceed almost directly to a full criminal conviction, with all its consequences, including sentencing before a judge. The SEC does not carry the big stick of an express route to full judicial (or administrative) remedies for the original violation—because it has no admission on the merits by the firm.

Return to the perspective of a hypothetical public enforcer looking at these two systems and deciding what to do in an instance of serious law violations within a corporation. The enforcer understands her mission to be to pursue the case in a manner that advances the basic objectives of punishment to deliver retribution to wrongdoers and efficiently reduce future production of social harm. She knows that retribution qua retribution is not a meaningful aim because a corporation cannot feel pain from deprivation of liberty or being labeled a criminal. Her only socially beneficial objective can be to enforce the law against the firm in a manner likely to reduce the incidence of future legal violations at justifiable cost.

On the one hand, the enforcer has a system that will assign a strong form of blame to the corporation that will communicate clearly to both outsiders and insiders the seriousness of what went wrong and the importance of working in the future to avoid occasions for such condemnation. This system will further provide a vehicle for tailoring remedies to the specific firm and wrongdoing. On the other hand, the enforcer has a system that rests primarily on the blunt instrument of a large monetary sanction. This system is supposed to discourage future law violations by pricing them higher. But this approach is not distinguishable from that of any civil liability mechanism. It has insufficient fealty to the idea that public law enforcement has any special role or potency in the projects of specific and general deterrence.

If the enforcer cares about more than churning cases and filling government coffers—if she hopes her efforts might lessen the future need for her and others' costly interventions—she is highly likely to choose the criminal remedy over the civil one, or at least choose it in addition to the civil one. The shortage of special features in the civil regulatory proceeding will be a major motivation for her choice. Her choice becomes even more likely if the particular firm or peer firms have been subject to civil sanctions for past instances of the same or similar violations. In that case it becomes almost undeniable that a civil proceeding's slack message effects will not substantially affect the firm's or the industry's behavior. (Of course, in the current system there is no such single enforcer choosing between civil and criminal liability, even though criminal enforcers are directed to consider the adequacy of available civil remedies before charging. But, as Brandon Garrett discusses in this volume, there is extensive dialogue between the SEC and DOJ over enforcement and litigation decisions.)

A straightforward way to alter the public enforcer's incentives is to adjust the nature of the civil proceeding so that it approximates more the criminal proceeding. To do so, one need not render the civil proceeding criminal. Indeed, the criminal proceeding has already done some of this work by altering itself through DPA practice to become more civil in nature. Why has the criminal proceeding been moving in the civil direction? Because of the concern about the overpotency of corporate criminal liability that has produced so much of the criticism of the doctrine and practice that lead to criminal charges against firms.

Likewise, we should move the civil proceeding in the direction of the criminal proceeding, to provide enforcers with a more attractive alternative to criminal liability for firms. Doing so promises further to reduce excessive costs that can result from the imposition of criminal liability, which has potentially beneficial message effects but can unleash uncontrollable and overly harsh reputational consequences.[20] If the criminal and civil regulatory forms of enterprise liability were to meet halfway—in the space that everyone, including the DOJ, seems to be seeking between simple monetary sanctions and the potential "corporate death sentence" of a prosecution—then a more supple and efficient enforcement scheme could emerge. If, however, a large chasm remains between criminal and civil proceedings, then the relative weakness of civil regulatory liability is likely to continue to make civil liability its own worst enemy, causing public enforcers to find it inadequate in cases of serious wrongdoing.

I will now consider measures necessary to push civil regulatory liability in the direction of criminal liability.

II. Reform Measures

Returning to the three distinctive characteristics of criminal enterprise liability, civil regulatory liability should be refashioned so that it has greater reputational consequences, decides more, and requires more of firms. Again choosing SEC enforcement of the securities laws as my example, several changes in law and practice could accomplish these objectives.

I will start with the third objective—requiring more of firms—because it is the simplest to adjust. The Securities Act of 1933 and the Exchange Act of 1934 have always included broad grants of power to the SEC to seek injunctive relief in federal court in response to fraud violations.[21] Injunctions in SEC enforcement actions, as well as the exercise by federal district courts of equitable powers, have long been available in any enforcement case in which the SEC can demonstrate "a reasonable likelihood of further violations in the future"—a condition that explicitly rests on the deterrence-based justification for including forward-looking remedies in a scheme of corporate enforcement.[22] A feature of the Sarbanes-Oxley Act of 2002 made this power more explicit and extended it, by authorizing the SEC to ask a federal court to grant "any equitable relief that may be appropriate or necessary for the benefit of investors."[23] This equitable power easily encompasses measures designed to prevent future wrongdoing, such as requiring a firm to alter business practices, institute compliance programs, submit to monitoring for future violations, and encourage and protect whistle-blowers.

DOJ prosecutors, who enjoy a high degree of independence from bureaucratic controls (especially in decentralized U.S. Attorneys' offices),[24] have been more innovative and freewheeling in developing remedies and settlement schemes. With the criminal charge at their disposal, they also enjoy greater leverage to force these measures into settlements. SEC enforcement lawyers are more tightly controlled by a central bureaucracy within the Enforcement Division, and their charging and settlement decisions require express approval of the five-member commission. This can slow things down substantially, which can greatly reduce the effectiveness of an enforcer's efforts to persuade firms to agree to extensive settlement terms.

One might be pessimistic that institutional redesign can dramatically alter SEC behavior in the face of pressures on the SEC staff to fall under the capture of those they regulate. Regulatory capture is a potential problem for any agency, prosecution offices included. The relevant issue is relative vulnerability to capture. The SEC has a strong tradition of independence compared with many other agencies that regulate more narrowly and with greater intimacy. The SEC's jurisdiction and mandate are broad. The Enforcement Division in particular is accustomed to taking a more adversarial posture toward the industries within its domain.[25] And the new director of enforcement, a former prosecutor, has signaled his intent to press the division further in that direction.[26]

Remaining impediments to more far-reaching SEC settlements can be removed. In serious cases with important message implications and potential, SEC settlements should require a package of DPA-like remedial terms that include strong monitoring and *ex post* enforcement features. The commission—perhaps through formal rulemaking—should establish guidelines that specify objectives and measures for the settlement process that are designed to bring about forward-looking and lasting change in offending firms.[27] The commission should state that if firms refuse to pursue productive negotiation of such measures in cases in which they are appropriate, the SEC will seek federal court order of those measures in litigation. And, as the new director of enforcement has quickly recognized and stated, the SEC must internally streamline its enforcement process.[28]

That leaves the problem of how to make the SEC's litigation threat credible and sufficiently potent. Firms must believe that nonsettlement will lead to trial, that trial is likely to lead to loss, and that loss is likely to mean imposition of stronger sanctions. To generate this belief, the SEC must try some cases and be happy to try more of them. The Enforcement Division very rarely goes to trial, and virtually never in cases against large corporations. Its attorneys who work in the courts (who in turn are separated, unlike DOJ lawyers, from the attorneys who investigate the cases) more closely resemble the "litigators" of large corporate law firms than the trial lawyers who staff U.S. Attorneys' offices. Changes in culture, hiring practices, and internal review mechanisms and incentives at the SEC are necessary to make the SEC a trial-ready and trial-eager operation that can credibly threaten firms in settlement negotiations. The SEC should move away from its current enforcement culture of aiming toward a press conference at which the agency announces another large payment from a corporation.

Firms must also believe that remedies imposed by a court after trial are likely to be more onerous than the conditions of a settlement with the SEC. The criminal liability that awaits a firm that refuses a DPA of course cannot be imposed in an SEC enforcement lawsuit. But a court can impose very large monetary sanctions. Outside the settlement context, firms exert little control over the size of that penalty, meaning that an enforcement action looms much larger over the financial future of a firm when the potential of a trial and court-ordered penalties increases uncertainty. The SEC should be prepared to bargain away some of the potential monetary penalty, in addition to uncertainty about that penalty, in exchange for remedial measures more likely to avert further wrongdoing and harm. Large settlement numbers are impressive in *Wall Street Journal* headlines, but they may not have adequate lasting effect.

There is another possible explanation for the SEC's less active role than DOJ in settlements that require changes in the conduct of firms. The agency might believe it lacks the expertise and, even more, the resources to implement an enforcement regime that resembles the DOJ's DPA scheme. An obvious rejoinder is to say that the specialized SEC ought to be, if anything, more confident than the generalist DOJ in its ability to design systems for reducing fraud in corporations and financial markets. If the DOJ can do it, so can the SEC.

The resource concern is more serious. As the DOJ has demonstrated, some of the costs of such a system can be outsourced to corporations, as, for example, through the appointment of private monitors funded by the firm. Still, an Enforcement Division forced to try massive cases of financial reporting failure against large corporations more frequently, and tasked with ongoing monitoring and enforcement of complex settlements, might grind to a halt, leaving unaddressed many important cases of individual and enterprise wrongdoing in markets.

But the DOJ has limited resources too. It rarely tries a corporate case, yet its threats are credible. The potency of the criminal remedy explains much of that credibility, but that does not mean the SEC would have to try many cases to obtain greater settlement leverage. An occasional trial against a large defendant, followed by the imposition of severe court-ordered remedies, should be sufficient to encourage forceful settlement agreements in the lion's share of SEC cases against firms. If the Enforcement Division needed some additional resources to accomplish this—such as the funding of a small trial unit dedicated to taking a few big cases all the way—the money would be well spent.

Now to the harder part of reforming SEC enforcement against firms. To make enforcement cases decide more and impose greater reputational effects (of course also enhancing the SEC's ability to lever remedial measures in settlements), one would want to eliminate the "neither admit nor deny" feature of the SEC enforcement case. This practice is pernicious because it gives away much of what distinguishes a public enforcement case from one of private liability.

In private litigation, almost all of which settles in the context of securities fraud, plaintiffs are generally happy to bargain away any finding or admission of wrongdoing by the defendant because plaintiffs are in it for themselves. If they obtain the compensation they seek, they care not whether the firm tells the world it did something wrong. Regulatory enforcement is pursued on behalf of the public, who for good reasons would very much like to be told whether the firm is a lawbreaker and, if so, exactly how and to what extent. The public would much prefer to learn this from an admission or a careful adjudicatory process than from the mere allegation of it in a federal agency's complaint that, beyond at most a motion to dismiss, is never subject to the scrutiny of legal process.

Trying more enforcement cases would recover a bit of this loss of the law's communicative potential. But message effects should not be squandered in the settlement process either. The SEC, like the DOJ, should require firms to admit liability and the facts of wrongdoing when it seeks to sanction them for serious violations of the securities laws. It is practically an abdication of responsibility for a public enforcer to resolve almost all its cases with no conclusion by the legal process as to whether wrongdoing occurred—especially an enforcer that professes to be in the business of making examples and communicating messages to market participants about norms of behavior and legal compliance. The most that can be said for current practice is that "everyone knows" that when the SEC alleges a violation, that means the firm really did it. Imagine if a criminal prosecutor were to rest her enforcement practices on such a foundation: "I mostly just indict cases without requiring an admission, plea, or trial because the indictment itself speaks clearly enough and imposes ample sanction."

Of course I am being quite unfair. The SEC's "neither admit nor deny" practice has a good rationale. The obvious reason for the SEC to forgo requiring admissions by firms is that firms would mightily resist settlements with devastating potential in collateral civil litigation. Securities fraud class action lawsuits lead to billions of dollars of recovery against corporations every year. Given that Rule 10b-5 affords a right of action to both investors and the government, a civil class action lawsuit is certain in any case in which the SEC brings a significant enforcement action for fraud.

Because of the huge cost of trying a large, complex fraud action, defendant leverage in the settlement of such suits comes mostly from the motion to dismiss. The Private Securities Litigation Reform Act ("PSLRA") sought to reduce the costs of securities fraud class actions for defendants, especially the costs of settling "strike suits" to avoid the expense of discovery and summary judgment litigation, primarily by making the motion to dismiss easier to win. To survive a motion to dismiss, plaintiffs must plead particular facts giving rise to a strong inference (meaning one at least as strong as any alternative) that the defendant acted with the requisite state of mind ("scienter") for fraud liability.[29] This affords defendants a powerful weapon because state of mind is difficult to establish, even by inference, in the absence of access to a firm's records and witnesses through discovery.

Requiring firms to admit fraud in public enforcement proceedings obviously would remove not just the PSLRA's barriers but also potentially all barriers to private liability, including trial risk for the plaintiff. Class action plaintiffs could simply print a copy of the settlement documents in the SEC enforcement proceeding, take them to a judge and if necessary a jury, and offer them as admissions to support denial of a motion to dismiss or for summary judgment, or even to support a jury verdict.

It is not an acceptable answer to this problem to throw up one's hands and say that the "neither admit nor deny" practice in SEC settlements is unavoidable. Possibilities exist for dealing with the preclusive problem that admission-based settlement practices would present. Among the powers that the SEC enjoys but private plaintiffs do not is the ability to bring a case for securities fraud under Section 17 of the Securities Act rather than (or in addition to) a case under Rule 10b-5 of the Exchange Act.[30] The law of Section 17, unlike 10b-5 law, does not require proof of scienter for liability.[31] The SEC could ask firms to settle enforcement actions for fraud by admitting violation of section 17 but not violation of 10b-5.

This approach would have two limitations. Firms might still strongly resist settlement because they do not want to concede other elements of section 17 liability, such as materiality, that would also in part establish 10b-5 liability. And the message effects of a Section 17 settlement would be weaker than those of a 10b-5 settlement. This is precisely because the enforcement action would not communicate anything about the mental state accompanying the fraud, which is arguably the chief culpability measure for fraud and the one most commonly used to distinguish "mere" civil fraud from more serious fraud meriting regulatory or criminal sanctions.

Another approach would be to ensure that the SEC settlement does not precede resolution of the class action lawsuit. But this would be an ill-advised means of dealing with worries about collateral consequences. Public enforcement actions should rarely if ever be held hostage to private lawsuits. Delay can greatly weaken the benefits of public law enforcement, and unwelcome incentives are likely to develop, causing defendants to slow down civil litigation to avoid public sanctions.

More fundamental change would be needed to do away effectively and beneficially with the "neither admit nor deny" settlement. More direct responses to the problem would be to bar collateral use of an SEC settlement or, as many are arguing for a host of reasons, to couple the private lawsuit for securities fraud with the SEC enforcement action. Both approaches likely would require legislation, as well as new rulemaking, and would occasion comprehensive reevaluation of the private and public enforcement scheme for securities fraud.

An amendment to the existing PSLRA scheme could dictate that liability concessions and factual statements in litigation initiated by the SEC are inadmissible in civil class action lawsuits. Civil plaintiffs would retain the burden of producing facts sufficient to establish a strong inference of scienter at the motion to dismiss stage, as well as the burden of ultimately convincing a jury of the facts of the defendant's fraudulent conduct.

These protections might not be sufficient to encourage defendants to accept settlements with the SEC that include admissions of fraud. Even with evidentiary protections, defendants would not want to admit fraud in court on the record. Their concerns would include that judges and juries deciding related private lawsuits would inevitably learn of these admissions and could not be expected to keep them from affecting their decisions, and that it would be at the very least awkward for the firm's counsel to maintain: "Yes we said this was a fraud in our SEC settlement but let me show you why the plaintiffs can prove no such thing." Placing firms in this legal posture potentially would dilute the same message effects of the regulatory proceeding I am arguing should be nurtured and exploited.

This analysis leads to the conclusion that the private action for securities fraud needs rethinking and reform of a larger order. This may be a welcome conclusion because it dovetails with several recent arguments by scholars of securities law that the public and private liability scheme for securities fraud is badly suboptimal in deterring fraud.[32] My contention that existing incentives for public enforcers also are suboptimal adds another justification for recrafting the full liability scheme.

The envisioned reform is not of the PSLRA variety. The objective is not simply to tinker with the weights on the existing liability scale, making it a bit harder here and there for the private plaintiff to bring her case. The objective is to design a full scheme of fraud liability that gets all four forms of civil liability working together to produce effective deterrence: public liability of firms, public liability of individuals, private liability of firms, and private liability of individuals.

Present law and practice sometimes pursue all four forms of liability in seemingly arbitrary ways that do not recognize interactive effects. For example, settlement of class action suits for securities fraud will often impose huge liability on a firm without imposing significant individual liability on managers responsible for the fraud. This arguably fails to advance deterrence because firm liability falls on the innocent shareholders not lucky enough to have disposed of their equity stakes before revelation of the fraud. In the future, managers who decide whether to pursue fraud know they will not bear liability costs for fraud. At worst, they will lose employment. But that same fear of employment loss may be the motive for fraud.

Some have argued that the SEC ought to be granted review and approval powers over private securities fraud litigation in order to improve coordination among sanctioning mechanisms.[33] The SEC might be given the authority to veto the filing of a securities fraud class action and the consummation of a settlement of such a case when the case or settlement does not advance the public interest in deterring fraud. Among other things, such a power would enable the SEC to bargain with firms over private liability in the settlement of enforcement actions. For example, the SEC could offer resolution of private liability in exchange for a real admission of serious wrongdoing and meaningful remedial measures, as well as a substantial monetary penalty to go to a compensatory fund for harmed investors.

A simpler means of eliminating the problem of the preclusive effect of SEC settlements is to do away with the private right of action under 10b-5. The elimination of private civil liability would be an overly sweeping measure, at least as a first step. Enforcement resources for the SEC already are a major concern, and invigorating SEC enforcement against firms to any degree, as I am advocating, will require additional resources. Privatizing some securities fraud enforcement is likely to remain attractive to many, not least the SEC itself.

But if a sensible liability scheme includes a foundation of widely available private liability supplemented by public enforcement for a select and important group of cases, it makes little sense to continue to pursue such a scheme without empowering a knowledgeable body to sit in review of the system and make rational and well-informed decisions about which cases merit public enforcement. The involvement of such a body promises not only to spend enforcement resources more wisely but also to ensure that cases of public enforcement stigmatize more, decide more, and require more of firms.

III. Potential Problems with Reform

I have argued for extensive change in regulatory enforcement practice, in the name of more judicious use of the criminal enterprise sanction. Dramatic institutional change, especially in an area as large and hotly contested as securities enforcement, ensures big complications and big fights. For example, consideration of whether to supplement much of criminal enforcement against corporations with enhanced civil enforcement would need to include empirical analysis, to the extent feasible, of the relative costs of the civil versus criminal processes, to both the state and firms. This brief chapter is not the place to engage fully with such implications.

I will consider just two complicating questions at the conceptual level. First, who is to say that a renovated SEC enforcement practice would not produce the same potentially cataclysmic and uncontrollable reputational sanction against firms that is said to be a principal flaw of corporate criminal liability? Second, if another flaw of existing corporate criminal practice is the questionable competence of criminal enforcers at reforming business enterprises, who is to say that the SEC would be any better at the job?

The first question is particularly hard to answer, or even speculate about, because it involves a huge counterfactual. Reputational sanctions resist measurement and explanation. We know that in general firms experience substantial reductions in equity value when it is revealed that they have engaged in fraud. We can be reasonably sure that a large portion of those reductions are explained not by the expectation that the firm will suffer legal sanctions but by what new information about fraud reveals about a firm's reliability as a potential supplier, customer, partner, or investment. We also can easily observe that, at least within reputationally sensitive firms, firm managers believe that serious legal proceedings, especially criminal ones, can have potentially devastating effects on business.

We do not know, however, how much the legal process adds to reputational sanctions other than serving as a source in some cases for first revelation of the wrongdoing. Other than watching how rational managers run from it, we do not know how much more of a reputational sanction the criminal process imposes on firms than a civil regulatory process. Reasons for absence of knowledge include that a firm's publicly traded equity price—

the measure of reputational sanction that empiricists have used—is only one measure of an event's economic effects on a firm, and that equity markets do not fundamentally reflect the true value of enterprises.

Lack of evidence makes it difficult to say how much the mere label "criminal"—whether imposed by a court or admitted by a firm—explains the potential oversanctioning, as through collapse of the firm, that can occur when the DOJ proceeds fully in a criminal action. There are grounds for doubt. The "criminal" label alone cannot be enough to destroy a firm. Without killing firms, that label has been attached to reputationally sensitive firms in DPA settlements, along with serious inculpatory admissions. Why should an indictment, which represents only a probable cause finding, be *more* reputationally damaging than a full admission of criminality? The only conceivable reason is fear that the criminal process could put the firm out of business by leading to revocation of licensure. But revocation of licensure affects only some firms and is routinely bargained away in settlement of criminal cases.

While waiting for definitive evidence about reputational sanctions that may not be forthcoming, it makes sense to explore reputational effects experimentally. We currently have a system of imposing criminal liability on firms, or at least putting them in criminal liability's shadow, that is criticized for being too potent because it may impose a crippling reputational sanction that the legal system cannot forecast or control. Given this status quo, there is no good reason not to see what would happen to reputational sanctions if we began to replace some of those criminal or shadow-criminal proceedings with civil regulatory actions that aimed, among other things, to impose a greater reputational sanction than current civil practice. At the very worst, we would end up no better off because the enhanced civil process would turn out to have the very same effects as the existing criminal one. But this seems doubtful. More likely, we would discover a middle ground where the enforcement process would better exploit the beneficial influences of reputational sanctions without the same risk of letting loose an uncontrollable force that produces oversanctioning.

The second question I have raised is whether SEC enforcement personnel would be subject to the same criticism currently leveled at DOJ lawyers in corporate criminal practice: that they are not equipped to engage in corporate governance. Imposing remedial measures on firms through DPAs can waste corporate assets, interfere with efficient management of the firm, and perhaps even make control of wrongdoing within firms more difficult. This critique has at least two components. One is that enforcers act *ex post* in response to wrongdoing, whereas governance design is better conducted from an *ex ante* perspective. In other words, it is a bad idea to regulate by prosecution. The other component is that criminal prosecutors do not know anything about how to manage businesses.

The first element of the critique applies equally to SEC lawyers as to DOJ lawyers. If engaging in firm-specific *ex post* regulation is detrimental, then no enforcement practice should do anything other than impose sufficiently large monetary penalties on firms to deter future wrongdoing. On this argument, even the Sentencing Guidelines should steer judges away from imposing probationary conditions on firms.

This position does not directly engage with the debate I have entered. The purpose of enhancing regulatory enforcement against firms, I contend, is to do a better job at lower cost than would a practice dominated by criminal enforcement—*given* agreement about an objective of reforming firms to avert future violations.

In any event, reforming firms *is* a worthy project. To reject the idea that changing an organization can be an effective way to make wrongdoing less likely is to disregard a fundamental fact about corporate crime. Especially in the most serious and damaging cases that involve widespread unlawful practices, organizational structure and culture can be major causal factors in wrongdoing by a firm's agents.

I have argued elsewhere that corporate criminal enforcement ought to focus above all on cases of genuine *institutional* production of wrongdoing.[34] Those are cases in which ascribing blame at the institutional rather than individual level is most justified and most likely to send useful messages about how institutions ought to arrange themselves so as not to produce lawbreaking. If holding firms responsible for their agents' violations is, in some instances at least, an ascription of responsibility to organizational culture, practices, and structure, then it makes little sense to miss an opportunity in that process to correct problems in culture, practices, and structure. Those problems can be much more clearly visible from an *ex post*, wrongdoing-centered perspective than from a generalized *ex ante* perspective. It might be true in the context of individual punishment that, with rehabilitation, "nothing works." But we have not yet learned that to be true for corporations.[35]

That leaves the question of who ought to be doing the rehabilitation. It cannot be the firm itself, at least not alone, because by definition a case of public enforcement is a case in which self-regulation has failed. Three choices remain: the executive branch enforcer, a court, or a private third party. The DOJ's current DPA practice combines the executive branch enforcer with a private third party hired to serve as an outside monitor of the firm's efforts to reform its practices. An enhanced SEC enforcement process of the type I suggest would be superior at least because it would combine all three possible actors.

In a settlement in a district court injunctive action, the SEC could, like the DOJ, require a firm to make changes, and it could delegate some or most of the monitoring function to a private third party. But unlike a DPA, such a settlement would require the approval of a federal judge and could, through reporting requirements, include oversight of the monitoring and compliance process by the federal court. This would address a major objection to current DPA practice: the almost complete lack of judicial review.[36] In addition, the SEC might improve upon present DPA practice by seeking third-party monitors with industry expertise suited to the firm in question. (Another alleged fault of DPA practice is to give the monitor job to litigation attorneys at large law firms, many of them former DOJ prosecutors.)

Having the SEC handle most cases of reform-based enforcement against firms might offer additional improvements over the present DOJ-driven practice. An objection to the DPA regime, at least among those representing firms, has been that individual prosecutors' offices, as well as Main Justice, have been inconsistent in their crafting and application of DPA settlements and that firms lack predictability when dealing with the DOJ over a case of serious wrongdoing. The SEC is more bureaucratized. The commission must approve settlements of cases brought by the Enforcement Division. That centralized process—as well as potential rulemaking and other guidance by the commission—could generate, over time, clearer and more consistent standards for the content and form of corporate settlements. This would fill a gap in current SEC policies, which include no such guidelines.

The objection would certainly remain that the SEC ought not be in the business of dictating matters of corporate governance that are the proper concern of state corporate law. But that objection tends to rest on a theoretical and unrealistic division between federal and state regulation of business enterprises.[37] The truth is that, by pursuing its core mission of regulating disclosure, the SEC inevitably regulates primary behavior within corporations. For the SEC to settle a case of fraud in financial reporting by requiring a firm to alter its financial reporting practices is only to do more directly what it already does indirectly. Arguably the SEC's commissioners and professional staff are better equipped not only than DOJ lawyers but also than Delaware judges to determine how a firm might change its practices at acceptable cost to avoid future violations of the securities laws.

IV. Conclusion

A scheme for behavior control that includes overlapping forms of liability must account for the incentives that determine the choices enforcers and litigants make about which cases to pursue. A valid objective of a scheme with multiple layers of liability is to impose graduated incentives on actors whose behavior is subject to control, so that increasingly more serious (and increasingly fewer) instances of wrongdoing are met with increasingly more severe sanctions. In a scheme with such an objective, incentives are perverse if they encourage enforcers to bypass lower levels of control in favor of higher ones, leading to harsh treatment of more cases than are treated less severely.

At least in the enforcement of the securities laws—and possibly in other areas in which criminal liability for firms overlaps regulatory liability—the current liability scheme produces perverse incentives for enforcers. The DOJ has been proceeding more frequently with criminal investigations, charges, and settlements against firms in part because the civil process does not offer a package of remedies that fully occupies the regulatory tier between private civil and public criminal enforcement. Reforming the SEC enforcement process against firms so that the SEC process stigmatizes more, decides more, and requires more of firms would help that process occupy the vacant regulatory space. The result would be more judicious use of the criminal sanction against firms. That appears to be a common goal among judges, academics, practitioners, and business enterprises.

NOTES

1. *E.g.*, Jennifer Arlen, *Corporate Crime and Its Control*, *in* 1 The New Palgrave Dictionary of Economics and the Law 492, 493 (Peter Newman ed., 1998); Lewis A. Kornhauser, *An Economic Analysis of the Choice Between Enterprise and Personal Liability for Accidents*, 70 Cal. L. Rev. 1345 (1982); Alan O. Sykes, *The Economics of Vicarious Liability*, 93 Yale L.J. 1231 (1984); Reinier H. Kraakman, *Corporate Liability Strategies and the Costs of Legal Controls*, 93 Yale L.J. 857 (1984).

2. Jennifer Arlen, *The Potentially Perverse Effects of Corporate Criminal Liability*, 23 J. Legal Stud. 833 (1994).

3. *E.g.*, Pamela H. Bucy, *Corporate Ethos: A Standard for Imposing Corporate Criminal Liability*, 75 Minn. L. Rev. 1095 (1991); Jennifer Arlen & Reinier Kraakman, *Controlling Corporate Misconduct: An Analysis of Corporate Liability Regimes*, 72 N.Y.U. L. Rev. 687 (1997); Samuel W. Buell, *The Blaming Function of Entity Criminal Liability*, 81 Ind. L.J. 473 (2006); William S. Laufer & Alan Strudler, *Corporate Intentionality, Desert, and Variants of Vicarious Liability*, 37 Am. Crim. L. Rev. 1285 (2000).

4. *See* Brandon L. Garrett, *Structural Reform Prosecution*, 93 Va. L. Rev. 853 (2007).

5. U.S. Dep't of Justice, U.S. Attorneys' Manual, § 9–28.1100 (Principles of Federal Prosecution of Business Organizations), *available at* http://www.usdoj.gov/opa/documents/corp-charging-guidelines.pdf.

6. Ian Ayres & John Braithwaite, Responsive Regulation: Transcending the Deregulation Debate 19–53 (1992).

7. *E.g.*, U.S. Dep't of Justice, U.S. Attorney, Southern District of New York, KPMG—Deferred Prosecution Agreement (Aug. 26, 2005), *available at* http://www.usdoj.gov/usao/nys/pressreleases/August05/kpmgdpagmt.pdf; U.S. Dep't of Justice, U.S. Attorney, District of Florida, UBS AG—Deferred Prosecution Agreement, *available at* http://www.usdoj.gov/tax/UBS_Signed_Deferred_Prosecution_Agreement.pdf.

8. *E.g.*, Press Release, U.S. Sec. & Exch. Comm'n, Commission Settles Civil Fraud Action Against Vivendi Universal, Release No. 2003–184 (Dec. 23, 2003), *available at* http://www.sec.gov/news/press/2003-184.htm; Press Release, U.S. Sec. & Exch. Comm'n, SEC Announces Agreement with Canadian Imperial Bank of Commerce, Release No. 2003–180 (Dec. 22, 2003), *available at* http://www.sec.gov/news/press/2003-180.htm.

9. Cindy R. Alexander, *On the Nature of the Reputational Penalty for Corporate Crime: Evidence*, 42 J. L. & Econ. 489 (1999).

10. U.S. Sentencing Guidelines Manual Ch. 8 §§ 8B1.2, 8D1.3 (2008).

11. *Id.* § 8C2.5.

12. *E.g.*, KPMG DPA, *supra* note 7.

13. *See supra* note 8. The SEC recently produced a publicly available manual providing guidance to its attorneys about how to handle enforcement matters. The manual, however, focuses on investigative practices and says almost nothing about settlement of cases. U.S. Sec. & Exch. Comm'n, Division of Enforcement, Enforcement Manual (Oct. 6, 2008), *available at* http://www.sec.gov/divisions/enforce/enforcementmanual.pdf.

14. Jonathan M. Karpoff, D. Scott Lee & Gerald S. Martin, *The Cost to Firms of Cooking the Books*, 43 J. Fin. & Quant. Analysis 581 (2008); *see also* Stephen Choi & Marcel Kahan, *The Market Penalty for Mutual Fund Scandals*, 87 B.U. L. Rev. 1021 (2007).

15. The best current effort to tease these two factors apart, Jonathan M. Karpoff, D. Scott Lee & Gerald S. Martin, *The Legal Penalties for Financial Misrepresentation* (Working Paper, May 1, 2007), *available at* http://papers.ssrn.com/sol3/papers.cfm?abstract_id=933333, relies on the obviously debatable assumption that the reputational effect independent of the government's involvement is measured by a firm's overall decline in market value less any legal penalties ultimately imposed. *Id.* at 19–21.

16. *See id.* at 11.

17. SEC v. Bank of America Corp., 2009 WL 2916822 (S.D.N.Y. Sept. 14, 2009).

18. These developments are thoroughly catalogued and summarized in two works: Jayne W. Barnard, *Corporate Therapeutics at the Securities and Exchange Commission*, 3 Colum. Bus. L. Rev. 793 (2008), and Jennifer O'Hare, *The Use of the Corporate Monitor in SEC Enforcement Actions*, 1 Brook. J. Corp. Fin. & Com. L. 89 (2006).

19. A typical recent settlement is *In re Applix, Inc.*, Securities Act of 1933 Release No. 8651, 2006 SEC LEXIS 8 (Jan. 4, 2006), which required a firm charged with improper revenue recognition to hire and follow the recommendations of a consultant that would review its financial policies. Among the most ambitious recent settlements have been those involving "market timing" and "late trading" in the mutual fund industry. These settlements have required firms not only to hire and follow the recommendations of consultants but also to

appoint new independent trustees to their boards who undertake an obligation to report to the SEC on firms' reform progress. *See, e.g., In re* Banc of America Capital Management, LLC, Securities Act of 1933 Release No. 8538, 2005 SEC LEXIS 291 (Feb. 9, 2005).

20. Buell, *supra* note 3.

21. 15 U.S.C. §§ 77t, 78u(d) (2009).

22. SEC v. Savoy Indus. 587 F.2d 1149, 1168 (D.C. Cir. 1978) (quoting SEC v. Commonwealth Chem. Sec., Inc., 575 F.2d 90, 99–100 (2d Cir. 1978)).

23. 15 U.S.C. § 78u(d)(5).

24. *See* Daniel Richman, *Prosecutors and Their Agents, Agents and Their Prosecutors*, 103 Colum. L. Rev. 749 (2003); Daniel C. Richman, *Federal Criminal Law, Congressional Delegation, and Enforcement Discretion*, 46 U.C.L.A. L. Rev. 757 (1999).

25. *See* John C. Coffee, Jr., *The Spitzer Legacy and the Cuomo Future*, N.Y.L.J., Mar. 20, 2008, at 5.

26. *See* John Herzfeld & Phyllis Diamond, *Khuzami Unveils Broad Reorganization of Enforcement Divisions, New Subpoena Powers*, BNA Corp. Accountability & Fraud Daily, Aug. 7, 2009. The enforcement director's August 5, 2009, speech is available at http://www.securitiesdocket.com/wp-content/uploads/2009/08/speechfirst-100-days.pdf.

27. The only guidance the SEC has provided of this type is a recent statement about general factors the SEC will consider in deciding whether to impose a monetary penalty on a firm. Press Release, U.S. Sec. & Exch. Comm'n, Statement Concerning Financial Penalties (Jan. 4, 2006), *available at* http://www.sec.gov/news/press/2006-4.htm. This statement and related policies are currently subject to criticism and might be revised or revoked. *See* Mark K. Schonfeld, *Back to the Future: Chairman Shapiro Ends Pilot Program for Corporate Penalties, Eliminates Commission Pre-authorization, Allows Staff to Negotiate*, 41 BNA Sec. Reg. & L. Rep. 307 (Feb. 23, 2009).

28. *See supra* note 26.

29. 15 U.S.C. § 78u-4(b)(2).

30. Maldonado v. Dominguez, 137 F.3d 1, 6–8 (1st Cir. 1998); Landry v. All Am. Assur. Co., 688 F.2d 381, 387–92 (5th Cir. 1982).

31. Aaron v. SEC, 446 U.S. 680, 691 (1980).

32. Merritt B. Fox, *Civil Liability and Mandatory Disclosure*, 109 Colum. L. Rev 237 (2009); Amanda M. Rose, *Reforming Securities Litigation Reform: Restructuring the Relationship Between Public and Private Enforcement of Rule 10b-5*, 108 Colum. L. Rev. 1301 (2008); Jennifer H. Arlen, *Public Versus Private Enforcement of Securities Fraud* (2007) (working paper on file with author); John C. Coffee, Jr., *Reforming the Securities Class Action: An Essay on Deterrence and Its Implementation*, 106 Colum. L. Rev. 1534 (2006).

33. *E.g.*, Rose, *supra* note 32.

34. Buell, *supra* note 3.

35. *But see* Kimberly D. Krawiec, *Organizational Misconduct: Beyond the Principal-Agent Model*, 32 Fl. St. U. L. Rev. 571 (2005); Kimberly D. Krawiec, *Cosmetic Compliance and the Failure of Negotiated Governance*, 81 Wash. U. L.Q. 487 (2003).

36. Garrett, *supra* note 4.

37. *E.g.*, Paul G. Mahoney, *Mandatory Disclosure as a Solution to Agency Problems*, 62 U. Chi. L. Rev. 1047 (1995); Robert B. Ahdieh, *Trapped in a Metaphor: The Limited Implications of Federalism for Corporate Governance*, 77 Geo. Wash. L. Rev. 255 (2009); Mark J. Roe, *Washington and Delaware as Corporate Lawmakers*, 34 Del. J. Corp. L. 1 (2009).

5

Inside-Out Enforcement

LISA KERN GRIFFIN

A distinct regulatory characteristic of corporate fraud cases is the interaction between government agents and private enforcement and the outsourcing of some investigative functions. The increasing use of DPAs between the federal government and corporate defendants provides a key mechanism for regulation by prosecutors. DPAs are hybrids of plea agreements, consent decrees, and private contracts. They offer corporations an intermediate sanction that averts some of the collateral consequences of indictment and conviction, but they require in exchange full cooperation with the investigation and remedial measures after settlement. When corporations commit to assisting government agents, perform critical investigative tasks like employee interviews, and undertake prosecutor-mandated compliance programs, the boundaries between public and private roles blur. Those lines ordinarily are clearly drawn in the criminal realm, and crossing them creates some distortions. While there are significant advantages to outsourcing in light of the resource constraints and complexity of corporate criminal investigations, these partnerships tend to exacerbate a major drawback of settling cases by DPA: the piecemeal nature of the resolution. Reliance on the private sector also imports one of the most problematic features of regulatory partnerships into criminal adjudication, which is the potential for self-dealing.

To negotiate and sustain a DPA, corporations must remove legal and informational barriers between the government and their employees. In effect, prosecutors enlist the target corporation as a co-enforcer. When they do so, prosecutors cede some discretionary authority to corporations to identify culpable employees and affect the course of the investigation. The result can be ad hoc targeting of individual defendants. In addition, DPAs are less visible than adjudication, which detracts from both the coherence of the government's enforcement strategy and the accountability of prosecutors. Prosecutors also extract inside information by capitalizing on assistance from compliance industry professionals retained by the corporation itself, including lawyers, public accountants, private investigators, business consultants, and risk-management experts. Reliance on these intermediaries in the private sector raises both quality-control issues about the evidence and some of the concerns about capture that regulators confront in civil enforcement. Some DPAs further require corporations to retain third-party monitors to design, implement, and oversee remedial measures. The installation of monitors mandated and selected by prosecutors forces outsiders into a corporate governance role and risks added conflicts of interest.

This chapter will explore the nature of the collaboration between public enforcers and private parties that stems from current corporate enforcement strategies, the costs and benefits of those partnerships, and whether the experience of DPAs suggests that prosecutors should yield some remedial functions back to regulators. It will address as well the changing conceptions of public and private interests developing out of the 2008 economic crisis and the bailout of financial institutions and how those new entanglements might affect next steps.

I. Outsourcing: Strategies to Address Personnel and Expertise Constraints

Some level of private-sector participation in the administration of criminal law is necessary and standard. The government outsources many public functions, including important aspects of the criminal justice system like forensic analysis and prison management. In corporate enforcement, however, the government does not simply hire contractors; rather, prosecutors require corporations to use their own resources to investigate wrongdoing and oversee compliance with settlements.

Prosecutors turn to private-sector partners because they simply do not have the resources to go it alone when conducting complex, expensive corporate investigations. Federal agents cannot replicate the work of corporate internal investigators, who may spend millions of dollars and review hundreds of thousands of documents to prepare a report.[1] Federal Bureau of Investigation ("FBI") staffing levels effectively account for the participation of private-sector partners. Although the Bush administration declared a "war on corporate crime" in 2002, it had already begun shifting FBI agents from domestic criminal investigations to national security assignments in response to the events of 9/11. More than 1,800 agents, including one-third of those assigned to white-collar investigations, have been transferred to counterterrorism and intelligence duties.[2] There was an initial surge in high-profile corporate prosecutions following the Enron and WorldCom scandals of 2001 and 2002, but the number of cases has since declined, and recent proposals to augment the enforcement budget will not fully replenish the ranks of investigators and prosecutors.

The 2009 budget, the last of the Bush administration, added 100 new FBI agents for criminal investigations, including white-collar enforcement,[3] and the Obama administration's first budget included increased funding for both white-collar investigations and mortgage fraud enforcement, as well as a 13 percent increase in the SEC's budget.[4] The recently enacted Fraud Enforcement and Recovery Act and the pending Supplemental Anti-Fraud Enforcement for Our Market Act ("SAFE Markets Act") will also expand the number of prosecutors, agents, and analysts devoted to financial crimes and increase the enforcement budgets of both the FBI and the SEC.[5] This buildup is roughly comparable to the response to the savings and loan crisis of the 1980s. In its wake, strike forces in twenty-seven cities were staffed with more than 1,000 federal agents. But the $100 billion lost in the savings and loan crisis in the 1980s and the billions in losses stemming from the 2001 Enron bankruptcy and other corporate accounting restatements of that period all pale in comparison to the multi-trillion-dollar figures associated with shoring up the collapsed financial system. New funding can only support a limited number of investigators, and the administration has committed to maintaining counterterrorism staffing at the current level rather than reassigning agents within the FBI.[6] No conceivable increase will be sufficient to keep pace with the anticipated case inventory and intensified enforcement activity. The FBI is opening new corporate fraud investigations at a rate of about one per day, and there are approximately 560 related investigations already pending,[7] including large-scale inquiries into potential wrongdoing at Fannie Mae, Freddie Mac, AIG, Lehman Bros., Bear Stearns, and many subprime mortgage lenders.

The economic conditions that led to the federal bailout of troubled financial institutions have also exacerbated issues of institutional competence. Even with sufficient resources, federal agents would depend on some level of outsourcing to conduct investigations. They face an unwieldy number of cases, and they confront the expanding variety and complexity of corporate fraud as well. Financial instruments grow ever more intricate, and white-collar crime tends to be private. Both of those features place enforcers at a critical informational disadvantage relative to corporate insiders. The business environment also crosses multiple jurisdictions, and technology increases the specialized knowledge required to evaluate economic crime.

Setting aside the issue of forensic expertise, the sheer volume of evidence makes every case of accounting fraud or financial statement manipulation labor-intensive. Agents could not review millions of pages of documents and interview hundreds of potential witnesses in each investigation on their own.

Moreover, the infusion of trillions of dollars in taxpayer funds into the financial system requires more oversight and opens up new avenues for criminality. Any rapid distribution of government resources—recent examples include the Iraq reconstruction and the aftermath of Hurricane Katrina[8]—risks waste and abuse. The unprecedented scope of the cash outlay to financial institutions, combined with complex initiatives like government subsidies to private investors buying toxic assets, necessitates significant policing. The Special Inspector General for the Troubled Asset Relief Program ("SIGTARP") has expressly outsourced some investigative functions in the conventional way, by retaining outside legal, consulting, and accounting firms at government expense. Those firms, however, will assist primarily with internal controls at TARP. SIGTARP already is launching broader investigations into the misuse of bailout funds, and ground-up forensic accounting on this scale would be impossible. For these new initiatives as well, regulators will supplement limited enforcement resources by commandeering the fruits of corporations' own internal investigations.

II. Drawing Insiders Out: Cooperating Employees and Compliance Professionals

Without the assistance of corporate insiders, prosecutors would find it difficult if not impossible to identify which individuals within a firm are involved in criminal activity. Responsibility may be shared among departments, documents may be spread among different locations, and employees may be transferred. The DOJ has acknowledged that, because of these obstacles, corporate cooperation is "critical in identifying culprits and locating relevant evidence."[9]

That corporations' own compliance efforts should augment government inquiries has long been recognized and is codified in the organizational sentencing guidelines, which provide for reduced penalties where corporations cooperate by providing sufficient information "for law enforcement personnel to identify the nature and extent of the offense and the individual(s) responsible for the criminal conduct."[10] DOJ policies on DPAs, however, go a step further in terms of prosecutors' ongoing access to corporations and the assistance prosecutors require with identifying culpable employees and completing investigations. DPAs effectively convert private investigative activity into a prosecutorial entitlement. The Thompson Memo and its successors—which set forth the factors prosecutors should consider in weighing a corporation's cooperation and determining whether to indict—cite both "the corporation's timely and voluntary disclosure of wrongdoing and its willingness to cooperate in the investigation of its agents."[11] And DOJ officials have described complete cooperation as nothing short of producing "all the witnesses the government will need to figure out exactly what happened."[12] The pressure on a corporation to avoid indictment, enter into a DPA, and comply with its terms creates heavy prosecutorial leverage.[13] Prosecutors use that power not only to obtain historical reports and the records of internal investigations but also to direct surrogate interviews with employees and impose managerial reforms.

Early criticisms of DPAs focused on potential abuses of prosecutorial authority and the lack of accountability. In a November 2006 editorial in the *Wall Street Journal*, Richard Epstein called them sinister, likened them to Stalinist purge trials, and decried their negative impact on corporate governance.[14] The coercion of individual employees has also been a significant concern. Compulsory cooperation becomes problematic when prosecutors are overcoming their comparative informational disadvantage by obtaining from corporate intermediaries evidence they could not lawfully seek themselves. In the KPMG prosecution, for example, the DPA required the corporation to produce "employees who would talk, notwithstanding their constitutional right to remain silent."[15] DPAs thus implicate prosecutors in possible Fifth Amendment violations, as well as demands that may run afoul of the Sixth Amendment, such as the requirement to waive attorney-client and work product protections, and pressure to withhold attorneys' fees from employees.

The perceived balance of power between firms and prosecutors has shifted somewhat, however. Few commentators would now describe corporations as hapless. Business interests effectively lobbied Congress and pressured DOJ to change its position with regard to privileges and indemnification.[16] The Second Circuit also ruled, in *United States v. Stein*, that a corporation's decision not to compensate employees for attorneys' fees, when it results from prosecutorial pressure, is unconstitutional.[17] Employees still find themselves the scapegoats in settlements between employer and enforcer, but it is increasingly clear that when prosecutors procure investigative assistance from corporations, the abuse of the government's bargaining position is only one side of the problem. Toward the end of the Bush administration, editorials began to accuse DOJ of "going soft on corporate crime" by *allowing* companies to enter into DPAs.[18]

With some blame for the financial crisis placed on inadequate regulatory enforcement, DPAs are now being scrutinized to see if firms, for their part, used them to mask systemic failures and avoid other forms of liability. The compliance industry is populated by former prosecutors and regulators with the expertise to head off scrutiny or preempt investigations, and outsourcing investigations may place excessive discretionary authority in their hands. Corporations acquiesce in DPAs because of a clear preference to avoid indictment, but there may be other advantages as well. All things considered, firms might prefer to partner with the government and to seek deferred criminal resolutions than to face broader civil enforcement and sanctions, or "private attorneys general" bringing bounty-hunter suits like shareholders' actions.[19]

Corporations may also benefit from what is ultimately an ad hoc approach to enforcement. Prosecutors' deep dependence on insider information can lead to charging decisions governed by the degree of a firm's cooperation and the employees it can deliver rather than compatibility with larger enforcement goals. Compliance professionals can also frame prosecutions in advantageous ways. Whether prosecutors already have engaged the corporation or the firm self-reports, blame is pushed down through organizations. Reliance on private partners to build cases means that the regulated entity exercises significant control over where that blame lands. Corporate influence over the course of the investigation arises, for instance, when corporations discover fraud by employees but choose to settle with culpable agents rather than summon regulators. Firms weigh the potential taint of a prosecution and the risk of a parallel civil suit against the internal deterrent effect of charges, the advantages of deploying mandatory federal restitution provisions, and the dangers of inviting prosecutors to discover wide-ranging misconduct. In some cases, firms determine that it is desirable to get the government's attention, either because the firm has exposure to liability and wants to establish early cooperation or because the firm is truly a victim of employee misconduct. To facilitate the approach to the government, corporations often retain private investigative and accounting firms to conduct inquiries, record witness statements, provide grand jury testimony to the government, and prepare "courtroom-ready" cases for FBI agents and prosecutors.

One risk consulting firm, for example, distributes training materials to private investigators on "packaging the corporate investigation for prosecution."[20] Kroll recommends that clients take actions that closely track a typical prosecutorial assessment: identifying applicable statutes, ensuring that the statute of limitations has not run on prosecution, determining how each element of the relevant statutes can be satisfied, and confirming that documentary evidence and witness statements are sufficient to prove the case. Prosecutors understandably favor cases where private investigators have thus minimized the necessary effort and expenditure and increased the likelihood of success.

Whether corporate misconduct even amounts to criminality and, if so, who ought to be charged are always difficult questions to answer.[21] Is it enough, for example, if financial analysts relay one opinion to clients and a different one to colleagues about an investment? Prosecutors ought to answer those questions with reference to legal interpretation and regulatory policy and not evidentiary ease. Yet corporate management can exploit its informational advantage to influence which investigations proceed, who gets prosecuted, and what wrongdoing remains concealed.

This direct link between corporations and the government is in part a consequence of the weak players self-regulatory organizations have become. Private sources of information independent of corporations—such as the National Association of Securities Dealers ("NASD") and the enforcement arm of the New York Stock Exchange ("NYSE") (consolidated in 2007 into the Financial Industry Regulatory Authority ("FINRA"))—atrophied in the deregulated environment of recent years. Other intermediaries who possess valuable information—such as credit ratings agencies (which may actually be incentivized now to cooperate in investigations because of their need for improved public relations)—have been discredited by the part they played in the financial crisis. As a result, the government has relied increasingly on compliance industry professionals, even though their role is ultimately to advocate for the corporations at issue.

Even setting aside the possibility of deliberate manipulation in a firm's favor, there is a question whether regulators and prosecutors have particular expectations for private cooperation and focus on information that comports with established views and comes packaged in a recognizable form. Whistle-blowers who are neither compliance professionals nor corporate insiders may have a hard time delivering their message. The most glaring recent example is the SEC's deference to industry insider Bernard Madoff. Harry Markopolos, a relative outsider, repeatedly warned the SEC about Bernie Madoff's multi-billion-dollar Ponzi scheme between 2000 and 2008, but the agency failed to verify Madoff's trades through any third parties.[22] The SEC, of course, is heavily overburdened, but it was also widely regarded as in thrall to the hedge funds during this period. Madoff had a close relationship with regulators, sat on an SEC advisory committee, and served as chairman of the NASDAQ. The inspector general's report on the Madoff investigation attributes some of the lackluster enforcement to agency bias in favor of reputable broker-dealers and notes that SEC staff discounted Markopolos's detailed complaints because of his outsider status.[23]

Some recent cases underscore other potential dangers of prosecutors' special relationships with particular private partners. In one instance, prosecutors filed charges that were not ultimately supported by the evidence after receiving the fruits of an investigation by Davis Polk & Wardwell, a private law firm representing the board of directors. Auto-parts manufacturer Collins & Aikman entered into a NPA with the government in 2007. In March 2007, the U.S. Attorney announced that agreement and the related criminal indictments of several individuals for misleading investors with false financial statements.[24] Charges against CEO David Stockman included securities fraud, bank and wire fraud, false statements, and obstruction. Prosecutors also charged J. Michael Stepp, the company's chief financial officer ("CFO"), David Cosgrove, its former controller, and Paul Barnaba, ex-director of financial analysis. According to the indictment, the executives conspired to falsify key financial metrics, including prematurely recognizing cost reductions from supplier rebates.[25] Four other Collins & Aikman executives pled guilty in the case. Almost two years later, in January 2009, the U.S. Attorney requested dismissal of the indictment against Stockman, Stepp, Cosgrove, and Barnaba. In filing for a *nolle prosequi*, prosecutors cited only their "renewed assessment of the evidence, including evidence and information acquired after the filing of the indictment."[26] Defense lawyers, however, placed blame for the precipitous charges on Davis, Polk & Wardwell's "fast, rushed" investigative report and the government's willingness to outsource the investigation to the firm.[27]

Compliance professionals not only seek to protect corporate clients by framing individual cases but also may have exposure to criminal or civil liability themselves. When they fail at their oversight responsibilities or participate in deceptive conduct, it is in their best interests to construct a narrative in which they are blameless. Consider, for example, the Metropolitan Mortgage & Securities case of 2007. In executive Thomas Turner's trial, one defense theory was that witnesses from accounting firm Ernst & Young accused Turner of misrepresenting the nature of transactions in order to minimize the firm's own negligence. In parallel civil proceedings, the accounting firm was exposed to hundreds of millions of dollars in potential liability.[28]

Furthermore, experts often have the incentive to shape prosecutorial strategies to maximize the market for their services. Legal intermediaries in the compliance industry are "self-interested private actors with a stake in the interpretation of regulatory policy."[29] To the extent they are successful at manipulating enforcement priorities, they may also appropriate "more than their fair share of the social benefits of legal policy, and undermin[e] its efficacy and efficiency in the process."[30]

The formation of investigative partnerships between private actors and the government imports the same flaws found on the private side, including self-dealing or inaccuracy, into any case pursued by the government. Although outsourcing solves the resource problem and bridges the informational divide, those gains may come at a cost. DOJ's great strength is its autonomy: federal prosecutors are not generally beholden to the regulated industry or prone to capture, and they are subject only to diluted political considerations. But turning to the private sector to complete significant investigative tasks means relying on evidence that third parties gathered and analyzed with a self-interested slant. With no formal guidelines for interaction with the private sector, whether cases are brought and how they are resolved turns too frequently on the serendipity of inside information and makes prosecutors susceptible to manipulation by the compliance industry.

This aspect of DPAs is ripe for reform, and some initiatives are under way to better calibrate public/private boundaries. Allocating additional resources to investigators and prosecutors will make them less reliant on private cooperators. The pending Accountability in Deferred Prosecutions Act of 2009 also calls for greater transparency, published guidelines on when to enter into DPAs, and an oversight role for the courts in approving agreements to ensure that they comport with DOJ's guidelines and the "interests of justice."[31] DOJ itself, however, is best positioned to establish guidelines and procedures that allow prosecutors to benefit from private compliance without depending on it.[32] Cooperators and compliance professionals can maximize efficiency, but prosecutors need some internal checks to help minimize inequities and maintain independence while partnering with them. The Filip Memo recently addressed some of the coercive aspects of the relationship with cooperating employees and corporations by directing prosecutors not to seek waivers of attorney-client privilege or work product protection and not to consider whether corporations have advanced legal fees to employees when evaluating cooperation. The more nuanced problem in the public/private corporate enforcement partnership is the makeshift way in which it can produce targets of prosecution. DOJ should also establish internal review procedures for both indictments in corporate fraud cases and DPAs. Applying some consistent standards could ensure the accuracy and quality of information from private partners and prevent the aggregation of too much discretionary authority in corporate hands.

III. Installing Outsiders in Corporations: Compliance Monitors

Another innovation of DPAs subject to substantial scrutiny is the use of monitors to oversee compliance with the terms of the agreement. Full consideration of the use of monitors is beyond the scope of this chapter and is addressed in more detail elsewhere in the volume.[33] But aspects of the monitor's role shed some light on the extent to which DPAs cross boundaries between prosecutorial decision making and corporate governance. Most DPAs mandate remedial measures, including prosecutor-designed compliance programs and, in some cases, personnel changes and structural reforms.[34] About half of all DPAs also include monitoring provisions that effectively install government representatives within corporations to review and evaluate internal controls. Once there, many monitors take on an intrusive role in corporate governance as well.

Requiring a regulated entity to enter into a private contract with a monitor as part of its settlement of criminal charges raises structural issues, particularly because monitors report to prosecutors and not to the courts. While corporations are not technically required to accept monitors' recommendations, prosecutors consider that response when making the ultimate determination whether the firm has complied with the terms of a DPA. The Obama administration's recent role in forcing out the General Motors CEO was viewed as a "dramatic government intervention[] in private industry,"[35] but prosecutors have been using DPAs to demand similar managerial changes for several years.[36] For example, the federal monitor overseeing compliance with the Bristol-Myers Squibb DPA successfully sought the CEO's ouster at a September 2006 board meeting.[37]

Installing a monitor allows DOJ to maintain a presence within the corporation without drawing on government resources. Monitors of DPAs are paid according to private contracts with the corporation. In theory, monitors also address the institutional competence issue because they have expert knowledge of the industry. According to the DOJ's defense of the use of monitors:

> [T]he appointment of a corporate monitor can have distinct advantages for the government and the public. Monitors allow the government to ver-

ify, through the work of an independent observer, whether a corporation is fulfilling the obligations to which it has agreed. A monitor also may provide specialized expertise to oversee and ensure compliance with complex or technical aspects of a corporate agreement, in areas where prosecutors may lack such skills.[38]

In practice, however, many monitors are former prosecutors, regulators, or retired judges, who generally bring the same set of skills—legal analysis rather than corporate governance—that prosecutors themselves have. Of the forty monitors appointed since 2000, thirty are former government officials.[39]

DPAs also fail to make clear the scope of the monitor's responsibilities. In some cases, monitors act as the eyes and ears of prosecutors and merely submit reports and recommendations; increasingly, they are the voice of the government as well.[40] The DPA for medical device company Zimmer Holdings, for example, states that the monitor is there on behalf of the government, empowers him to retain other professionals at the company's expense, and requires access to governance decisions.[41] Monitors gain these powers without accompanying duties to shareholders. Most monitors have neither the expertise nor the incentive to profit-maximize, yet corporations do not generally have the authority to terminate and replace them. And once monitors are installed, information flows directly through them to the government because no privileges apply to their consultations with the corporation.

In addition, monitors raise their own set of self-dealing concerns. The appointments can be highly profitable, and many DPAs specify the monitors that corporations must hire. Former Attorney General John Ashcroft's consulting firm notoriously received up to $52 million for monitoring Zimmer after the U.S. Attorney specified him in the DPA.[42] When prosecutors direct sole-source contracts to former colleagues in the private sector, questions about conflicts of interest arise.[43] Some structural suggestions for mitigating potential conflicts can be drawn from the EPA's efforts to maintain an arm's-length financial relationship when implementing Supplemental Environmental Projects ("SEPs"). SEPs often form part of settlements between the EPA and industry in Clean Air Act enforcement. They are "environmentally beneficial projects" that violators can undertake over and above their legal obligations under the injunction entered in the case. In exchange, companies can receive decreased penalties, at the discretion of the EPA. The EPA does not require or impose SEPs; the regulated entity makes a proposal for DOJ approval. The EPA's SEP policy provides that the agency "may not play any role in managing or controlling funds" set aside for performance of the SEP. The EPA allows the regulated entity to contract with third parties to implement the projects but will not itself endorse private organizations because "a close working relationship with such organizations could create the appearance that EPA is using the organization[s] as a means to indirectly manage or direct SEP funds."[44]

Similar measures could address the coercive appointments of monitors and also maximize their independence within the corporation. The Accountability in Deferred Prosecutions Act is one attempt to contend with this issue. It would require rules for the disinterested selection and compensation of independent monitors, including the creation of a national list of organizations and individuals with the necessary skills and expertise and development of a preapproved fee schedule.[45] DOJ has taken self-regulatory action, meanwhile, to address the structural flaws and underlying conflicts. The Morford Memo directs that Main Justice be notified of any DPAs specifying a monitor and instructs prosecutors to consider both the costs to the corporation and the impact of a monitor on its operations before imposing one. The Morford Memo also precludes individual prosecutors from making unilateral decisions to appoint or veto particular monitor candidates and requires instead that the deputy attorney general approve them. In terms of the scope of the monitor's authority and duties, the Morford Memo states that the monitor "is not an employee or agent of the corporation or of the government" and further clarifies that a monitor's chief responsibility is to prevent recurring misconduct rather than to investigate historical wrongdoing.[46]

One issue the Morford Memo does not address is the high level of compensation that monitors receive. The contracts are so lucrative that monitors' own independence is in doubt, and they may come to identify with the corporations they are supposed to be monitoring. Ratings agencies like Moody's, Standard & Poors, and Fitch provide an interesting analogue. Although in theory they serve as a check on financial institutions, they are compensated by the same firms whose products they rate, which has prompted proposals to shift fees to end users. The 2008 financial crisis exposed the fact that models could be gamed in favor of both issuers and investors, as many of the products that precipitated the market downturn received triple-A ratings from the agencies. To address these potential distortions in the appointment of monitors, proposals for published fee schedules, advance work plans, and reporting requirements all merit consideration.

Whether monitors are effective in ensuring compliance is also open to question. Take the example of AIG, the insurance company that received approximately $180 billion in federal funds—the largest government bailout of a private firm in U.S. history—after it sustained staggering losses from insurance policies on subprime mortgages. AIG had entered into two different DPAs and had an on-site monitor throughout the four-year period preceding its near collapse in September 2008. The monitor—who received $20 million in fees from the insurer—had oversight responsibility for the very same financial-products group that wrote billions in credit-default-swap contracts. He was also tasked with examining internal controls on financial reporting and overseeing compliance programs.[47]

IV. Signaling for Broader Compliance: The Impact of Partnerships on Deterrence

The AIG example is but one indication that, despite its efficiencies, regulation by prosecutors via third-party intermediaries may not be working all that well. DPAs increase cooperation against employee defendants and thus have an impact according to metrics of criminal adjudication, but they fall short with regard to the goals of regulation. There have been mixed results in terms of specific deterrence at corporations receiving DPAs, and general deterrence may actually suffer.

The nature of criminal enforcement is to punish, and the Corporate Fraud Task Force set out to "ensure just and effective punishment of those who perpetrate financial crimes."[48] The ability to deputize corporate insiders does expedite the prosecution of individual defendants and increases the total number of indictments and convictions. By exerting pressure to cooperate, DPAs have thus increased symbolic punishment and some retributive effects.

But DOJ's approach to corporate crime has evolved so that it is not solely, or even primarily, retributive. Prosecutors envision DPAs as mechanisms of industry-wide deterrence. The Thompson Memo and its successors describe enforcement as "a force for positive change of corporate culture."[49] In a recent defense of the agreements, DOJ officials further explained that "by requiring solid ethics and compliance programs, the agreements encourage corporations to root out illegal and unethical conduct, prevent recidivism, and ensure that they are committed to business practices that meet or exceed applicable legal and regulatory mandates."[50] As many commentators have detailed, DPAs have the structural potential to achieve prospective compliance and systemic reform.[51] The partnerships with private parties that DPAs facilitate are derived from regulatory models and should be similarly effective at establishing norms. In theory, they allow prosecutors to act as "norm entrepreneurs,"[52] not only setting standards but also communicating values.

It is not clear, however, that forming public/private partnerships has led to additional internalization of compliance norms. To date, there is little evidence that prosecutors have succeeded in filling the gaps left by deregulation. This is in part because prosecutors are oriented to a command-and-control approach—reflected, for example, in the demands placed on cooperating employees—rather than the collaborative ideals of horizontal negotiation described by administrative law scholars.[53] It is also because, despite their resemblance to regulation, DPAs are still piecemeal adjudications of individual corporate liability that only occasionally have industry-wide impact.

The limited expressive success of DPAs may in part be a product of the regulatory era in which they have operated. The financial crisis exposed the gaming that has flourished throughout corporate culture, and the availability of DPAs ultimately fosters this norm. DPAs suggest that corporate actors can "bear the risk of legally questionable business practices" and later cut a deal if discovered.[54] Many regulations are so lax, and loopholes so large, that corporations can profit-maximize by bending but not quite breaking rules. Compliance officers, ethics professionals, and risk assessors were virtual nonentities while financial institutions were leveraging heavily and signing off on collateralized debt obligations. The private side of the enforcement partnership has not held up its end as an overseer, and prosecutors have not been particularly good at distinguishing effective compliance programs from cosmetic ones. Up until this point, an insincere but facially adequate compliance program accomplished the goal of deflecting regulation and prosecution almost as well as a robust one.[55]

Events may have addressed this failure in hybrid enforcement in a way that no reform proposal could. The 2008 market meltdown provides an occasion to rethink enforcement strategies and correct for some of the distortions in DPAs. Rising fear and renewed understanding about the harm of corporate malfeasance create an opportune moment to transmit norms of compliance to firms. The partnership model requires, and has been missing, a sense of common cause. Public calls for increased regulation and a clamor to assign responsibility recall the post-Enron environment, but there is now a much more profound sense on the part of corporations themselves that compliance is linked to survival and not just a protection against indictment. Actively managing risk made the difference between some firms that minimized losses, such as teachers' pension fund TIAA-CREF and J. P. Morgan, and others that failed, such as Lehman Bros., Bear Stearns, and Merrill

Lynch. Goldman Sachs's announcement of blockbuster quarterly earnings in July 2009, the highest in its 140-year history, raises the question whether the firm internalized the lessons of its own ability to weather the risk-management storm.[56] The profits reflect record revenues in the units trading mortgage and other credit instruments, and a steady increase as well in the firm's value-at-risk (a statistical model of potential portfolio losses and exposure to market risk).[57] This is among the disheartening signals that whatever window the financial crisis opened for regulatory reform and increased compliance already has closed. The market collapse did, however, prompt at least a temporary suspension of the "bonus culture." In that ongoing conversation about shared interests in the health of financial firms, there is a chance to align personal, institutional, and governmental objectives through regulatory cueing.[58] A window has opened as well to the "publicization"—in terms of the extension of norms of accountability—of the private corporations enlisted as enforcers by the government.[59]

Although concerns about conflicts of interest arise when executives from the private sector move in and out of government positions, that process itself has some potential to extend norms of compliance in one direction while increasing financial expertise in the other. Investment bankers from Goldman Sachs occupy key regulatory positions, including leadership posts at the Treasury Department, TARP, the Commodity Futures Trading Commission, and the Federal Reserve. The extent of the firm's influence in the current administration has garnered particular attention, but it is only one example of the revolving door between the market and regulators. Prosecutors have long continued their careers as compliance professionals, and it now appears that if the ranks of federal regulators swell, the inflow will include some laid-off employees from the financial industry. At an April 2009 job fair in New York, the shift in financial power from Wall Street to Washington was visibly represented by hundreds of veterans of financial institutions lining up to interview with the SEC, the FBI, the Federal Deposit Insurance Corporation, and other agencies.[60]

V. Expanding the Role of Regulators: The Need for an Integrated Approach

Prosecutors are now better positioned to signal that the government and corporations have a mutual interest in preventing broader economic harm, but they may also have discovered that administrative enforcement best serves that interest. DOJ functionally makes regulation through DPAs by using them to establish what conduct merits sanction and to enlist corporations in preventing it. In the end, though, this only approximates regulation. Many DPAs are not published, and press releases do not make lasting policy. With rare exceptions like the medical device industry, regulation by settlement reaches only a fraction of the relevant firms, and enforcement is unpredictable and inconsistent.

Nor is it clear that prosecutors should address all wrongdoing associated with the failure of financial institutions. The crisis appears to be primarily the result of the uncalculated risk-taking and unbridled greed that flourished in a deregulated environment, rather than the product of criminality per se. A common response when economic declines coincide with revelations of corporate wrongdoing is to create new crimes. That may meet some political objectives and placate an angry public, but it only perpetuates the current model of ad hoc targeting and will not fill the enforcement gap. With more than 4,000 federal laws already on the books, there are adequate tools to address every species of fraud that may have been perpetrated. The existing mail and wire fraud provisions alone could be interpreted to fit thousands of cases of misfeasance, but it is not realistic or practical to criminally punish every bad actor who contributed to the economic collapse. Even with regulatory features, criminal enforcement focuses on people as causal agents; administrative regulation is better situated to deal with failed products, like credit default swaps and value-at-risk models. Just because prosecutors have a point of entry to approach corporate compliance criminally does not mean that they should pass through it. Some high-profile prosecutions of malfeasance will emerge, and to the extent restitution and asset recovery are possible retrospectively, prosecutors should bring charges against entities and individuals as necessary to accomplish it. But backward-looking criminal liability will do little to restore the economy, and hearings and investigations will more likely serve to set the stage for prospective civil regulation.

Although DPAs resemble regulation, they sometimes reproduce its worst features (like gaming and self-dealing) without the advantages of industry-wide reform through horizontal regulation. Regulators have been behind the scenes of many DPAs while pursuing parallel enforcement and have formed similar relationships with the compliance industry. If a staffed-up and better financed SEC takes a more active role in policing corporations,[61] and civil authorities assume responsibility for evaluating compliance programs,[62] public/private partnerships could become more productive. An expert regulatory response, framed with administrative accountability, might better establish self-regulation and achieve "synergy between punishment and persuasion."[63] Once relieved of the compulsion to operate as de facto government agents, corporate insiders, the private bar, and the compliance industry may be more effective at stimulating compliance. When self-regulation fails, professional regulators can adjust the rules accordingly and broadly enlist the assistance of the private sector in enforcing them. Criminal cases—including indictments and threatened indictments—should occupy the space at the top of the enforcement pyramid.[64] Prosecutors may function best as the "benign big gun" and send the strongest signals to comply with a few well-chosen indictments rather than many DPAs.

VI. Further Entangling Public and Private Interests: Regulators as Stakeholders

The market collapse shifts the paradigm not only of public and private roles but also of public and private interests. The government and corporations share common cause in economic health generally and in some companies specifically. Where the government now has partial ownership of companies, regulators are navigating new entanglements. The idea that the regulatory system involves arm's-length oversight of market actors making private investment decisions no longer holds. As former SEC chair Christopher Cox has explained, "When the government becomes both referee and player, the game changes rather dramatically for every other participant."[65] The government's role as enforcer and stakeholder combined introduces new complications, and addressing the variety of potential conflicts will be a difficult but important task as regulatory roles are redefined.

With its 80 percent stake in AIG, for instance, the government could literally get a seat in the boardroom, although the presence of regulators there might not be the most effective way to protect taxpayers' investment.[66] Officials have repeatedly disavowed any interest in making operational decisions for financial institutions accepting government funds, but curbs on executive compensation are one example of a pending intervention,[67] and action on investment preferences and corporate governance policies could follow.

Another recent example involves Bank of America's acquisition of Merrill Lynch and the role that the Treasury and the Federal Reserve may have played in negotiating the $50 billion merger. Chairman Bernanke and Secretary Paulson allegedly cautioned against disclosure of Merrill Lynch's deteriorated value to Bank of America shareholders, while threatening personnel changes and promising additional TARP funds.[68] As a growing number of financial institutions require scaffolding with government funds, questions arise whether regulators will reveal negative information that could jeopardize the replacement of federal investment with private capital. Disclosures that diminish the value of the government's stake harm taxpayers generally, but guarding material information exposes public shareholders to risk. The SEC is tasked with regulating from a layer above, scrutinizing transactions for the protection of shareholders even where the government's broader interest in stabilizing the financial markets counsels against regulation. Should a corporation in which the government has a substantial stake come under criminal investigation by DOJ, how that new dimension of the public interest factors into the calculus whether to indict, negotiate a deferred prosecution, or decline the case altogether also remains to be seen.

VII. Conclusion

Given the enormous variety and complexity of corporate crime and the tight resource constraints, prosecutors have taken the necessary step of enlisting corporations and compliance professionals in enforcement. DPAs enable them to commandeer the fruits of private investigations by making the threat of indictment a bargaining tool. Prosecutors not only appropriate inside information but also install outside observers in corporations. DPAs can impose monitors and specify detailed compliance provisions that approximate regulation. But despite the parallels to regulatory methods, DPAs retain the piecemeal resolution that characterizes adjudication and import as well as the conflicts of interest that are the most significant drawback of public/private partnerships in regulation. Nor have they achieved the advantages of industry-wide regulation or succeeded in inculcating broad norms of compliance. The financial crisis itself now sends a strong signal of mutual interest in risk management and good corporate citizenship and thus corrects for some of the expressive shortcomings of regulation by prosecutors. It also demonstrates, however, that selective criminal enforcement—even according to a regulatory model—cannot substitute for robust regulations themselves.

NOTES

1. *See, e.g.*, Interview with United States Attorney James B. Comey Regarding the Department of Justice's Policy on Requesting Corporations Under Criminal Investigation to Waive the Attorney Client Privilege and Work Product Protection, U.S. Att'ys' Bull., Nov. 2003, at 4, *available at* http://www.usdoj.gov/usao/eousa/foia_reading_room/usab5106.pdf.

2. *See* Eric Lichtblau, David Johnston & Ron Nixon, *FBI Struggling to Handle Wave of Finance Cases*, N.Y. Times, Oct. 19, 2008, at A1.

3. *See* David Johnston & Neil A. Lewis, *Obama Team to Keep Focus of Agencies on Terrorism*, N.Y. Times, Mar. 26, 2009.

4. *See* David Segal, *Financial Fraud Rises as Target for Prosecutors*, N.Y. Times, Mar. 12, 2009, at A1.

5. *See* Federal Enforcement and Recovery Act of 2009, P.L. No. 111–21 (2009); Supplemental Anti-fraud Enforcement for Our Market Act, S. 331, 111th Cong. (2009).

6. David Johnston & Neil A. Lewis, *Obama Team to Keep Focus of Agencies on Terrorism*, N.Y. Times, Mar. 26, 2009, at A16.

7. *See Federal and State Enforcement of Financial Consumer and Investor Protection Laws: Hearing Before the H. Comm. on Financial Services*, 111th Cong. (2009) (statement of John Pistole, deputy director, FBI).

8. *See The Need for Increased Fraud Enforcement in the Wake of the Economic Downturn: Hearing Before the S. Judiciary Comm.*, 111th Cong. (2009) (statement of Neil Barofsky, Special Inspector General, Troubled Asset Relief Program).

9. *See* Memorandum from Paul J. McNulty, Deputy Attorney General, U.S. Dep't of Justice, to Heads of Department Components and United States Attorneys, *Principles of Federal Prosecution of Business Organizations* (Dec. 12, 2006), http://www.usdoj.gov/dag/speeches/2006/mcnulty_memo.pdf.

10. U.S. Sentencing Guidelines Manual § 8C2.5 cmt. 12 (2004).

11. *See* Memorandum from Larry D. Thompson, Deputy Attorney General, U.S. Dep't of Justice, to Heads of Department Components and United States Attorneys, *Principles of Federal Prosecution of Business Organizations* (Jan. 20, 2003), http://www.usdoj.gov/dag/cftf/corporate_guidelines.htm.

12. *See* Comey Interview, *supra* note 1, at 1–2.

13. *See generally* Lisa Kern Griffin, *Compelled Cooperation and the New Corporate Criminal Procedure*, 82 N.Y.U. L. Rev. 311, 318–26 (2007).

14. Richard A. Epstein, *The Deferred Prosecution Racket*, Wall St. J., Nov. 28, 2006, at A14.

15. United States v. Stein, 440 F. Supp. 2d 315, 337–38 (S.D.N.Y. 2006).

16. *See* Memorandum from Mark Filip, Deputy Attorney General, U.S. Dep't of Justice, to Heads of Department Components and United States Attorneys, *Principles of Federal Prosecution of Business Organizations* (Aug. 28, 2008), http://www.usdoj.gov/dag/readingroom/dag-memo-08282008.pdf.

17. *See* United States v. Stein, 541 F.3d 130 (2d Cir. 2008).

18. Editorial, *Going Soft on Corporate Crime*, N.Y. Times, Apr. 10, 2008, at A26.

19. *See, e.g.*, Vikramaditya S. Khanna, *A Political Economy Theory of Corporate Crime Legislation* (Apr. 1, 2003) (unpublished paper), *available at* http://papers.ssrn.com/sol3/papers.cfm?abstract_id=392121.

20. John Kocoras, *Making a Federal Case Out of It: Packaging the Corporate Investigation for Prosecution*, 14 Corp. Governance Advisor 4, 21 (July/Aug. 2006).

21. *See, e.g.*, Samuel W. Buell, *Criminal Procedure Within the Firm*, 59 Stan. L. Rev. 1613, 1628–29 (2007); Geraldine Szott Moohr, *Prosecutorial Power in an Adversarial System: Lessons from Current White Collar Cases and the Inquisitorial Model*, 8 Buff. Crim. L. Rev. 165, 180–81 (2004).

22. *See* Report of Investigation, United States Securities and Exchange Commission Office of Inspector General, Case No. OIG-509, Investigation of Failure of the SEC to

Uncover Bernard Madoff's Ponzi Scheme, Executive Summary (Aug. 31, 2009), *available at* http://www.sec.gov/news/studies/2009/oig-509.pdf.

23. *See id.* at 17.

24. *See* Press Release, U.S. Attorney's Office, Southern District of New York, U.S. Charges David Stockman—Former CEO of Auto Parts Maker—And Other Former Executives with Securities Fraud; Company Not Charged (Mar. 26, 2007), *available at* http://www.usdoj.gov/usao/nys/pressreleases/March07/stockmanetalindictmentpr.pdf. One of this book's editors, Anthony S. Barkow, worked as a prosecutor on this case after it was charged. Thus, Rachel E. Barkow edited this chapter.

25. *See* Indictment, United States v. Stockman, Cr. No. 07–220 (S.D.N.Y. Mar. 26, 2007).

26. *See* Nolle Prosequi, United States v. Stockman, Cr. No. 07–220 (S.D.N.Y. Jan. 9, 2009).

27. *See* David Glovin, *Stockman, Reagan Adviser, Has Fraud Case Dropped*, Bloomberg.com, Jan. 9, 2009, *available at* http://www.bloomberg.com/apps/news?pid=20670001&refer=home.

28. *See* John Stucke, *Auditor Testifies Metropolitan Needed "Extra Attention,"* Spokane Rev., June 1, 2007. Federal prosecutors also unsuccessfully sought a stay of discovery to prevent depositions of Ernst & Young partners in the parallel SEC enforcement action. SEC v. Sandoval, No. C06–1631C (Dec. 11, 2006).

29. Kimberly D. Krawiec, *The Return of the Rogue*, 51 Ariz. L. Rev. 127, 148 (2009).

30. *Id.*

31. H.R. 1947, 111th Cong. (2009).

32. *See generally* Rachel E. Barkow, *Institutional Design and the Policing of Prosecutors: Lessons from Administrative Law*, 61 Stan L. Rev. 869 (2009).

33. *See infra* Vikramaditya S. Khanna, *Reforming the Corporate Monitor?*

34. Mary Jo White, *Corporate Criminal Liability: What Has Gone Wrong?*, 2 37th Ann. Inst. on Sec. Reg. 815, 818 (PLI Corp. Law & Practice, Course Handbook Series No. B-1517, 2005).

35. Neil King, Jr. & John D. Stoll, *Government Forces Out Wagoner at GM*, Wall St. J., Mar. 30, 2009, at A1.

36. *See, e.g.*, U.S. Dep't of Justice, U.S. Attorney, District of New Jersey, Bristol-Myers Squibb—Deferred Prosecution Agreement at 3 (June 13, 2005), *available at* http://www.usdoj.gov/usao/nj/press/files/pdffiles/deferredpros.pdf (specifying a government-approved board member); *see also* U.S. Dep't of Justice, U.S. Attorney, Eastern District of New York, Computer Associates—Deferred Prosecution Agreement at 7–13, *available at* http://www.usdoj.gov/dag/cftf/chargingdocs/compassocagreement.pdf.

37. *See* Brooke A. Masters, *Bristol-Myers Ousts Its Chief at Monitor's Urging: Dolan Had Led Firm Since 2001*, Wash. Post, Sept. 13, 2006, at D1.

38. Letter from Brian A. Benczkowski, Principal Deputy Assistant Attorney General, to John Conyers, Jr., Chairman, House Committee on the Judiciary (May 15, 2008) [hereinafter Benczkowski Letter].

39. *See id.*

40. Vikramaditya Khanna & Timothy L. Dickson, *The Corporate Monitor: The New Corporate Czar?*, 105 Mich. L. Rev. 1713, 1720 (2007).

41. U.S. Dep't of Justice, U.S. Attorney, District of New Jersey, Zimmer Holdings—Deferred Prosecution Agreement (Sept. 27, 2007), *available at* http://www.zimmer.com/web/enUS/pdf/Zimmer_DPA.pdf.

42. Eric Lichtblau, *In Justice Shift, Corporate Deals Replace Trials*, N.Y. Times, Apr. 9, 2008, at A1.

43. Editorial, *The Kindness of Cronies*, N.Y. Times, May 25, 2008.

44. Memorandum from John Peter Suarez, Assistant Administrator, EPA, to Regional Counsels, Enforcement Managers, Media Division Directors, and Enforcement Coordinators, *Guidance Concerning the Use of Third Parties in the Performance of Supplemental Environmental Projects (SEPs) and the Aggregation of SEP Funds*, pt. II, ¶ B (Dec. 15, 2003), *available at* http://www.epa.gov/compliance/resources/policies/civil/seps/seps-thirdparties.pdf.

45. H.R. 1947, 111th Cong. (2009).

46. Memorandum from Craig S. Morford, Acting Deputy Attorney General, U.S. Dep't of Justice, to Heads of Department Components and United States Attorneys, *Selection and Use of Monitors in Deferred Prosecution Agreements and Non-prosecution Agreements with Corporations* (Mar. 7, 2008), http://www.usdoj.gov/usao/eousa/foia_reading_room/usam/title9/crm00163.htm.

47. Peter Lattman, *The U.S.'s Fly on the Wall at AIG*, Wall St. J., Mar. 27, 2009, at C1.

48. Press Release, White House, Executive Order Establishment of the Corporate Fraud Task Force (July 9, 2002), *available at* http://www.usdoj.gov/dag/cftf/execorder.htm. This task force has since been renamed the Financial Fraud Enforcement Task Force. *See* Press Release, White House, Executive Order Establishment of the Financial Fraud Enforcement Task Force (Nov. 17, 2009), *available at* http://www.sec.gov/news/press/2009/2009-249-exec-order.pdf.

49. *See* Filip Memo, *supra* note 16.

50. Benczkowski Letter, *supra* note 38, at 3.

51. Brandon L. Garrett, *Structural Reform Prosecution*, 93 Va. L. Rev. 853, 858 (2007).

52. Pamela H. Bucy, *Moral Messengers: Delegating Prosecutorial Power*, 59 S.M.U. L. Rev. 321, 341–42 (2006); *see also* Jody Freeman, *Extending Public Law Norms Through Privatization*, 116 Harv. L. Rev. 1285, 1314–50 (2002).

53. *See, e.g.*, Jody Freeman, *The Private Role in Public Governance*, 75 N.Y.U. L. Rev. 543, 547–48 (2000).

54. Lichtblau, *supra* note 42 (quoting Vikramaditya S. Khanna).

55. *See, e.g.*, Donald C. Langevoort, *Monitoring: The Behavioral Economics of Corporate Compliance with Law*, 2002 Colum. Bus. L. Rev. 71, 106 (2002).

56. *See* Graham Bowley, *With Big Profit, Goldman Sees Big Payday Ahead*, N.Y. Times, July 14, 2009.

57. *See, e.g.*, Christine Harper, *Goldman Sachs VaR Reaches Record on Risks Led by Equity Trading*, Bloomberg.com, July 14, 2009, *available at* http://www.bloomberg.com/apps/news?pid=newsarchive&sid=anh9S6AJxcbY.

58. *See* Robert B. Ahdieh, *Law's Signal: A Cueing Theory of Law in Market Transition*, 77 S. Cal. L. Rev. 215, 255 (2004).

59. *See* Freeman, *supra* note 52, at 1351.

60. Tomoeh Murakami Tse, *Wall Street Workers Bank on a Federal Future*, Wash. Post, Apr. 25, 2009, at C4.

61. *See, e.g.*, Zachary A. Goldfarb, *SEC Chairman Requests Broad Investigative Power*, Wash. Post, July 16, 2009.

62. *See supra* Jennifer Arlen, *Removing Prosecutors from the Boardroom: Limiting Prosecutorial Discretion to Impose Structural Reforms.*

63. *See* Ian Ayres & John Braithwaite, Responsive Regulation: Transcending the Deregulation Debate 25 (1992).

64. *See id.* at 35–41.

65. Christopher Cox, Chairman, U.S. Sec. & Exch. Comm'n Address to Joint Meeting of the Exchequer Club and Women in Housing and Finance (Dec. 4, 2008), *available at* http://www.sec.gov/news/speech/2008/spch120408cc.htm.

66. *See* Epstein, *supra* note 14.

67. *See, e.g.*, David Cho et al., *U.S. Targets Excessive Pay for Top Executives*, Wash. Post, June 11, 2009, at A1.

68. *See* Letter from Andrew M. Cuomo, Attorney General, New York, to Christopher J. Dodd, Chairman, Sen. Comm. on Banking, Housing, and Urban Affairs, Mary L. Schapiro, Chairman, U.S. Sec. & Exch. Comm'n, Barney Frank, Chairman, H. Financial Services Comm., and Elizabeth Warren, Chair, Congressional Oversight Panel, Apr. 23, 2009, *available at* http://www.oag.state.ny.us/media_center/2009/apr/pdfs/BofAmergLetter.pdf.

6

The Institutional Logic of Preventive Crime

MARIANO-FLORENTINO CUÉLLAR

Most organized societies promise to punish unjustified violence.[1] An assassin wrapping up her latest job seems as deserving of criminal punishment as the underworld boss who hired her or the intoxicated driver who smashes into them. But crime control drives a hard bargain. As police walk their beats, investigators sift through evidence, and prosecutors charge, the machinery of criminal justice routinely reveals a darker side. Mass incarceration imposes severe fiscal burdens and social costs.[2] Police action often seems to reflect glaring inequities, sometimes degenerating into brutal episodes as violent as those used to justify criminal enforcement in the first place.[3] And the specter of wrongful convictions looms even in systems with elaborate adjudicatory constraints. When balancing this darker side with the value of punishing past harms, society confronts familiar and difficult trade-offs dominating much of criminal law scholarship and policymaking.

Yet the world is even more complicated than these trade-offs imply. With life constantly at risk from the very world that sustains it, society's well-being depends not only on punishing paradigmatic violent offenses but also on managing risks of adulterated food, faulty medical devices, complex and difficult-to-price financial products, toxic water supplies, and terrorist attacks. The impulse to manage those risks is a major factor fueling the emergence of a modern regulatory state in advanced industrialized countries.[4] Not surprisingly, the role of criminal enforcement in managing seemingly intangible, hidden risks inspires sharp debate among scholars and policymakers. Given these debates, at least three questions about the intersection of crime and preventive risk regulation deserve sustained attention: (1) Is preventive criminal enforcement in the regulatory or national security context an aberration, as some participants in recent debates have suggested? (2) Why do lawmakers and executive officials support preventive criminal enforcement in the first place? (3) In light of the institutional characteristics affecting the organizations implementing the law, what role can (or does) criminal justice play in the modern regulatory state?

My purpose here is to address these puzzles by showing how much organization theory, criminal law, and the study of the regulatory state have to learn from each other. My approach involves closely scrutinizing existing criminal law provisions to elucidate their relationship to risk regulation, rethinking the political economy of criminal enforcement in light of the crime-regulation connection, and applying organization theory to make sense of how criminal justice operates in regulatory and national security domains. In the course of pursuing this approach, the chapter challenges a number of widely accepted notions about the institutional realities of criminal justice. Scholars and policymakers often suggest that criminal justice is ill-suited to prevention,[5] that criminal enforcement bureaucracies are poorly equipped to manage risk-creating behavior in the domestic policy or national security domains,[6] or that pervasively dysfunctional political dynamics fuel ill-conceived expansive crime definition.[7] I find otherwise.

I. Legal Constraints and Organizational Capacity

Criminal law is supposed to regulate private conduct. But its scope also determines what organizations engage in risk regulation, and how they undertake that mission. Some forms of criminal liability, for example, could be described as "preventive" in orientation because they encompass prophylactic offenses such as record-reporting violations designed to prevent the realization of some ultimate harm, or inchoate conduct in preparation for the completion of problematic behavior. The creation of such liability allows bureaucracies with distinctive investigative and analytical capacities to take part in regulating social conduct. Capacity is what allows a bureaucratic organization to perform its ostensible function. Even if one dispenses with frequently unrealistic assumptions about bureaucratic "slack,"[8] attaining capacity tends to be costly. It requires individual and organizational investments of time, energy, and resources. Since individuals in public organizations often aim for a suboptimal aspirational standard instead of maximally effective performance (what Cyert and March describe as "satisficing"), organizations may miss opportunities to enhance their performance.[9] In some cases they may be deliberately engineered to fail.[10] All these factors make it unlikely that bureaucracies charged with preventive enforcement functions will naturally build all the capacity they can to perform in accordance with public expectations.

Yet not all organizational actors operate the same way. Organizations routinely differ in how they define their missions, what trade-offs their leaders consider acceptable, and how internal norms interact with external pressures to affect the allocation of rewards for organizational performance. For example, capacity investments are more likely in organizations whose performance is judged in large measure on the basis of their ability to meet external constraints by a politically relevant audience.[11] Drawing implications from this observation is difficult in a world where even law enforcement agencies are quite heterogeneous. While local beat cops, IRS criminal investigators, and federal prosecutors reflect such distinctions, however, they are similar in the fact that their career incentives and organizational environments force them to take into account legal constraints. Those constraints matter to law enforcement agencies whose behavior is readily observable by political constituencies concerned about (especially violent) crime rates.[12] Yet they also apply—in underappreciated ways—to federal law enforcement authorities given the career interests of agents and prosecutors whose advancement depends to a nontrivial extent on producing investigative results and convictions.[13]

There is little question that the conditions fomenting growth in agencies' capacity are context-dependent and worth further empirical scrutiny. Law enforcement capacity is contingent on the intersection between organizational incentives and culture, legal constraints, and public expectations. Not surprisingly, the extent of police and prosecutorial capacity is not the same at different points in history, or in different countries. Urban police departments in turn-of-the-century Chicago, for instance, had little regard for the law and built correspondingly meager capacity to navigate its constraints.[14]

Nonetheless, even in a world where criminal enforcement agencies are heterogeneous and the scope of criminal liability is broad (and growing), criminal justice bureaucracies are likely to be different from regulatory bureaucracies in critical ways likely to foment capacity. In particular, societies with more elaborate legal constraints governing police and prosecutorial behavior are more likely to generate capacity, and thereby more likely to end up with law enforcement bureaucracies that can add value to regulatory tasks. Law enforcement organizations must be capable of supporting their factual assertions sufficiently to convince an institutionally distinct, external (judicial) observer. They are more readily identified with popular missions that are relatively more salient to the public than most regulatory agencies. Even in the case of federal prosecutors, high-profile drug, fraud, or public corruption cases are likely to carry considerable prospects of career rewards that can be reaped both within and beyond the law enforcement system. The prospect of such rewards can provide a degree of motivation to law enforcement officials that is less likely to be present for regulatory staff. Finally, as noted in the next section, law enforcement entities tend to reflect characteristics making it easier for them to build and maintain organizational autonomy—allowing them greater latitude to shield their efforts to build and retain capacity from being eroded by pressure from organized interests.

These dynamics have had an effect on law enforcement bureaucracies. Despite their enormous power, many investigators and prosecutors work in an environment where they are expected to meet constraints imposed by legislators,[15] the mass public,[16] and the judiciary. Observers of federal prosecutors have often (and rightly) emphasized their striking degree of discretion in deciding what to charge and whom to charge.[17] But the limits and subtleties of such discretion—like the more general autonomy that tends to be associated with many law enforcement agencies—must be understood in context. Even U.S. Attorneys' Offices are under pressure to perform in particular ways. Federal prosecutors are free to pursue more complex cases, but not to lose them all. Congress and the executive branch pressure prosecutors to do more of one kind of case or less of another.[18] And individual federal prosecutors may often care not only about bureaucratic and political audiences but also about the demands of future employers. Moreover, despite the staggering breadth of federal criminal liability, if it is true that federal prosecutors have incentives to bring "knife-edge" cases involving conduct that is not obviously criminal,[19] the constraints associated with judicial evaluation of law enforcers' legal and factual arguments are likely to loom especially large.

Over time, the combination of pressures to investigate and achieve convictions in particular domains and legal constraints leads law enforcement to develop distinctive structural features and concentrations of skills. Drug and money laundering enforcement agencies have built up elaborate, measurable capacities to make arrests and achieve convictions relying on undercover investigations, informants, and police patrol methods where there are likely to be high concentrations of offenses (such as airports or inner-city neighborhoods).[20] By contrast, in the drug and money laundering context, the regulatory agency with primary responsibility for imposing civil penalties to encourage compliance with antilaundering regulations (the Financial Crimes Enforcement Network, or "FinCEN") struggled for many years to develop a capacity to effectively impose such penalties.[21] Detectives investigate and solve homicides because these offenses attract widespread attention and the absence of leads resulting in prosecutions can generate political pressures. Federal prosecutors adapt their routines to achieve convictions in complex cases, for which they tend to be individually accountable and to receive career rewards.[22] Investigative agencies also tend to develop distinct organizational routines, focused on following individuals and cases rather than focusing on (for example) geographic regions,[23] and local cops amass tacit knowledge relevant to identifying individuals committing chargeable offenses.[24] Though far from perfect, it is a striking contrast to the investigative capacities of many regulatory bureaucracies,[25] and even intelligence agencies.[26]

As an example of organizational contrasts in capacity, consider the story of the Central Intelligence Agency's ("CIA's") failure in tracking Khalid al-Mihdhar and al-Hazmi, two al-Qaeda suspects, in the months before the September 11 attacks. As the suspects traveled to Malaysia and then Thailand, CIA analysts tracking their progress faced considerable difficulties, ultimately resulting in the loss of the suspects.[27] Analysts failed to communicate effectively across bureaucratic lines of geographic jurisdiction within the CIA as the suspects traversed lines of international jurisdiction.[28] The CIA bureaucracy did not make a single person (or small team) accountable for following the whereabouts of these individuals,[29] nor did it attempt to gather systematic information about their associates or immediate future plans.[30] Despite information suggesting that the suspects might try to enter the United States to plan or commit criminal offenses, the intelligence agency failed to notify the FBI and immigration authorities.[31] By comparison, the FBI had investigative protocols in place to prevent the failures experienced by the intelligence agency.[32]

The contrast between the FBI's and the CIA's approach in the al-Mihdhar episode is not an accident. Because criminal justice bureaucracies tend to be subject to pressures that can be partially managed by building skills in investigation, interviewing, and analysis of evidence, their capacities are in demand in some regulatory and national security settings. Not only was the bombing of the USS *Cole* investigated by the FBI, but the question of who actually carried out the bombing (an attribution question on which crucial national security and foreign policy decisions depended) was repeatedly punted to the FBI.[33] This move is not irrational; despite the agency's considerable shortcomings, the agents' culture and career paths constantly forced them to work in environments likely to develop different (and distinctly valuable) investigative skills compared with those that might otherwise be available among national security bureaucracies. In a radically different context, California's Department of Occupational Safety and Health developed a team of criminal investigators for similar reasons—because they were likely to possess some of the distinctive skill sets that would elude ordinary regulatory analysts.[34]

In an account of the Food and Drug Administration's ("FDA's") efforts to regulate tobacco under the Food, Drug, and Cosmetics Act, former Commissioner David Kessler also acknowledges the unique contributions of criminal investigators.[35] When the FDA discovered cyanide-laced Sudafed capsules in March 1991, Kessler found the skills of experienced investigators particularly useful in pinpointing the extent of the tampering. Finding that the FBI had taken too long to respond, however, he rushed to "build an Office of Criminal Investigations to fill the huge gap in the agency's capabilities that Sudafed had revealed."[36] The value of filling those gaps was soon evident as the FDA received reports of syringes in Diet Pepsi cans. Unlike conventional regulatory inspectors, the FDA's newly enlarged team of criminal investigators proved to be keen interrogators, who ended up flying "from city to city to investigate tampering reports and soon . . . were eliciting confessions from people who had fabricated claims and were making arrests."[37]

Experienced criminal investigators also played a pivotal role in handling informants, such as the R. J. Reynolds employee that Kessler colorfully names "Deep Cough," whose leads helped the FDA strengthen its legal case for asserting regulatory jurisdiction over tobacco.[38] The thorny nature of the agency's relationship with "Deep Cough" led Kessler to reflect again on the value of individuals whose instincts were forged outside the realm of conventional regulatory policymaking. Here is what happened when Kessler learned about the potential source: "[I] knew we had to handle the informant delicately. I could not use the FDA scientists and lawyers who had taken the first tentative steps into the world of tobacco. *Instead, I needed professionals with law enforcement experience—bluff-proof investigators with the skills to test the credibility of a confidential informant*."[39]

The point of Kessler's account is not that regulatory goals depended exclusively on the availability of criminal *prosecution* as an option against the tobacco companies—though at one point he does suggest that overlapping criminal enforcement and regulatory mandates may have shaped the tobacco companies' willingness to disclose information to the FDA.[40] Instead, the centrality of criminal investigators to the FDA's fact-gathering efforts further demonstrates the demand among public bureaucracies for the abilities that investigators hone specifically in the context of the criminal justice system. Working with a mixture of discretion and constraints, criminal investigators tend to nurture skills crucial to the regulatory state. They are capable of helping regulators coax individuals to reveal false reports of syringes in soda cans, handle nervous tobacco company whistle-blowers, and discern the full extent of a tampering scandal. Unique skill sets and organizational cultures associated with law enforcement personnel also caused tensions within the FDA.[41] As he assigned greater responsibilities to his growing cadre of criminal investigators (in many cases tasks unrelated to prosecution), Kessler paid the price of incurring these tensions in exchange for the capacities his organization acquired.

In the meantime, if pivotal legislators and executive branch officials expect to face skeptical audiences, they may seek to encourage deployment of criminal sanctions.[42] Perhaps it is not entirely surprising, upon reflection, that following the September 11 attacks, a federal government that has consistently insisted it does not need to deploy criminal prosecutions to manage national security threats has nonetheless continued to do so in selected cases. British authorities, too, used criminal prosecution to mollify critics who were increasingly skeptical of an alleged terror plot to bomb aircraft using liquids thwarted by law enforcement.[43] Confronting a doubting public, British law enforcement officials chose a strategy of information dissemination and prosecution: "The decision to press formal charges came after days of growing public skepticism about the extent of the plot that the authorities announced on Aug. 10. At the time, the police warned that the purported conspirators had planned to commit mass murder on what one officer called an 'unimaginable scale.'"[44] The more skeptical the relevant audiences monitoring government policy, the less likely they are to accept that regulatory and national security actions that can be imposed on a near-discretionary basis provide any indication of the government's capacity to detect and respond to legitimate threats.

No doubt my rendition of some of the distinctive capacities of criminal justice bureaucracies seems difficult to reconcile with a spate of problems revealed in particular cases or investigations. The *Hamdi* trial produced a striking array of missteps.[45] The Chandra Levy investigation in Washington, D.C.—burdened by bureaucratic failures and glaring media attention—long disappointed even the most ardent defenders of police conduct.[46] Yet part of the argument is precisely that such shortcomings (at the margin) are more likely to become apparent among criminal justice bureaucracies than regulatory or national security bureaucracies. And when the problems do emerge, prosecutors, investigators, and their senior managers operate in an environment that makes it more difficult to neglect the shortcomings than does the environment in which regulators or national security officials work.

The key point is not that criminal justice bureaucracies will always have more capacity in absolute terms than traditional regulatory bureaucracies.[47]

Instead, it is that investigative and prosecutorial techniques, honed in an environment where the discretionary culture at least occasionally focuses on meeting external legal constraints, can play a constructive role. In light of those constraints and their organizational cultures, law enforcement entities tend to develop distinctive investigative, operational, and analytical capacity relevant to the central task of investigation, persuasively adjudicating liability, and developing responses to threats. Because of such characteristics associated with law enforcement entities, executive authorities' decisions to deploy criminal enforcement to manage risks (including those involving corporate misbehavior or national security) can allow government to signal its competence to the public.

II. Criminal Justice and Organizational Autonomy

If organizational realities in institutional cultures, incentives, and resources distinguish criminal justice from ordinary regulatory agencies, then surely one specific dimension along which these bureaus differ involves how they relate to their larger political environment. Criminal justice agencies tend to be characterized by people with relatively similar goals and professional backgrounds. Although they are politically responsive in a number of underappreciated ways—especially the state and local ones—the reigning conventional wisdom about these agencies among policy elites and members of the mass public is that they should be relatively independent from the interference of representative politicians.[48] Though regulatory agencies vary in their missions, priorities, organizational cultures, and institutional structures, they are not ordinarily identified with a relatively popular mission the way law enforcement agencies are, nor do they boast the professional cohesion and identity that law enforcement agencies possess.[49]

These differing characteristics can lead some legislators and executive branch officials to expect that many law enforcement agencies will be characterized by greater autonomy—that quality of bureaucracies that allows them to better resist interference from external sources such as organized interests.[50] Criminal justice bureaucracies may be better insulated from the pressures of organized interests, who may have multiple ways of dissuading regulators from severe enforcement activity and whose own members and staffs may end up running traditional regulatory agencies.[51]

Consider first a pronounced example of autonomy. By design, federal prosecutors enjoy a distinct measure of political independence, with the recent investigations involving U.S. Attorney firings in the Bush administration poignantly demonstrating the political risks of interference in this domain.[52] In California, prison officials leveraging the alleged centrality of their public safety mission managed to successfully cut back on nettlesome quantitative and qualitative reviews geared toward advancing more ambitious rehabilitation objectives.[53] In short, despite interest group dynamics affecting crime definition and even enforcement, criminal justice agencies seem to achieve a different degree of independence compared with the typical regulatory agency.

Law enforcement agencies differ in their precise extent of autonomy. The U.S. Attorney's Office for the Southern District of New York is not a typical, but perhaps a prototypical, example of how criminal justice bureaucracies can forge autonomy. What Manhattan federal prosecutors have created over several decades is a more exaggerated version of the political environment that a host of other law enforcement agencies can promote—a high-visibility, publicly popular overall mandate, officials with considerable prestige and a strong (and strongly shared) professional identity, along with "coalitions of esteem" outside the agency from former officials in other important positions, elites supportive of the agency's mission, and staff who perceive career rewards from expending major efforts to undertake the agency's particular function.[54] Together these factors place the Southern District, and to a lesser extent law enforcement agencies generally—at the center of a web of expectations supportive of the office's relative independence from the interference that would be more familiar to an ordinary administrative agency.[55] Even for the Southern District, autonomy is not the same thing as absolute freedom from external constraints, which play an important role in shaping agency capacity. Instead, within the context of the constraints described in the previous section, the contention is that law enforcement agencies are likely to have greater autonomy in deciding what targets to pursue, and how to do it.

While many law enforcement agencies will fail to achieve the Southern District's unusual degree of independence, they are likely to fare better at forging autonomy in comparison to ordinary regulatory entities. In California, the Circuit Prosecutor Project—promoted independently by the California District Attorneys Association—was explicitly designed to take up occupational safety and environmental cases that were too technically complex or taxing for other prosecutors' offices.[56] By creating the project, prosecutors apparently hoped to supplement the activities of California's occupational safety regulatory agency and to bolster its capacity to deploy (in conjunction with prosecutors) criminal sanctions that might otherwise be routinely and effectively opposed through pressure from organized interests. In a larger sense, it is telling that, historically, one of the signature scholarly and policy preoccupations regarding regulatory agencies such as California's occupational safety enforcement or its federal equivalent was subjecting them to political controls,[57] while the corresponding concern involving criminal enforcement bureaucracies has been (broadly speaking) to foment their relative independence from ordinary political interference.[58]

The costs of such political interference vary not only in terms of the specific agency but also in its broader legal context. French investigative magistrates, for example, historically faced powerful executive controls. These were particularly strong, ironically, in the domain of public corruption investigations.[59] As a result, at least under the Fifth Republic's heavily presidential system, magistrates (who roughly combine the functions of prosecutors and investigators) historically faced unique difficulties in achieving autonomy. When a spate of political scandals came to light during the late 1980s and 1990s, the magistrates seized on the opportunity to appeal to public concerns about corruption. The magistrates began to leverage their criminal investigation mission and the presence of the scandals to argue for greater independence and increase politicians' costs of direct interference with the investigations.[60] As politicians faced increasing difficulties and even risks of criminal sanctions when seeking to engage in traditional patterns of interference with investigations, the magistrates began to increase the rate of investigations, thereby bringing additional scandals to light and affecting public perceptions of the frequency of illicit financing of political activities. The magistrates pursued this agenda while building on a reputation for impartiality by investigating figures across the political spectrum. Between 1990 and 1995, the number of French politicians in important positions placed under investigations went from about five to fifty, and thereafter the number remained between thirty and fifty.[61] Ultimately, their actions began to change norms among French politicians and contributed to passage of new campaign financing legislation establishing more realistic (but nonetheless constrained) mechanisms through which parties and candidates could fund their activities.[62]

In contrast, American law enforcement agencies tend to begin from a higher level of autonomy, particularly federal prosecutors in a post-Watergate environment.[63] The relative political independence of law enforcement agencies has, for example, facilitated state-level occupational safety prosecutions over interest group objections.[64] Criminal enforcement agencies' deep connection to a mission considered both crucially important and in need of protection from political interference has facilitated local prosecutors' own political influence over policymaking, electoral contests, and judicial selection.[65]

State and federal law enforcement officials routinely impact the legislative process.[66] State, local, and federal law enforcement agencies generate some of their revenues through forfeiture actions, arguably insulating them from some of the constraints associated with the politics of legislative budgeting.[67] Federal criminal agencies, though not uniformly invested with the degree of autonomy associated with the U.S. Attorney's Office for the Southern District of New York, display even more flexibility and discretion.[68] In particular, the FBI has a long tradition of effectively advocating for its interests in Congress.[69]

Even in a system assigning such importance to law enforcement, American criminal justice enjoys nothing like complete political autonomy. State and local law enforcement authorities certainly face political constraints because these agencies are held responsible for local crime control, especially violent crime.[70] But as long as these agencies comply with the basic political imperative of satisfying the implicit threshold for effectiveness that politically responsive constituencies impose on state and local law enforcement agencies, these organizations retain considerable autonomy to choose the strategies they will deploy, including (for instance) "broken windows" type policing strategies.[71]

The situation tends to be different for traditional regulatory agencies. Only rarely (if ever) do regulators at the EPA, OSHA, or Customs and Border Protection enjoy the full complement of advantages helping criminal justice organizations foster bureaucratic autonomy. Despite the different missions of the Bureau of Citizenship and Immigration Services, the Federal Communications Commission, or the California Coastal Commission, their missions are often explicitly recognized as involving critical policy trade-offs that merit political oversight, if not control.[72] The OSHA, EPA, National Labor Relations Board ("NLRB"), and other regulators charged with quasi-legislative missions that are routinely described as meriting political oversight remain more readily subject to political control.[73]

Criminal justice agencies tend to benefit from the perceived importance of their crime-fighting mission. Accordingly, some observers question whether the expanding scope of criminal sanctions would eventually erode the relevance of criminal law as a distinct category of social regulation, and therefore the distinctive features of criminal enforcement agencies in the regulatory process.[74] In fact, the process through which the public modifies its overall impressions of the criminal justice system is likely to evolve gradually and in response to a host of countervailing pressures. Even if some members of the public are constantly updating their perceptions of what precise law enforcement missions criminal enforcement agencies are carrying out, large fractions of the mass public are likely to harbor impressions that remain "sticky."

Experimental evidence suggests people resist disconfirming evidence when evaluating the nature of criminal justice and related matters.[75] Many members of the public, moreover, possess quite limited information about prosecutors' and investigators' work.[76] In the short term, fixing the "crime" label onto a regulatory mandate is likely to leave public perceptions of law enforcement bureaucracies relatively unchanged—particularly when enforcement is initially relatively restrained.[77] Over time, the expanding scope of criminal liability may tend to expand the range of conduct many members of the public consider problematic because it is criminal.[78] Yet in the shorter run, the expanding scope of regulatory crimes is unlikely to entirely dilute criminal enforcement agencies' autonomy advantages.

III. Interaction of Criminal and Noncriminal Enforcement

Still other institutional rationales can support politicians' decisions to invest criminal justice authorities with power to engage in preventive enforcement. These rationales may hold valid even if it turns out criminal justice authorities have little power to proceed on their own because they depend (as is the case in domains such as occupational safety) on the investigative work of regulatory agencies facing constraints from organized interests. Greater enforcement may result from competition between traditional regulatory agencies with authority to investigate preventive criminal violations (such as the EPA) and law enforcement agencies sharing investigative authority (the FBI).[79]

As institutional designers weigh these implications, some will recognize how the presence of overlapping criminal and civil jurisdiction can facilitate the imposition of more severe civil penalties. Regulatory agency staff may be affected by what psychologists describe as a context-dependent reaction, or a moderation bias.[80] Decisions about penalty severity might by affected by the existence of an even more severe layer of (criminal) penalties and a formal review structure for analyzing whether an agency should impose (or recommend) maximally severe (criminal) penalties. Adding a layer of maximally severe criminal penalties may lead agency staff to view its most severe civil penalties as more appropriate than it would in the absence of the availability of criminal sanctions. This effect may play a role even if the criminal penalties are not routinely used.[81] In addition, the bureaucratic entities representing the state gain additional negotiating leverage from the presence of criminal sanctions. Regulators can advance environmental compliance goals by leveraging criminal penalties to negotiate occupational disqualification provisions for company executives.[82] The presence and use of criminal penalties can help generate considerable publicity about regulatory violations, raising private actors' costs of noncompliance. Together, these factors almost certainly impacted the behavior of chronic occupational safety violators like McWane, Inc. McWane faced repeated civil sanctions as stray machinery injured its workers and placed their lives at risk, but it did not materially change its practices until it faced severe criminal prosecution.[83]

Over time, the occasions where criminal penalties *are* used may shape public perceptions regarding the underlying harmfulness of particular conduct—an outcome that could in turn favorably influence the political context of legislators who can then reap political rewards for supporting regulation in domains that initially would not have garnered substantial public attention. As Friedman observed:

> Many acts become regulatory crimes…for administrative reasons, rather than because they involve "real" criminality—that is, what we define as evil, guilt, blameworthiness. But the line is hard to draw. And getting harder. People in our times feel themselves dancing on the deck of a doomed ship. They hear that the air is poisoned, the water full of muck, resources shrinking, forests shriveling, the planet collapsing from consumer debauchery and wanton material waste. In this climate, some regulatory crimes—polluting water and air—get redefined as real crimes, as crimes against the human race. What started out as *malum prohibitum* ends up as *malum in se*.[84]

With a steady progression from *malum prohibitum* to *malum in se* under way, groups and individuals protesting against the existence of criminal penalties may become stigmatized. This feature of criminalization warps conventional pluralist politics, a detail that may not be lost on politicians trying to change the traditional interest group bargaining constraining legislative and bureaucratic action.

As this evolution plays out, criminal enforcement itself may also justify limited but material expansions in regulatory policy. Because of the distinctive constraints associated with criminal prosecution (described earlier as being instrumental to the development of capacity in criminal justice bureaucracies), criminal prosecutions motivated by preventive objectives may require special resources. Given these needs and the perception among relevant constituencies that preventive criminal prosecution is indispensable to target the most severe offenders, the perceived needs of criminal enforcement agencies can become a rationale for regulatory bureaucracies to expand the scope of their own detection capacity. For example, the gradual moves made to regulate criminal financial activity were largely driven by the goal of creating the capacity for preventive criminal enforcement (first, specialized conspiracy cases, and eventually, money laundering cases).[85] The California occupational safety regulator's unit of criminal investigators, whose creation was primarily justified as a means of facilitating criminal prosecutions, also refers situations with suspicious facts for special attention to civil authorities.[86]

A version of the preceding dynamic—where the criminal law label becomes capable of changing the policy environment over time—is present when law enforcement organizations with criminal jurisdiction press for expansions in regulatory policies designed to disrupt criminal offenses. In many cases, as with money laundering, the criminal offenses themselves constitute a prophylactic measure with some ambiguous (though rarely, if ever, entirely implausible) connection to some activity considered harmful (e.g., terrorism, or supplying domestic illegal drug markets).[87] In the early 1970s, when the bureaucratized system for disrupting criminal finance was just getting under way, the new Currency Transaction Reporting requirements governing banks had proved difficult to pass and were vigorously opposed by the banking industry.[88] By the late 1980s, the situation had changed. Although interest in disrupting organized and drug crime remained high throughout the 1970s and 1980s, lawmakers and executive branch officials in the 1980s had the benefit of newly enacted statutes explicitly criminalizing money laundering. Rather than explaining the potentially problematic consequences of financial activities, advocates for greatly expanded regulations could simply emphasize the existing difficulty of fighting the crime of money laundering.[89] The existence of new, highly salient criminal offenses facilitated the substantial expansion of the regulatory system to include suspicious activity reporting and money services businesses.[90]

Take these factors together, and we can begin to see why coalitions of politicians could have subtle organizational incentives to support preventive criminal enforcement even without necessarily being able to sell such enforcement as part of broadly popular crime-fighting initiatives, and even if, in an ideal world, enacting majorities preferred to spur strict civil enforcement rather than a mixture of civil and criminal enforcement. Legislators cannot entirely prevent or assure that particular bureaucracies develop sufficient autonomy to protect their ability to enforce sanctions against unwilling and potentially threatening organized interests. What power legislators and executive branch officials *do* have to enhance autonomy, moreover, comes with the cost that such independence may lead to what some politicians consider to be unwelcome expansions in regulatory power. Creating preventive criminal provisions and encouraging their enforcement can allow legislators to spur preventive enforcement overall, leveraging the autonomy and capacity of criminal enforcement bureaucracies.

Plainly, the benefits of using criminal enforcement to advance regulatory policy goals must involve some combination of actual prosecutions and sanctions as well as the *potential* for them. Settlements and deferred prosecution agreements are unlikely to work without a credible threat of criminal prosecution. On the other hand, much of what is described focuses on the potential impact of criminal investigation rather than merely regulatory review and the threat of civil sanctions. While the organizational conditions giving rise to criminal investigations must include the credible possibility of prosecution, in the course of routine practice (e.g., in "equilibrium") deferred prosecution agreements and settlements are an important part of the picture and have the added social benefit of limiting the need for routine costly imposition of imprisonment and other sanctions.

Moreover, the approach described here suggests that regulators are the central players in elaborating ultimate regulatory goals, or at least filling the details left by legislatures. Although law enforcement officials must often make general interpretive judgments across policy domains, they are unlikely to be in an adequate position to harmonize the technocratic capacity and pluralistic political participation that result in reasonable regulatory policies. Indeed, some of the benefits involve the *interplay* of regulatory power and criminal enforcement jurisdiction, including the conveyance of appropriate matters from one bureaucracy to another. Hence, for the most part the approach here describes law enforcement officials working in concert with regulators rather than supplanting them. The one caveat here involves situations where law enforcement officials' greater degree of political autonomy allows them to pursue important regulatory missions (e.g., as with occupational safety in local contexts) where conventional regulators find it more difficult to do so. But, overall, the picture is one of complementarities between civil regulatory and criminal enforcement, rather than replacement.

IV. Conclusion

Government has always found occasions to deploy the strategic advantages of criminal sanctions in risk regulation, and it will continue to do so. Far from reflecting only recent encroachment into regulatory territory, criminal law has long had a "regulatory edge" encompassing the management of social and economic risks, rendering the criminal justice system "both more and less than the moral steward of society."[91] But to cite our law's doctrinal structure and historical legacy in this area in very general terms hardly settles the matter of *how* the criminal justice system should be used to regulate risks in a democratic, advanced industrialized state. The relevant question for policymakers is precisely when and to what degree we should deploy this "regulatory edge" of criminal justice to manage a world where privately sponsored brutality and grave yet unseen risks exert a major impact on our lives. A close look at the work of key players in the system reveals a complex interplay of organizational, political, practical, and doctrinal reasons for the entanglement of crime control and regulatory policy. Only through careful appreciation of these institutional dynamics can we hope to establish a proper role for criminal justice in the regulatory state.

NOTES

1. *See* Lawrence M. Friedman, Crime and Punishment in American History 172 (1993) ("In [American] society, and in all modern societies, there is an ideal form or image of criminal justice. Only the state, the law, has the right to use force. The state is supposed to have a 'monopoly of legitimate violence.' And the only rightful use of force is against force . . . ."); Jonathan Simon, Governing Through Crime: How the War on Crime Transformed American Democracy and Created a Culture of Fear (2007).

2. *See Mass Incarceration in the United States: At What Cost?: Hearing Before the Joint Economic Committee*, 110th Cong. (2007); Bernard E. Harcourt, *Reflecting on the Subject: A Critique of the Social Influence Conception of Deterrence, the Broken Windows Theory, and Order-Maintenance Policing New York Style*, 97 Mich. L. Rev. 291, 298–99 (1998) (linking New York City's increased use of misdemeanor arrests to higher numbers of police brutality complaints and disproportionate minority arrests); Tracey L. Meares, *Social Organization and Drug Law Enforcement*, 35 Am. Crim. L. Rev. 191, 205–11 (1998) (arguing that a drug enforcement strategy of mass incarceration only exacerbates social ills related to drug use).

3. *Cf.* Susan Bandes, *Patterns of Injustice: Police Brutality in the Courts*, 47 Buff. L. Rev. 1275 (1999) (describing numerous incidents of police brutality as support for the claim that patterns of brutality often go unrecognized by courts).

4. *See, e.g.*, Charles Tilly, Coercion, Capital, and European States (1992).

5. *See, e.g.*, John C. Coffee, *Paradigms Lost: The Blurring of the Criminal and Civil Law Models—And What Can Be Done About It*, 101 Yale L.J. 1875, 1877 (1992) ("[I]f we measure the success of the criminal law exclusively in terms of the number of crimes prevented, we could wind up, in Herbert Packer's memorable phrase, 'creating an environment in which all are safe but none is free.'" (quoting Herbert L. Packer, The Limits of the Criminal Sanction 65 (1968))); Claire Finkelstein, *Positivism and the Notion of an Offense*, 88 Cal. L. Rev. 335, 376–77 (2000). *But see* Carol S. Steiker, *Foreword: The Limits of the Preventive State*, 88 J. Crim. L. & Criminology 771, 774 (1998).

6. *See generally* Richard H. Pildes, *Conflicts Between American and European Views of Law: The Dark Side of Legalism*, 44 Va. J. Int'l L. 145, 162 (2003); Ronald J. Sievert, *War on Terrorism or Global Law Enforcement Operation?*, 78 Notre Dame L. Rev. 307 (2003); John J. Farmer, *The 2004 Paul Miller Distinguished Lecture: The Rule of Law in an Age of Terror*, 57 Rutgers L. Rev. 747 (2005).

7. *See generally* William J. Stuntz, *The Pathological Politics of Criminal Law*, 100 Mich. L. Rev. 505 (2001).

8. *See* William Niskanen, Bureaucracy and Representative Government (1971).

9. *See generally* Richard M. Cyert & James G. March, A Behavioral Theory of the Firm (1963).

10. *See* Terry M. Moe, *The Politics of Bureaucratic Structure, in* Can the Government Govern? 267, 268 (John E. Chubb & Paul E. Peterson eds., 1989) (discussing how agency structures cater to political ends more than the interests of efficiency and effectiveness).

11. *Cf.* Matthew C. Stephenson, *Bureaucratic Decision Costs and Endogenous Agency Expertise*, 23 J.L. Econ. & Org. 469 (2007) (modeling the circumstances under which imposing decision costs on regulatory bureaucracies—akin to those involved in prosecuting criminal offenders—can cause them to develop endogenous expertise).

12. *See* Stuntz, *supra* note 7, at 543 ("[T]he public's priority is violent crime . . .").

13. The cases may be different—and in particular, the willingness of prosecutors to push the envelope in making more novel and complex legal arguments, *see id.* at 544—but prosecutors and investigators who fail to produce results are unlikely to have the same range of career and professional advancement options as those who do produce results. *See generally* James Q. Wilson, The Investigators: Managing FBI and Narcotics Agents 165 (1978); Michael Edmund O'Neill, *Understanding Federal Prosecutorial Declinations: An Empirical Analysis of Predictive Factors*, 41 Am. Crim. L. Rev. 1439, 1444–45 (2004).

14. *See* Mark H. Haller, *Historical Roots of Police Behavior: Chicago, 1890–1925*, 10 Law & Soc'y Rev. 303, 309 (1976).

15. *See* Luis Garicano & Richard A. Posner, *Intelligence Failures: An Organizational Economics Perspective*, 19 J. Econ. Persp. 151, 163 (2005) (discussing the 9/11 Commission Report's finding that Congress gave the FBI insufficient resources to fulfill its mandate); *see also* Wilson, *supra* note 13, at 197.

16. *See* Wilson, *supra* note 13, at 214.

17. *See, e.g.*, Stuntz, *supra* note 7, at 508 & n.4 ("[E]nforcement discretion, particularly for vice crimes, makes law enforcers into lawmakers.").

18. *See* Wilson, *supra* note 13, at 15.

19. *See* Stuntz, *supra* note 7, at 549 (highlighting the risk of "criminal lawmaking" whereby prosecutors use broad statutes to charge differently than legislators would wish).

20. *See* Mariano-Florentino Cuéllar, *The Tenuous Relationship Between the Fight Against Money Laundering and the Disruption of Criminal Finance*, 93 J. Crim. L. & Criminology 311, 365 (2003); William J. Stuntz, *Race, Class, and Drugs*, 98 Colum. L. Rev. 1795 (1998).

21. *See* Cuéllar, *supra* note 20, at 369.

22. *See* Stuntz, *supra* note 7, at 533, 543.

23. *See* Wilson, *supra* note 13, at 19–21 (comparing the work of a uniformed patrol officer to that of an investigator).

24. *See* Peter K. Manning, *Rules in Organizational Context: Narcotics Law Enforcement in Two Settings*, 18 Soc. Q. 44, 48 (1977) (describing the unspoken understanding among narcotics enforcers about the distinction between "major violators" and "street junkies").

25. *See* David Barstow, *California Leads in Making Employer Pay for Job Deaths*, N.Y. Times, Dec. 23, 2003, at A1.

26. *See* Richard A. Best, Intelligence Issues for Congress, CRS Issue Brief for Congress (2009), *available at* http://ftp.fas.org/sgp/crs/intel/RL33539.pdf (noting that Congress has often criticized the weaknesses of intelligence analysis since 9/11).

27. *See Report of the Joint Inquiry into the Terrorist Attacks on September 11, 2001: Report of the S. Select Comm. on Intelligence and H. Permanent Select Comm. on Intelligence*, 107th Cong. 144–48 (2002), *available at* http://www.gpoaccess.gov/serialset/creports/pdf/fullreport_errata.pdf; *see also* Amy B. Zegart, *"CNN with Secrets": 9/11, the CIA, and the Organizational Roots of Failure*, 20 Int'l J. Intelligence & Counterintelligence 18, 18 (2007).

28. *See* Zegart, *supra* note 27, at 19–20.

29. *See id.* at 23 ("Above all, surveillance of the three terrorists faltered because the CIA's internal structure left no single person or office in charge of the case. . . . [T]he CIA's field office structure focused on where, not who; it was designed to cover broad territory rather than track specific terrorists.").

30. *See* Final Report of the National Commission on Terrorist Attacks upon the United States 268–70 (2004) [hereinafter 9/11 Commission Report], *available at* http://www.gpoaccess.gov/911/pdf/fullreport.pdf.

31. In retrospect, these performance failures proved costly to the intelligence agency and to some of its personnel. Such costs, however, are almost entirely an *ex post* consequence of the September 11 attacks themselves and the subsequent investigation. The more relevant distinction between intelligence and law enforcement agencies concerns their routine tasks, organizational structures, and capacities. In the case of the CIA and other intelligence agencies, these characteristics seem to have been affected by the relative lack of rewards analysts and managers received for ensuring that individuals' whereabouts, actions, and plans could be known and that such information could be validated through presentation to a relatively neutral observer such as a court.

32. Zegart, *supra* note 27, at 25 (quoting an FBI agent as stating, "We had the predicate for a [deleted] investigation if we had that information. . . . [W]e would immediately go out and canvass the sources and try to find out where these people were. . . . [T]hey were very close—they were nearby—[and] . . . [w]e would have used all available investigative techniques. We would have given them the full court press." (citation omitted)). These observations must, of course, be taken with a grain of salt. Nonetheless, they are consistent with deeper structural characteristics of the FBI involving the priority assigned to tracking suspects and gathering information that reflect its role as a criminal enforcement agency.

33. President Clinton was reluctant to launch a reprisal attack without officials being "willing to stand up in public and say, we believe that he [Bin Laden] did [the attack on the U.S.S. *Cole*]." *See* 9/11 Commission Report, *supra* note 30, at 193. The FBI played a critical role in the investigation. *Id.* at 192–93. The CIA had "no definitive answer on [the] crucial question of outside direction of the attack . . . ." *Id.* at 195. Meanwhile, CIA Director Tenet was "surprised to hear that the White House was awaiting a conclusion from him on responsibility for the *Cole* attack . . . ." *Id.* at 196.

34. *See* Barstow, *supra* note 25.

35. The Food, Drug, and Cosmetic Act ("FDCA" or "Act"), 21 U.S.C. § 301 *et seq.*, grants the FDA the authority to regulate, among other items, "drugs" and "devices," §§ 321(g)–(h), 393, defined as such in relevant part on the basis of whether their manufacturers intend them to affect "the structure or any function of the body." 21 U.S.C. § 321(g)(1)(C). In order to determine whether regulation under the FDCA would be possible, the FDA was forced to gather extensive information regarding the pharmacological effects of cigarettes and nicotine, as well as the knowledge of and extent of efforts to manipulate such effects by tobacco companies. *See generally* David Kessler, A Question of Intent (2001).

36. *See* Kessler, *supra note* 35, at 26. Recognizing that the goal of such an office was not necessarily criminal prosecution (even though it would plainly leverage the capacities and cultures that individuals had forged working in an environment favoring prosecution), Kessler identified the objectives of the 100 criminal investigators he was hiring as "meet[ing] the needs not only of law enforcement but of public safety." *Id.* at 26–27.

37. *Id.* at 79.

38. *Id.* at 81–84; *see also* FDA v. Brown & Williamson Tobacco Corp., 529 U.S. 120 (2000).

39. Kessler, *supra* note 35, at 80 (emphasis added).

40. *See id.* at 377–78. Kessler also notes the value of criminal penalties in discussing his eventual response to the Pepsi syringe scare. After his criminal investigators confirmed the incidents involved hoaxes, Kessler "went on national television to underscore that such actions were criminal and to warn that we would prosecute every case. Almost immediately, the torrent of claims slowed to a trickle." *Id.* at 79. Note that threatening prosecution in such cases made it easier to address behavior from disaggregated groups of individuals not acting through private firms generally more sensitive to economic sanctions.

41. *See id.* at 100–01.

42. Obviously, executive officials (and some legislators) may also be concerned about the risk of embarrassment (e.g., resulting from acquittal).

43. *See, e.g.*, Alan Cowell, *Britain Files Charges for 11 Tied to Plot*, N.Y. Times, Aug. 21, 2006, at A1.

44. *See id.*

45. *See* Frank W. Dunham, *Where Moussaoui Meets Hamdi*, 183 Mil. L. Rev. 151 (2005) (describing the uncertainty and the numerous appeals that preceded Hamdi's being able to file a *habeas* petition).

46. *See* Sari Horwitz, Scott Higham & Sylvia Moreno, *Who Killed Chandra Levy: Epilogue*, Wash. Post, July 27, 2008, at A1.

47. It is not even obvious that organizational capacity can be coherently defined in absolute terms rather than relative to specific goals. *See, e.g.*, Mariano-Florentino Cuéllar, *"Securing" the Nation: Law, Politics, and Organization at the Federal Security Agency, 1939–1953*, 76 U. Chi. L. Rev. 587, 638–39 (2009).

48. *See* Friedman, *supra* note 1, at 360.

49. *See* Patrick Roberts, How Bureaucracies Control Change: Autonomy in the FBI and CIA 11 (Apr. 6, 2006) (unpublished CISAC Social Science Seminar Paper) (on file with author); *see also* James Q. Wilson, Bureaucracy: What Government Agencies Do and Why They Do It 181 (1989).

50. *See generally* Daniel P. Carpenter, The Forging of Bureaucratic Autonomy: Reputations, Networks, and Policy Innovation in Executive Agencies (2002).

51. *See generally* John P. Heinz et al., The Hollow Core: Private Interests in National Policy Making 105–55 (1993) (providing empirical data about the career trajectories of Washington representatives).

52. *See* Dan Eggen, *Gonzalez Ready to Leave the Stage*, Wash. Post, Sept. 14, 2007, at A11 (describing Attorney General Alberto Gonzalez's departure from the DOJ following revelations about the politicized firings of federal prosecutors).

53. Karen M. O'Neill, *Organizational Change, Politics, and the Official Statistics of Punishment*, 18 Soc. Forum 245, 246 (2003).

54. On the independence of the Southern District, see Daniel C. Richman, *Prosecutors and Their Agents, Agents and Their Prosecutors*, 103 Colum. L. Rev. 749, 753 n.17 (2003). For a discussion of the organizational factors promoting agency autonomy, see Carpenter, *supra* note 50, at 14. Too much autonomy may be undesirable in the context of sentencing, however, since agencies can be more effective by working within political spheres. *See generally* Rachel E. Barkow, *Administering Crime*, 52 UCLA L. Rev. 715 (2005).

55. *Cf.* Roberts, *supra* note 49, at 27.

56. *See* Barstow, *supra* note 25.

57. *See generally* Richard Stewart, *The Reformation of American Administrative Law*, 88 Harv. L. Rev. 1667, 1672 (1975) ("Coercive controls on private conduct must be authorized by the legislature, and, under the doctrine against delegation of legislative power, the legislature must promulgate rules, standards, goals, or some 'intelligible principle' to guide the exercise of administrative power.").

58. The perceived importance of the criminal justice system's independence might encompass two conceptually distinct dimensions: one involving the protection of the integrity of criminal investigations, *see, e.g.*, Thomas Newcomb, *In from the Cold: The Intelligence Community Whistleblower Protection Act of 1998*, 53 Admin. L. Rev. 1235, 1253–54 (2001), and another emphasizing the importance of ensuring that law enforcement–related policies and activities in general are not diluted or manipulated for unrelated political purposes. *See, e.g.*, Einer Elhauge, *Preference-Estimating Statutory Default Rules*, 102 Colum. L. Rev. 2027, 2139 (2002); David A. Sklansky, *Police and Democracy*, 103 Mich. L. Rev. 1699, 1819 (2005). *But see* William J. Vizzard, In the Cross Fire: A Political History of the Bureau of Alcohol, Tobacco, and Firearms 217 (1997).

59. *See* Ari Adut, *Scandal as Norm Entrepreneurship Strategy: Corruption and the French Investigating Magistrates*, 33 Theory & Soc'y 529, 530–32 (2004).

60. *See id.* at 555.

61. *Id.* at 553.

62. *See id.* at 564–65; *see also* Violaine Roussel, *Changing Definitions of Risk and Responsibility in French Political Scandals*, 29 J.L. Soc'y 461 (2002).

63. *See generally* Ken Gormley, *Impeachment and the Independent Counsel: A Dysfunctional Union*, 51 Stan. L. Rev. 309 (1999).

64. *See* Barstow, *supra* note 25.

65. *See* Simon, *supra* note 1, at 37–39.

66. *See* Stuntz, *supra* note 7.

67. *See* Karis Ann-Yu Chi, *Follow the Money: Getting to the Root of the Problem with Civil Asset Forfeiture in California*, 90 Cal. L. Rev. 1635, 1647–48 (2002).

68. *See* Athan Theoharis, *FBI Wiretapping: A Case Study of Bureaucratic Autonomy*, 107 Poli. Sci. Q. 101 (1992).

69. *See generally* Daniel C. Richman, *Federal Criminal Law, Congressional Delegation, and Enforcement Discretion*, 46 UCLA L. Rev. 757 (1999).

70. *See* Stuntz, *supra* note 7, at 546 ("When making criminal law, Congress has the same...incentive[] as state legislatures—to pay attention to the needs and wants of prosecutors and the police.").

71. For a theoretical critique of the "broken windows" policing strategy, see Harcourt, *supra* note 2.

72. It is a heightened version of this notion that seems so profoundly entrenched in some classic administrative law cases favorably disposed toward political control of regulatory agencies. *See, e.g.*, Chevron U.S.A., Inc. v. Natural Res. Def. Council, 467 U.S. 837, 865 (1984); Motor Vehicle Mfrs. Ass'n v. State Farm Mut. Auto. Ins. Co., 463 U.S. 29, 57 (1983) (Rehnquist, J., concurring in part and dissenting in part).

73. *See, e.g.*, Terry M. Moe, *Integrating Politics and Organizations: Positive Theory and Public Administration*, 4 J. Pub. Admin. Res. & Theory 17 (1994); Peter Cleary Yeager, *Industrial Water Pollution*, 18 Crime & Just. 97 (1993). Note that such control may affect the distribution of criminal prosecutions because of regulatory agencies' role in detecting offenses. Still, criminal investigations can sometimes have their own detection strategies (including, for instance, whistle-blowers, citizen suit provisions, and referrals raising concern among law enforcement officials). Indeed, it is perhaps the prospect of impacting the distribution of punishment that probably leads some actors to focus on shaping detection by targeting weaker regulatory agencies instead of risking apparent manipulation of criminal justice agencies.

74. *See, e.g.*, United States v. Weitzenhoff, 35 F.3d 1275, 1293 (9th Cir. 1993) (Kleinfeld, J., dissenting).

75. *See generally* Matthew Rabin & Joel L. Schrag, *First Impressions Matter: A Model of Confirmatory Bias*, 114 Q.J. Econ. 37 (1999); Charles S. Taber & Milton Lodge, *Motivated Skepticism in the Evaluation of Political Beliefs*, 50 Am. J. Poli. Sci. 755 (2006).

76. *See, e.g.*, Katherine Beckett, *Setting the Public Agenda: "Street Crime" and Drug Use in American Politics*, 41 Soc. Probs. 425 (1994); Julian V. Roberts, *Public Opinion, Crime, and Criminal Justice*, 16 Crime & Just. 99 (1992).

77. *Cf.* Lawrence M. Friedman, *Legal Rules and the Process of Social Change*, 19 Stan. L. Rev. 786 (1967).

78. *See, e.g.*, Cuéllar, *supra* note 20, at 351–63.

79. *See, e.g.*, Wilson, Bureaucracy, *supra* note 49, at 352 (describing how competition between sheriff departments in California led to more efficient law enforcement outcomes).

80. *See* Mark Kelman, Yuval Rottenstreich & Amos Tversky, *Context-Dependence in Legal Decision Making*, 25 J. Legal Stud. 287 (1996).

81. *Cf.* Mukesh Bhargava, John Kim & Rajendra K. Srivastava, *Explaining Context Effects on Choice Using a Model of Comparative Judgment*, 9 J. Consumer Psych. 167 (2000).

82. *See* Joseph F. Dimento, *Criminal Enforcement of Environmental Law*, 525 Annals of Am. Acad. of Pol. & Soc. Sci. 134, 138 (1993).

83. *See When a Worker Is Killed: Do OSHA Penalties Enhance Workplace Safety?: Hearing Before the S. Comm. on Health, Education, Labor & Pensions*, 110th Cong. 3, 6 (2008) (statement of David M. Uhlmann), *available at* http://help.senate.gov/imo/media/doc/uhlmann.pdf.

84. *See* Friedman, *supra* note 1, at 289–90.
85. *See* Cuéllar, *supra* note 20, at 348.
86. *See* Barstow, *supra* note 25.
87. *See* Cuéllar, *supra* note 20, at 393–95.
88. *Id.* at 444–47.
89. *See id.* at 393–96.
90. *See id.* at 328–29.
91. Lawrence M. Friedman, A History of American Law 592 (Simon & Schuster, 2d ed. 1985).

7

Collaborative Organizational Prosecution

BRANDON L. GARRETT

This chapter begins a discussion about the merits of "regulation by prosecution" by framing the increasingly close but complex relationship between prosecutors and regulators in corporate cases. The Supreme Court has held that parallel administrative and criminal penalties against the same firm do not raise double jeopardy issues.[1] As a result, corporations may face parallel proceedings by civil regulatory authorities and criminal prosecutors in the same matter, including in multiple jurisdictions. Commentators have long debated the significance of such blurring of the civil and criminal distinction. Less examined has been the institutional relationship between civil and criminal enforcers as they adjudicate organizational cases. One might argue that as a normative matter, although they are vested with overlapping authority, civil and criminal enforcers should try to maintain separate roles, where prosecutors enforce criminal prohibitions and civil authorities employ a broader regulatory function. However, this chapter questions any rigid institutional distinction between civil and criminal enforcement. The relationship between federal regulators and prosecutors has grown surprisingly close, and a largely collaborative approach has emerged, in three respects that this chapter describes.

First, single prosecutions can have a deterrent effect extending beyond the single case. When settling a prosecution with one firm in a deferred or nonprosecution agreement, prosecutors typically require that the firm adopt compliance reforms, a subject that I have written about previously and termed as efforts to accomplish "structural reform."[2] Such actions are forward-looking, and thus more like a regulation in the sense that future conduct is altered, than an action seeking merely to penalize past criminal conduct.[3] The settlement of a single prosecution can influence the conduct of other similarly situated firms. After all, they know that prosecutors have in the past rewarded certain types of compliance reforms and cooperation. Federal prosecutors also promote broader deterrence. They issue guidelines stating the goals and purposes of organizational prosecutions, and in doing so, prosecutors say they hope to "send a message" to influence change in "corporate culture." Prosecutors also regularly give speeches announcing such goals to industry groups. Regulatory agencies have adopted parallel civil enforcement approaches that reward similar compliance and cooperation by firms. In that sense, regulators and prosecutors operate in tandem.

Second, prosecutors and regulators collaborate in joint adjudication. What has been little recognized is that many federal organizational prosecution agreements were negotiated jointly with regulatory agencies. Many were first investigated by regulators and then referred to federal prosecutors, although the precise nature and scope of the collaboration are typically not public.[4] While such broad-reaching agreements do not constitute "regulation" in the sense that an entire industry is bound by a rulelike norm, they do create a structural reform approach for remedying violations. They should not, however, typically be seen as an extension of the underlying adjudicatory goals of the agency. While there may be close collaboration in individual cases, referrals are not typically made in any consistent or strategic way. Agencies often refer matters on an informal and ad hoc basis, and prosecutors retain discretion to initiate matters on their own. Enforcement dynamics are further complicated where regulators or prosecutors may or may not have a clear agenda in an area and where one actor or another may have greater resources, expertise, or independence. Criminal adjudication, because it is far more infrequent, may not as clearly announce enforcement priorities in the way that regulatory agencies often do through adjudication. Further, prosecutors have not typically consciously sought to use criminal adjudication to accomplish regulatory goals. Prosecutors are divided between state and federal offices with considerable autonomy. As a result, criminal adjudication does not usually exhibit regulatory priorities of prosecutors, much less those of regulators. However, regulators and prosecutors use an informal collaborative approach to increase the deterrent effect of adjudication and to preserve their discretion, flexibility, and resources.

Third, in some unusual cases prosecutors adopt a different and specific regulatory goal—general deterrence of all organizations situated similarly to the target entity, perhaps even entire industries, by using adjudication to cement a rulelike norm or industry reform. In literature citing tort cases as examples of "regulation through litigation," commentators have focused on mass tort cases targeting entire industries and often negotiating global settlements that include regulatory changes outside the rule-making process.[5] In the past few years, as organizational prosecutions have increased in number from a handful to close to a hundred, the approach of federal prosecutors has evolved. Prosecutors typically do not seek to influence entire industries, but there are a few fascinating examples of such an approach. While any corporate prosecution raises important questions regarding coordination with regulators, when prosecutors take part in efforts to accomplish regulatory ends, particularly novel questions are raised about the prosecutorial role. Perhaps for that reason, prosecutors in each example cooperated with regulators in pursuing industry reform.

This chapter concludes that our complex system of overlapping enforcement authority has many benefits, and despite a sometimes tense partnership between prosecutors and regulators, it is no surprise that none have sought to fundamentally restructure that relationship. In practice, prosecutors work closely with regulators, and they now share many of the same goals. As a practical matter, this status quo could only be altered with difficulty and with real costs. Both regulators and prosecutors benefit from both informality and collaboration. The great surprise is the degree to which regulators and prosecutors have coordinated their approaches, typically through informal means. Where regulators and prosecutors have fundamentally different structures, adjudicatory procedures, and underlying enforcement goals, there will be some disconnect between their efforts. However, the Financial Fraud Enforcement Task Force, agency guidelines, and other informal agency interactions can aim to improve cooperation between regulators and prosecutors, without unduly constraining their discretion.

I. Organizational Prosecutions and the Regulatory Context

On first blush, the notion that an individual prosecution could "regulate" seems counterintuitive. After all, prosecutions involve highly individualized facts, varying employee conduct, state of mind requirements, all litigated on a case-by-case basis, often resulting in negotiated resolutions in which little is made public. All those features of prosecutions make them awkward vehicles for regulation. However, prosecutions of corporations are often different than typical criminal cases. I say often because the overwhelming majority of corporations prosecuted are small firms that may be alter egos of individuals participating in a criminal enterprise. In contrast, large corporations are typically legitimate businesses that seek to comply with the law. Unlike other types of criminal actors, large corporations may be particularly attentive to patterns of prosecutions as they seek to comply and avoid the potentially dire consequences of a prosecution. The prosecution of a large corporation affects others, particularly firms subject to similar prohibitions, in a manner similar to that in which administrative agencies use civil adjudication to regulate. Before turning to the outsized impact of an organizational prosecution, I discuss how organizational prosecutors proceed, briefly, because others in this volume will have discussed this.

In response to a series of corporate governance scandals, the DOJ created a Corporate Fraud Task Force (since renamed as the Financial Fraud Enforcement Task Force) and fostered more frequent federal investigation and prosecution of corporate conduct than in the past.[6] The task force was created to foster collaboration and coordination between prosecutors and regulatory agencies; it includes ten federal agencies, as well as federal prosecutors.[7] It is unclear how much substantive coordination the task force conducts. Dan Richman has, for example, called it chiefly a "branding device" to take credit for the work of the various U.S. Attorneys' offices and agencies, without assuming significant oversight.[8] Perhaps not due to the task force's efforts, the prosecution approach that emerged in the years since is one that I have called a structural reform approach, and one that I have described elsewhere in some detail.[9] The DOJ has followed revised guidelines for organizational prosecutions under which prosecutors typically defer prosecution or agree not to prosecute if a firm will enter into an agreement.[10] The guidelines are nonbinding and contain a series of charging factors to be considered; as a result, the settlements that result provide additional information about decision making. The settlement agreements are consistent in their broad outlines. They typically require that a firm adopt a compliance program, retain an independent monitor, admit guilt, and cooperate with any investigation or prosecution of current or former employees. The overriding goal of the agreements is the institutional reform of the target firm and not general deterrence of an entire industry.

While the DOJ's guidelines do not specify in advance the type of compliance that it seeks from organizations, the agreements themselves suggest the types of compliance programs that prosecutors seek to implement. In doing so, the DOJ may foster the adoption of such compliance efforts throughout corporate America. Doing so does not take the form of a regulation, but corporations may structure their behavior in anticipation of the DOJ's enforcement approach. The DOJ guidelines on compliance mirror and reference the requirements of the Organizational Sentencing Guidelines, which provide more detail regarding sought-after compliance than the DOJ's memos or agreements. Corporations have paid close attention to those DOJ memos (and have successfully advocated for a range of modifications to them). The result does not clearly define criminal prohibitions or provide notice to industry regarding what interpretations of regulations or associated criminal prohibitions are advanced. However, predictable steps can be taken to obtain leniency. No matter the context, corporations have strong incentives to cooperate and create rigorous compliance programs.

Taking strong action against a single firm can also impact an industry to the extent that the firm behaved in a manner common to other similarly situated firms. The DOJ in its Thompson Memo cited the ability of an indictment to encourage not just specific deterrence but also "deterrence on a massive scale" as the rest of the industry responds. In the Filip Memo, the DOJ put it slightly differently, stating that "corporations are likely to take immediate remedial steps when one is indicted for criminal misconduct that is pervasive throughout a particular industry, and thus an indictment can provide a unique opportunity for deterrence on a broad scale."[11]

Similarly, in a deferred prosecution agreement, a large fine may be designed to send a message to the industry that criminal violations will be taken seriously. For example, after ITT was fined $100 million and pleaded guilty to compromising night vision technology in violation of the Arms Export Control Act, the government announced that the fine was "one of the largest ever paid in a criminal case," and that the prosecutors hoped, at least, that "the agreement reached with ITT will send a clear message that any corporation who unlawfully sends classified or export-controlled material overseas will be prosecuted and punished."[12]

DOJ has also avoided seeking indictments with the express interest in *not* harming an entire industry. Attorney General Alberto Gonzales explained that the DOJ did not indict KPMG in part because of the concern with "protecting innocent workers and others from the consequences of a conviction."[13]

II. Interaction Between Regulators and Prosecutors

On its face, the current DOJ approach avoids a regulatory role except in the sense that firms have incentives to generally cooperate and adopt a range of compliance practices, or face potentially dire consequences of an indictment or conviction. Corporate prosecutions also often involve offenses that are "regulatory" in nature, in that they involve crimes defined as willful or knowing violations of regulations, such as securities or bank regulations. An additional feature of the current regime could reinforce regulation: federal prosecutors usually work arm in arm with regulators when pursuing organizational prosecutions. This should be no surprise; the stated purpose of the Task Force is to coordinate federal organizational prosecutions with the SEC and other relevant regulatory agencies. Constitutional criminal procedure explains still additional coordination. Should a case go forward to a trial, prosecutors may be "charged with knowledge" of the parallel civil investigation. Courts have held that prosecutors possess a duty under *Brady v. Maryland* to obtain investigation materials from civil regulators and to disclose any material potentially exculpatory information to the defense.[14] Further, the SEC and other agencies share a parallel approach to their parallel litigation. They have adopted similar enforcement guidelines rewarding cooperation and compliance. Many DPAs and NPAs incorporate similar terms from civil settlements with regulators, and many arose from collaboration between prosecutors and regulators. While we can learn from settlement agreements that there was collaboration between prosecutors and regulators, and we can discern something as to the nature of that collaboration, from the outside, we know few details about the precise nature of the work. Relationships between prosecutors and regulators should be studied further, and they may vary quite a bit depending on the prosecutor and the regulator involved, as well as the type of case.

Why do regulators refer cases to prosecutors, and when and how do they refer cases? First, stepping back, regulators themselves face an initial choice whether to regulate conduct by rulemaking or adjudication.[15] That policymaking choice is broad and often largely unconstrained. That is, they may issue regulations to interpret a federal statute (or they must do so if Congress required promulgation of regulations). Alternatively, they may use adjudication in administrative actions or civil enforcement actions in court to resolve issues in a case-by-case fashion. Each method has its merits and disadvantages. Rulemaking is today "a labor-intensive enterprise," requiring agency deliberation, "notice and comment," including hearings involving the public, and availability of judicial review.[16] However, rulemaking results in generally applicable rules. Adjudication is flexible and fact-specific, involves trial-like proceedings, and is far less burdensome and faster. While adjudication does not involve the same transparency or clarity, some agencies must conduct public hearings before entering into a consent decree.[17] Finally, agencies often issue "guidance documents" that do not involve rules or adjudication, but rather explain agency interpretations, positions, or enforcement priorities in a nonbinding fashion.[18] The Thompson Memo and the SEC's Seaboard Report are examples of such documents, which each provide guidance regarding principles for enforcement against corporations.[19]

Adjudication against corporate entities may often occur in cases involving potentially criminal conduct, in which not only were regulations violated, but in a manner involving a more-than-negligent state of mind by high-level corporate actors. Agencies often seek consent decrees and civil penalties in such cases—and they typically obtain them, with, for example, more than 90 percent of SEC enforcement actions resulting in settlements.[20] Indeed, Congress has stepped in to increase the power of the SEC to obtain equitable relief in its enforcement actions. The Sarbanes-Oxley Act provided the SEC with the power to obtain from courts not just relief to remedy a violation but also "any equitable relief that may be appropriate or necessary for the benefit of investors."[21] Monitors retained by the SEC as part of consent decrees have acted with broad authority to reform corporate governance. Richard Breeden's work in the WorldCom case is a particularly high-profile example of such an undertaking.[22] Breeden, after being appointed by Judge Jed S. Rakoff, assumed a wide-ranging role in reshaping the governance of WorldCom, including by reviewing the budget, executive compensation, and facilitating its merger with MCI and helping to choose the new board of directors.[23]

Such regulatory adjudication is intended to accomplish both specific and general deterrence goals. The SEC, for example, states that fines should be assessed against corporations not only to deter the repetition of the conduct but also with consideration of the likelihood that the penalty "will serve as a strong deterrent to others similarly situated."[24] Where the agency observes pervasive misconduct, recidivism, or complicity of high-level officials, it may then conclude civil penalties may not be sufficient to deter future violations. Or it may conclude that in some cases the entity is intransigent, concealing its conduct, and will remain unwilling to cooperate unless prosecutors become involved. Thus, some subset of cases adjudicated by an agency may be determined appropriate for referral to prosecutors.

Regulatory adjudication can proceed case by case, but it can sometimes also take the following form: the agency announces an enforcement priority in an area where the regulation is not clear. The agency initiates a series of enforcement actions to corral industry players and ensure compliance with the new norm. Such efforts resemble rulelike regulation far more than the typical case-by-case adjudication, in that they seek as their goal to promote a new industry norm by using a series of cases litigated as part of an adjudicatory strategy. The EPA, for example, has pursued such a strategy in the area of petroleum refinery compliance with the Clean Air Act.[25] Since 2000, the EPA has sought to enter into settlement agreements one by one with every refinery, and it has successfully done so. The EPA "has entered into 22 settlements with U.S. companies that refine nearly 87 percent of the Nation's petroleum refining capacity" and notes that negotiations "are continuing with other refiners representing an additional 6 percent of domestic refining capacity and investigations are underway on others."[26] The settlements thus cover almost the entire petroleum refining industry, and they require a range of structural reforms, adoption of new technologies, as well as fines, and "supplemental environmental projects."[27] Thus, the EPA announced its policymaking goal and then pursued it using a concerted adjudication effort.

If the DOJ were to take a set of formal referrals from regulatory agencies, then firms could simply look to the regulatory agency for information about enforcement priorities. It would be no departure from the EPA's already-announced policymaking effort if the EPA referred a case of an egregiously noncomplying refinery to the DOJ. But that is an unlikely "if."

The current approach does not look like such an ideal view of regulatory adjudication buttressed by prosecutorial adjudication. Federal prosecutors and federal regulators have separate and independent authority to file actions against firms, if the conduct violates both civil and criminal prohibitions. Under the current approach, prosecutors typically enter into agreements that resemble regulatory consent decrees in many respects, and they do it with the cooperation of regulators. Joint investigations often result in joint settlement agreements, including agreements that give regulators a crucial role, even in selecting the independent monitor, monitoring compliance, and deciding whether the agreement has been successfully completed. The substantial role of regulatory agencies in investigating, negotiating, and also implementing most DPAs and NPAs is underappreciated.[28] The DOJ's approach was modeled on and complements the self-reporting, disclosure, and compliance regimes that a series of federal agencies currently use to secure compliance (as well as the U.S. Sentencing Commission Organizational Sentencing Guidelines). Such regulatory regimes establish remedial norms and involve regulators in monitoring firms. The DOJ often learns of cases from civil investigators. The regulators often participate in the negotiation of a settlement. The independent monitor is often selected in consultation with the regulators and reports to the regulators, and thus the entire compliance effort is conducted in conjunction with regulators.

It would be entirely natural, then, to see such prosecutions as extensions of the regulatory agency's adjudicatory goals. The agency uses adjudication to pursue its regulatory agenda and then refers selected egregious cases for additional criminal punishment (often in conjunction with a civil regulatory enforcement action). However, while substantial collaboration often does exist between prosecutors and regulators, it is typically not formalized or consistent. Regulatory agencies themselves may not have clearly defined adjudicatory strategies. Indeed, coordination within enforcement agencies can raise substantial challenges for administrators.[29]

Nor have prosecutors announced any intention to collaborate with regulators in accepting referrals based on the adjudicatory priorities of regulators. Prosecutors have their own priorities, which include obtaining convictions of individual wrongdoers, leveraging their enforcement resources, and pursuing criminal enforcement priorities set by the DOJ or the president. The various U.S. Attorneys' offices are decentralized, unlike a single regulatory agency, and so perhaps could not be expected to effectively coordinate a single adjudicatory approach with a regulatory agency.

Regulatory agencies, due to their complexity, may have internal disagreements about how to investigate or handle a matter. While U.S. Attorneys' offices may also have such disagreements, they have a simpler structure granting far greater discretion to line attorneys. In some contexts, prosecutors are long used to working on their own cases, to enforce criminal laws and not based on outside regulatory priorities. In other contexts, prosecutors routinely collaborate. Even when they do so, prosecutors are long used to deference from civil investigators and regulators. In some respects this may be undesirable, if prosecutors undermine regulatory consistency. In other respects this may be highly desirable, if prosecutors are less subject to industry capture and can more effectively marshal investigative resources.

The interaction between agencies and prosecutors is often ad hoc and not the product of any formalized referral procedure—and the degree of collaboration does not lend itself to generalization but depends very much on which federal agency is involved, in which type of matter, and with which prosecutors. To continue with the EPA example, the EPA has a voluntary disclosure program that in many respects resembles the DOJ's approach to organizational prosecutions. Indeed, most federal agencies have adopted over the past several decades quite similar adjudicatory regimes rewarding self-reporting, cooperation, and the adoption of compliance programs.

The EPA program states that firms providing full cooperation under the program will not receive a formal criminal referral. Those assurances may hold true for the most part in practice. However, as a formal matter, a firm cannot count on any such assurance against prosecution. Prosecutors ultimately retain their own discretion to initiate action. First, firms may or may not be found not to have fully cooperated, and if not they would then be eligible for a referral. Second, even cooperating firms may be subject to an investigation that leads to an informal referral to the DOJ, such as a sharing of information during an investigation to pique prosecutorial interest in the case. Further, the DOJ may open a criminal investigation based on information learned from the voluntary disclosure program but absent any EPA referral, formal or informal.[30]

Other agencies also regularly use informal exchange of information and consultation as a supplement to formal referral processes. The SEC has a formal referral process in which a report is prepared and presented to the commission, which then decides whether to refer the case.[31] Yet "in practice, this formal referral process is rarely used."[32] Informal discussion of cases is far more common, and the DOJ may make a written request for investigative files. U.S. Attorneys may also initiate their own prosecutions, and they often do. SEC staff may bring cases to prosecutors' attention without preparing any reports or bringing the cases to the attention of the commission itself. The SEC does not document such informal referrals.[33]

Agencies must also be disaggregated. Line regulators may have different priorities than distant supervisors at the top of the hierarchy. Large agencies have problems tracking enforcement, managing enforcement priorities, and coordinating internal communications. Resolving such issues with respect to outside agencies, much less decentralized prosecutors' offices, poses even greater challenges.

At the other end of the spectrum, the IRS has the most formalized procedures for investigation and referral of criminal matters, in part because it must follow certain rules regarding confidentiality of tax return information. Civil audits by revenue agents are suspended if the agent finds a "firm indication of fraud" and are transferred to the IRS Criminal Investigation Division ("CID"), which will in its discretion assign a special agent to investigate the case.[34] Procedures permit that special agent to prepare a report and make a recommendation about a possible prosecution only if the evidence is "sufficient to establish guilt beyond a reasonable doubt."[35] Next, CID sends the case to the IRS Counsel's Office, the taxpayer has an opportunity to present evidence, and the case may be transferred to the DOJ Tax Division.[36] However, despite those multilayered investigation and referral procedures, the IRS permits "the necessary solicitation of advice and assistance with respect to a case prior to formal referral of the entire case to the Justice Department for defense, prosecution, or other affirmative action."[37]

Some offices, like agency offices of inspectors general, conduct only investigations, after which they may refer matters to agencies or to prosecutors for further action.[38] Thus, the U.S. Department of Housing and Human Services' Office of Inspector General ("OIG") adopted a Provider Self-Disclosure Protocol rewarding voluntary reporting and compliance, adopted in conjunction with the DOJ and the U.S. Attorneys' offices.[39] However, the OIG cannot guarantee that compliance with the program will ensure that there will be no referral to the DOJ. After all, prosecutors could simply decide to take a case. Thus, the OIG advises that "[b]ecause a provider's disclosure can involve anything from a simple error to outright fraud, the OIG cannot reasonably make firm commitments as to how a particular disclosure will be resolved or the specific benefit that will enure to the disclosing entity."[40]

There are many reasons why both regulators and prosecutors might prefer an informal referral regime. Indeed, both might oppose any effort to require an agency referral as a prerequisite to an organizational prosecution. Informal interactions facilitate the use of joint and interagency investigations of potentially criminal conduct, which might tend to occur well before any decision about a referral was to be made. Less formality permits less bureaucratic work; it means fewer memos and reports and less time spent administering the referral process. As noted, dysfunctional communication within agencies may lead to lack of coordination both with civil enforcement groups and with outside enforcers. Adding new complexity to the process of communicating with prosecutors might simply hamper effective enforcement. Our largely informal process is more flexible and faster. Agency staff may desire legal advice from prosecutors long before they decide whether a case is ripe for a referral.

Other aspects also benefit enforcers but at the expense, perhaps, of the target firms. Less transparency means firms cannot complain that they were improperly selected. Firms also cannot rest secure that they will be subject only to civil penalties; a criminal referral may occur informally if the case piques a prosecutor's interest. Finally, and perhaps most important, the unique power and discretion of federal prosecutors explains the current approach. Federal prosecutors rarely precommit to abstain from prosecuting firms under any internal formal procedure, much less that of an agency.

Since prosecutors can take a case on their own initiative, they can short-circuit any formal referral process. As a result, the current regime, while unlikely to change, is not a transparent process designed to optimally further a clear adjudicatory agenda (should such an agenda exist). Instead, regulators and prosecutors often work together, and perhaps quite effectively, but not by formally coordinating their discretion. The result, some complain, makes it less predictable which cases will ultimately be referred for criminal prosecution. On the other hand, the public may also benefit from the current approach. An agency can become captured, and leadership can stymie civil enforcement. One can imagine occasions where the relatively greater political independence of prosecutorial offices could be a benefit if an agency was not sufficiently pursuing certain enforcement objectives. Indeed, informal referrals to prosecutors may become more common if agencies attempt to centralize oversight to unduly constrain enforcement.

III. Organizational Prosecutions and Regulatory Norms

Prosecutors have not announced any intention to formally complement a regulatory adjudication regime. They do often cooperate with regulators, and guidance documents of the DOJ and agencies share the same focus on self-reporting, cooperation, and compliance. At times, prosecutors have gone further and sought to shape and enforce their regulatory priorities. What is most interesting about the few noteworthy examples of such ambitious actions is that most involve close collaboration with regulators.

A. The Global Research Settlement

Perhaps the most well-known and ambitious effort to date to prosecute an entire industry was lead by the then NY AG Eliot Spitzer against top investment firms. Of course, that office functioned as not only a prosecutor but also a regulator pursuing civil enforcement for the State of New York. The office viewed (and still views) its role as that of a regulator, much unlike the way federal prosecutors view their role. This investigation began with an investigation of fraudulent reporting by research analysts at Merrill Lynch, which was settled in 2002.[41] An early critic of that settlement called the case "a prime example of regulation by prosecution. Although the settlement does not by its terms apply to the entire securities industry, there are similar ongoing investigations of other firms that could result in similar settlements."[42] That fear came to pass; the investigation by Spitzer revealed more widespread positive reporting on securities despite known negative information.

The NY AG joined forces with the SEC, stock exchanges, and other regulators to reach a global research settlement. The enforcement agencies announced in 2003 that "enforcement actions against ten of the nation's top investment firms have been completed, thereby finalizing the global settlement."[43] The ten leading firms were to pay $875 million in penalties and disgorgement, much of which was placed in a fund to compensate customers, together with $432.5 million to fund independent research.[44] The agreement also required that for five years "each of the firms will be required to contract with no fewer than three independent research firms that will make available independent research to the firm's customers."[45] The agreement required adoption of structural reforms as well, including retention of an independent monitor for eighteen months. Each firm agreed to "separate research and investment banking, including physical separation, completely separate reporting lines, separate legal and compliance staffs, and separate budgeting processes."[46] The firms needed to alter compensation of analysts so that it would not be linked in any way to investment banking revenue and had to adopt a range of policies, including "firewalls," to ensure no investment banking influence on research.[47]

Perhaps even more resembling a form of new regulation than each of those industry-wide structural reforms, the settlement also adopted what was in effect a series of new disclosure requirements. Those requirements included publication each quarter of analyst performance, disclosures on each research report that the firm "does and seeks to do business with companies covered in its research reports," and a requirement that the firm "issue a final research report discussing the reasons for the termination" of an issuer.[48] North American Securities Administrators Association ("NASAA") President Christine Bruenn described the settlement in those terms, stating that the prosecutors "worked with national regulators on enforcement actions and market-wide rule changes."[49]

Some regulations on the subject had already been adopted by the time of the settlement.[50] When Congress passed the Sarbanes-Oxley Act in 2002, additional rulemaking was required on the subject of research analyst conflicts of interest, though unlike the settlement, Congress simply requested that regulators adopt additional rules, which the SEC and the exchanges then did.[51]

Indeed, the NY AG specifically cited the failure of regulators to address the problem, stating that "the SEC was not doing enough."[52] Of course, the SEC not only actively cooperated but publicly stated, at least, that it welcomed prosecutors' efforts.[53] The Global Research Settlement can be criticized for adopting the wrong sorts of regulations, but more of interest here, it can also be criticized for regulating outside the political process and for creating regulations inconsistent with those adopted through the political process. To the extent that Sarbanes-Oxley led to the adoption of regulations that incompletely address the problem, because there was no need to duplicate elements of the Global Research Settlement, the prosecution may have short-circuited the regulatory process. To the extent that regulators joined in the effort, it could be because they welcomed the shortcut, but perhaps also because if they did not join, they would lose any voice in what amounted to a binding industry regulation. Such an effort raises very difficult questions about the legitimacy of attempting to cement regulation through prosecution and also regarding the proper coordination of regulation and prosecution.

B. KPMG

Federal prosecutors have been loath to use organizational prosecutions to cement regulatory norms. However, the KPMG case provides an example in which prosecutors and regulators appear to have tried to use a deferred prosecution agreement to bolster a regulatory norm—though the case also serves as a cautionary tale regarding the potential pitfalls of relying upon the criminal process to accomplish regulatory ends without resort to the regulatory process.

The criminal case had been referred to the DOJ by the IRS, which had for some time been investigating the use of tax shelters by KPMG, including by convening congressional hearings. The IRS had listed the shelters as suspect but had not adopted regulations prohibiting their use. The IRS apparently then sought, in conjunction with the DOJ, to use a prosecution as an adjudication to cement the illegality of the listed shelters. The DPA was negotiated in conjunction with the IRS. The agreement included detailed factual findings regarding the criminality of particular tax shelters, nicknamed BLIPS, FLIP, OPIS, and SOS, that had previously neither been found illegal by a court nor been made illegal by an IRS regulation.[54] The DOJ included similar factual admissions in the related German bank HVB deferred prosecution agreement.[55]

Those admissions that the tax shelters in question were illegal were presumably included to use criminal adjudication to further establish the illegality of the shelters. Tax experts predicted that, using those stipulated findings, "[t]he IRS and Justice Department will attempt to use KPMG's admissions as evidence in litigation with taxpayers on the merits of the shelters."[56] In doing so, the IRS could avoid the regulatory process, with its time-consuming notice and comment rules. Perhaps, then, the IRS drove its regulatory agenda, using the prosecution as its vehicle.

However, any effort to use the prosecution to cement the illegality of the shelters ran aground in several respects that suggest greater difficulty using prosecutions to achieve the goals of rulemaking or regulatory adjudication.

New questions were raised about those admissions when a document surfaced indicating that there was "substantial debate within the I.R.S." about whether such shelters had to be registered with the agency.[57]

Further, the prosecutions of individuals continued after the DPA was signed, and showing fraud required showing state of mind and not simply the illegality of the shelters. Those prosecutions faltered for reasons unrelated to the issue of the shelters' legality, but instead related to a series of criminal procedure rulings by District Judge Lewis A. Kaplan. Ultimately, only three of the sixteen defendants were convicted, with thirteen indictments dismissed.[58] Entity prosecutions are often accompanied by individual prosecutions, in which the prosecutors must prove guilt beyond a reasonable doubt and in which criminal procedure protections apply. Such individual prosecutions, should they fail to result in convictions, may cast doubt on the plea agreement or settlement of the entity, which after all can only have committed a crime through one of its agents. A civil regulatory action, in contrast, has none of those complicating factors.

C. Foreign Corrupt Practices Act

An area in which industry-wide prosecutions are becoming increasingly common is in Foreign Corrupt Practices Act ("FCPA") enforcement.[59] Two commentators note that "[i]nstead of merely targeting persons for their own conduct, in FCPA cases, the government is using the more aggressive strategy of subpoenaing all players in an industry."[60] In this area, the SEC administers the reporting requirements of the FCPA, and though it may refer a case if potential criminality is uncovered in an investigation, Main Justice exclusively prosecutes violations of prohibitions on bribing foreign officials. Thus, the DOJ alone sets enforcement priorities in the area, and in particular, Main Justice exclusively handles FCPA bribery matters.[61]

The DOJ has proceeded by often pursuing entire industries, in the same way that, say, the EPA targets an industry to cement a rule. For example, an industry-wide investigation is currently pending into Swiss logistics conglomerate Panalpina World Transport and payment of bribes to officials in Nigeria. Panalpina recently completely withdrew its operations from Nigeria, perhaps due to concerns regarding SEC and DOJ investigations.[62] The investigation has become, however, "an unprecedented industry-wide investigation," with examination of companies that did business with Panalpina.[63]

Similarly, the investigation of the DOJ and the SEC into oil companies participating in the United Nations Iraq Oil for Food program expanded to include a vast number of industry participants. One commentator called it "conceivably the largest international anti-corruption investigation ever," and the investigation, led by former Federal Reserve Chairman Paul Volcker, has "implicated 2,253 companies worldwide and $1.8 billion in alleged 'kickbacks' to the Iraqi regime of Saddam Hussein," involving in addition to the DOJ and the SEC, "two U.S. Attorney's Offices, four congressional committees, the Manhattan District Attorney's Office, the Department of Treasury's Office of Foreign Asset Control, the United Nations, and at least six foreign governments, to date."[64] Unlike the other examples described, the Independent Inquiry Committee that initially led the investigation and that produced a series of reports was convened by the United Nations, with an international membership.[65] The findings, however, led to investigations in a number of countries. DOJ investigations have resulted in a series of FCPA prosecutions of organizations that had participated in the Iraq Oil for Food program, many of which were settled with DPAs.[66]

This approach is logical. Where no regulatory agency handles the task of broadly interpreting the FCPA using rulemaking or adjudication, the DOJ must itself define priorities and cast a wider net. Unlike in other areas, the DOJ does, however, have the ability to partner with regulators in foreign countries. The DOJ has made increasing efforts to do so, and perhaps such a strategy can result in a targeted adjudicatory approach. To date, though, Main Justice has announced enforcement priorities in speeches and press releases, in the general sense that it has announced that it will aggressively prosecute FCPA violations and will not tolerate noncompliance. However, no more specific priorities have been announced. Instead, the DOJ has proceeded against related firms and industry groups, in the fashion it would were it prosecuting cartel behavior, and as a matter of convenience and logic as investigations unfold and not due to any targeting of specific industry conduct. Thus, one lesson from the FCPA context is that centralization of enforcement authority does not necessarily bring about consistency.

There are few other examples of industry-wide approaches. In a related area involving domestic and not foreign kickbacks, the DOJ prosecuted five corporations that together constitute almost the entire market for hip and knee replacements. The companies, Biomet, Inc., DePuy Orthopaedics, Smith & Nephew, Inc., Zimmer, Inc., and Stryker Orthopedics, Inc., each entered into DPAs with the U.S. Attorney for the District of New Jersey. According to one commentator, the False Claims Act theory in the case, that kickbacks "necessarily give rise to false claims," is "a theory that is not tested."[67] As with other negotiated resolutions, such legal questions are not resolved. However, this industry supervision was not established absent cooperation of regulators. The prosecution agreements were entered simultaneously with corporate integrity agreements with the OIG.[68] Any regulation was the product of collaboration between prosecutors and regulators.

IV. Conclusion

The relationship between prosecutors and regulators remains collaborative, but between partners with different goals. Prosecutors do not often seek to accomplish wide-ranging industry regulation, but in rare cases when they do, they turn to regulators. More typically, however, prosecutors regulate firms in different senses and in a different form than regulators do. While prosecutors and regulators may both seek to reform the same firm, prosecutors may have only a modest interest in any industry regulation agenda, and regulators may have only a modest interest in seeking punishment of responsible parties. That should be no surprise. The real surprise may be the extent to which prosecutors and regulators now collaborate and cooperate even absent formalized procedures for doing so.

The effectiveness of a prosecution and regulatory partnership depends on the performance of each partner and on the exercise of their independent discretion. Regulators select only a subset of possible violators for investigation, then select a subset for adjudication, and may also select an even smaller subset for referral to prosecutors. Regulators can obtain the same types of remedies as prosecutors, and indeed their consent decrees are often more ambitious, though also court-supervised, but they may also pursue reform through regulation. Since few cases are referred to prosecutors, referring the right cases could be important, although the selection of those cases may depend on the goal of the adjudicatory strategy. If the purpose is to cement a disclosure regime, then referring only noncooperating firms would make sense. If the purpose is to additionally punish the most willful wrongdoers, then an assessment of whether high-level employees were involved would make sense. If the purpose is to accomplish specific deterrence, then an assessment of which conduct might most typically evade detection would make sense. Perhaps due to the difficulty of confining decisions to any short list of considerations, agencies often rely on informal contacts and joint investigations.

Prosecutors also retain discretion to initiate a case absent a referral, or to accept or decline a case that is referred. Prosecutors in U.S. Attorneys' offices may not be aware of the underlying goals of the agency's regulatory agenda, nor may they share the same goals. Independent exercise of discretion by prosecutors, including the ability of prosecutors to initiate matters absent an agency referral, may benefit the public. Prosecutors may have more expertise in detecting potential criminality, they may be less subject to industry capture, and they may be able to leverage additional investigative resources. Prosecutors have additional goals, particularly successful prosecution of individual wrongdoers. However, criminal procedure rules can introduce complexities that regulators do not face. It may in practice be quite difficult for prosecutorial discretion to truly complement a regulatory adjudication regime. Criminal cases involve case-specific facts and procedural complexities that may make them hard to use to broadly cement industry norms. For those reasons, few organizational prosecutions display a regulatory agenda. The work by prosecutors often has a one-shot flavor, and the added value of a prosecution may lie more in the cases of unusually intransigent firms and in cases in which prosecutions of individual employees are a high priority.

When prosecutors do seek to promote industry change on their own, they may be on thinner ice, and as a result federal prosecutors have proceeded cautiously and alongside regulators. In some areas, like the FCPA, there is no regulatory agency conducting civil adjudication, so the DOJ sets its own priorities by necessity. In other areas, however, prosecutors and regulators typically cooperate to pursue adjudicatory ends, but with sometimes mixed success, as in the KPMG case, because prosecutions may simply not be as effective for cementing adjudicatory goals. Finally, as others in this volume will discuss, state prosecutors who have civil regulatory authority do directly pursue regulatory ends, raising questions regarding federalism.[69]

Formalizing interactions between federal regulatory agencies and prosecutors would provide more notice to firms whether they face not only a civil enforcement action but also the possibility of a prosecution. The current flexible approach leaves such decisions opaque. This may serve the interests of both regulators and prosecutors, and perhaps also the public. Prosecutors and regulators retain the flexibility to exercise their discretion as justified in each case. Formalized procedures might stifle needed enforcement. Or formalized referrals might lead to more expansive regulation by prosecution, not less, which may be why firms have not called for a change in the current approach. Regardless, in the unlikely event that Congress sought to require such formal coordination, separate enforcement authority, the lack of a double jeopardy bar on successive administrative and criminal proceedings, and diverging priorities would still make for a mismatched relationship.

Despite their structural differences and the challenges of coordination, regulators and prosecutors have been following a path that brings them closer together. It is often difficult to know from the outside where the involvement of prosecutors ends and that of regulators begins. What lies ahead on this path? Another way to improve the quality of cooperation between prosecutors and regulators would be to enhance the role of the Financial Fraud Enforcement Task Force. Prosecutors and regulators could continue to communicate about enforcement priorities. Prosecutors could more clearly establish informal guidelines delineating the respective roles of prosecutors and regulators. The referral process could be documented. Finally, prosecutors could more clearly explain the circumstances in which a substantive policy-oriented agenda influences their discretion.

A Herculean task confronts any who seek to enhance coordination within and between regulatory agencies, among the U.S. Attorneys' offices, with Main Justice, and with other state and local regulators and prosecutors in complex organizational crime cases. Fully centralizing control over enforcers with independent discretion might be undesirable, and it is regardless highly unlikely. Instead, the Financial Fraud Enforcement Task Force is the logical place to consider improving joint work between prosecutors and regulators, since that coordination problem is central to its mission. The task force can create new opportunities for engagement between prosecutors and regulators, just as future collaborations may help to harmonize enforcement between prosecutors and regulators. In the years ahead, the development of such relationships, protocols, and coordination efforts will be worth watching carefully. While prosecutors and regulators may not work together in harmony, they will likely continue to productively collaborate in remarkable large-scale corporate enforcement efforts.

NOTES

1. Hudson v. United States, 522 U.S. 93 (1997).
2. Brandon L. Garrett, *Structural Reform Prosecution*, 93 Va. L. Rev. 853 (2007).
3. *See* Kenneth Abraham, *The Insurance Effects of Regulation by Litigation*, *in* W. Kip Viscusi, Regulation Through Litigation 212, 231 (2002).
4. I discuss this feature of then-extant deferred and nonprosecution agreements by federal prosecutors in Garrett, *supra* note 2.
5. W. Kip Viscusi, *Overview*, in Viscusi, *supra* note 3, at 1, 3.
6. *See* Stephen Labaton, *Downturn and Shift in Population Feed Boom in White-Collar Crime*, N.Y. Times, June 2, 2002, at A1; Garrett, *supra* note 2.
7. *See* Corporate Fraud Task Force, Report to the President (2008), *available at* http://www.usdoj.gov/dag/cftf/corporate-fraud2008.pdf.
8. Daniel Richman, *Federal Sentencing in 2007: The Supreme Court Holds—The Center Doesn't*, 117 Yale L.J. 1374, 1383 (2008).

9. For a description of this approach and analysis of agreements entered through 2007, see Garrett, *supra* note 2. The agreements themselves have been posted on a UVA Law Library resource website, together with updated data concerning the agreements. *See* University of Virginia School of Law—Library, http://www.law.virginia.edu/agreements.

10. *See* Memorandum from Larry D. Thompson, Deputy Attorney General, U.S. Dep't of Justice, to Heads of Department Components and United States Attorneys, *Principles of Federal Prosecution of Business Organizations* (Jan. 20, 2003), http://www.usdoj.gov/dag/cftf/corporate_guidelines.htm.

11. *See* Memorandum from Mark Filip, Deputy Attorney General, U.S. Dep't of Justice, to Heads of Department Components and United States Attorneys, *Principles of Federal Prosecution of Business Organizations* (Aug. 28, 2008), http://www.usdoj.gov/dag/readingroom/dag-memo-08282008.pdf.

12. Press Release, U.S. Immigration & Customs Enforcement, ITT Corporation to Plead Guilty (Mar. 27, 2007), http://www.ice.gov/pi/news/newsreleases/articles/070327washingtondc.htm.

13. Press Release, U.S. Dep't of Justice, KPMG to Pay $456 Million for Criminal Violations in Relation to Largest-Ever Tax Shelter Fraud Case (Aug. 29, 2005), http://www.usdoj.gov/opa/pr/2005/August/05_ag_433.html.

14. *See, e.g.*, United States v. Reyes, 577 F.2d 1069, 1078 (9th Cir. 2009); United States v. Bhutani, 175 F.3d 572, 577 (7th Cir. 1999).

15. M. Elizabeth Magill, *Agency Choice of Policymaking Form*, 71 U. Chi. L. Rev. 1383, 1386–98 (2004); David L. Shapiro, *The Choice of Rulemaking or Adjudication in the Development of Administrative Policy*, 78 Harv. L. Rev. 921, 954–58 (1965).

16. Magill, *supra* note 15, at 1390.

17. *See* Garrett, *supra* note 2, at 885 n.136.

18. Magill, *supra* note 15, at 1391.

19. *See* Thompson Memo, *supra* note 10; Report of Investigation Pursuant to Section 21(a) of the Securities Exchange Act of 1934 and Commission Statement on the Relationship of Cooperation to Agency Enforcement Decisions, Exchange Act Release No. 44,969, 76 SEC Docket 296 (Oct. 23, 2001), *available at* http://www.sec.gov/litigation/investreport/34-44969.htm. The district court in the *Stein* litigation imprecisely characterized such memos, stating that "[t]he Thompson Memorandum in substance was a regulation." United States v. Stein, 495 F. Supp. 2d 390, 412 (S.D.N.Y. 2007).

20. Jayne W. Barnard, *Corporate Therapeutics at the Securities and Exchange Commission*, 2008 Colum. Bus. L. Rev. 793 (2008); Jennifer O'Hare, *The Use of the Corporate Monitor in SEC Enforcement Actions*, 1 Brook. J. Corp. Fin. & Com. L. 89, 90 (2006).

21. Securities Exchange Act of 1934 § 21(d)(5) (codified at 15 U.S.C. § 78u(d)(5)).

22. *See* O'Hare, *supra* note 20.

23. *See* Yuki Noguchi, *The "Sheriff" of MCI; Watchdog Laid Down Laws Now Affecting Merger Talks*, Wash. Post, Apr. 28, 2005, at E01.

24. Press Release, U.S. Sec. & Exch. Comm'n, Statement of the Securities and Exchange Commission Concerning Financial Penalties (Jan. 4, 2006), http://www.sec.gov/news/press/2006-4.htm.

25. EPA—Petroleum Refinery National Priority Case Results, http://www.epa.gov/compliance/resources/cases/civil/caa/oil/index.html (2009).

26. *Id.*

27. *Id.; see also* EPA—Enforcement and Compliance Assurance Returned to Core: Petroleum Refining, http://www.epa.gov/compliance/data/planning/priorities/petrol.html.

28. Daniel Richman, *Institutional Competence and Organizational Prosecutions*, 93 Va. L. Rev. In Brief 115 (2007); *see* Garrett, *supra* note 2, at 896; *see also* Brandon L. Garrett, *United States v. Goliath*, 93 Va. L. Rev. In Brief 105 (2007).

29. *See* Daniel Richman, *Political Control of Federal Prosecutions: Looking Back and Looking Forward*, 58 Duke L.J. 2087, 2119 n.152 (2009).

30. *See* Jacqueline C. Wolff, *How to Protect Your Client Under the EPA's Voluntary Disclosure Policy, in* Bus. Crimes Bulletin: Compliance & Litig., Dec. 1998, at 1–2.

31. 17 C.F.R. § 202.5(a)–(b) (2006).

32. Roger M. Adelman, The Securities Enforcement Manual: Tactics and Strategies (2008).

33. *See* U.S. Gov't Accountability Office, GAO-07–830, Securities and Exchange Commission: Additional Actions Needed to Ensure Planned Improvements Address Limitations in Enforcement Division Operations 34 (Aug. 2007), *available at* http://www.gao.gov/new.items/d07830.pdf.

34. IRM 9.1.1.2, 25.1.2.1.

35. *Id.* at 38.3.1.3.

36. Leandra Lederman & Stephen W. Mazza, Tax Controversies: Practice and Procedure §14.02 (2002).

37. Staff of Joint Comm. on Taxation, 94th Cong., 2d Sess., General Explanation of the Tax Reform Act of 1976, at 322 (Comm. Print 1976) ("Blue Book"); *see* 26 U.S.C.A. § 6103(h)(3) (contemplating release of tax return information when a case has been "referred" to the DOJ); *see also* United States v. Bacheler, 611 F.2d 443 (3d Cir. 1979); Memorandum from Christopher H. Schroeder, Acting Assistant Attorney General, Office of Legal Counsel, to Assistant Attorney General, Tax Division (Oct. 8, 1996), http://www.usdoj.gov/olc/undercovop.htm#N_2.

38. For a proposal that, in the procurement fraud context, OIGs be permitted to pursue enforcement, see National Procurement Fraud Task Force Legislation Committee, Procurement Fraud: Legislative and Regulatory Reform Proposals (2008), *available at* http://pogoarchives.org/m/co/npftflc-white-paper-20080609.pdf.

39. OIG's Provider Self-Disclosure Protocol, 63 Fed. Reg. 58,399 (Oct. 30, 1998).

40. *Id.* at 58,400.

41. Charles Gasparino, *Merrill, Spitzer Near Settlement in Research Case*, Wall St. J., Apr. 18, 2002, at C1.

42. Roberta S. Karmel, *Reconciling Federal and State Interests in Securities Regulation in the United States and Europe*, 28 Brook. J. Int'l L. 495, 520 (2003).

43. Press Release, U.S. Sec. & Exch. Comm'n, Ten of Nation's Top Investment Firms Settle Enforcement Actions Involving Conflicts of Interest Between Research and Investment Banking (Apr. 28, 2003), http://www.sec.gov/news/press/2003-54.htm.

44. *Id.*

45. *Id.*

46. *See* U.S. Sec. & Exch. Comm'n, SEC Fact Sheet on Global Analyst Research Settlements, http://www.sec.gov/news/speech/factsheet.htm.

47. Press Release, *supra* note 43.

48. SEC Fact Sheet, *supra* note 46.

49. Press Release, *supra* note 43.

50. *See SEC Gives Nod to Analyst Rules Aimed at Boosting Independence*, 34 Sec. Reg. & L. Rep. (BNA) 749 (May 13, 2002); Order Approving Proposed Rule Changes by the NASD and NYSE, Exchange Act Release No. 34–45,908, 67 Fed. Reg. 34,968 (May 15, 2002).

51. Sarbanes-Oxley Act of 2002, Pub. L. No. 107–204, 116 Stat. 745 (codified as amended in scattered sections of 15 U.S.C.); NASD and NYSE Rulemaking, Exchange Act Release No. 34–48252 (July 29, 2003), *available at* http://www.sec.gov/rules/sro/34-48252.htm; Regulation AC—Analyst Certification, 17 C.F.R. §§ 242.500–.505 (2006); Selective Disclosure and Insider Trading, Securities Act Release No. 33–7881, Exchange Act Release No. 34–43154, Investment Company Act Release No. 24599, 65 Fed. Reg. 51,716 (Aug. 24, 2000). For an excellent in-depth account, see Jill E. Fisch, *Fiduciary Duties and the Analyst Scandals*, 58 Ala. L. Rev. 1083 (2007).

52. *See* Jenny Anderson, *New Cops on the Beat*, Instit. Investor, July 2002, at 77, 78.

53. *See* Michael Schroeder, *SEC Welcomes Prosecutions*, Wall St. J., June 11, 2002, at A2.

54. U.S. Dep't of Justice, U.S. Attorney, Southern District of New York, KPMG—Deferred Prosecution Agreement (Aug. 26, 2005), *available at* http://www.law.virginia.edu/pdf/faculty/garrett/kpmg.pdf.

55. U.S. Dep't of Justice, U.S. Attorney, Southern District of New York, HVB—Deferred Prosecution Agreement (Feb. 13, 2006), *available at* http://www.law.virginia.edu/pdf/faculty/garrett/germanbankhvb.pdf.

56. Scott D. Michel & Kevin E. Thorn, *Deferred Prosecution Agreements: Implications for Corporate Tax Departments*, 58 Tax Executive 49, 52 (2006).

57. *See* Lynnley Browning, *Document Could Alter KPMG Case*, N.Y. Times, Sept. 15, 2006, at C1.

58. Chad Bray, *Former KPMG Executives Convicted of Tax Evasion*, Wall St. J., Dec. 18, 2008, at C4.

59. For a more in-depth discussion, see Brandon L. Garrett, *Globalized Corporate Prosecutions* (draft in progress).

60. Virginia A. Davidson & Eric S. Zell, *The Foreign Corrupt Practices Act: Pitfalls in Doing Business Overseas*, 55 Fed. Law. 20, 22–23 (2008).

61. In contrast, the DOJ and SEC may engage in parallel investigations in civil matters. *See, e.g.*, SEC v. Dresser Indus., 628 F.2d 1368 (D.C. Cir. 1980); United States v. KPMG-Siddharta, 4 FCPA Rep. 699.8273 (S.D. Tex. 2001); *see also* Marika Maris & Erika Singer, *Foreign Corrupt Practices Act*, 43 Am. Crim. L. Rev. 575 (2006).

62. Press Release, Panalpina, Panalpina Reports Dynamic Growth in the First Half Year (July 30, 2008), http://www.panalpina.com/www/global/en/media_news/news/news_archiv_2/08_07_30.html.

63. *To Host or Not to Host: Approving Travel and Entertainment Expenses Under the FCPA After Lucent*, FCPA Insights, Apr. 2008, at 19.

64. *Id.*; *see* Indep. Inquiry Comm. into the U.N. Oil-for-Food-Programme, *Report on the Manipulation of the Oil-for-Food Programme by the Iraqi Regime* (Oct. 27, 2005), *available at* http://www.iic-offp.org/story27oct05.htm.

65. Independent Inquiry Committee—About the Committee, http://www.iic-offp.org/about.htm.

66. Examples include the AB Volvo, Chevron, El Paso, Flowserve, Ingersoll-Rand, Textron, and York International deferred prosecution agreements. *See* University of Virginia School of Law—Library, http://www.law.virginia.edu/agreements.

67. James P. Ellison, *DOJ Settles with Five Hip and Knee Replacement Companies*, FDA Law Blog, http://www.fdalawblog.net/fda_law_blog_hyman_phelps/2007/10/nj-us-attorneys.html.

68. *See* Press Release, U.S. Dep't of Justice, Five Companies in Hip and Knee Replacement Industry Avoid Prosecution by Agreeing to Compliance Rules and Monitoring (Sept. 27, 2007), http://www.justice.gov/usao/nj/press/files/pdffiles/hips0927.rel.pdf.

69. *See infra* Rachel E. Barkow, *The Prosecutor as Regulatory Agency*; *infra* Sara Sun Beale, *What Are the Rules If Everybody Wants to Play? Multiple Federal and State Prosecutors (Acting) as Regulators.*

8

The Prosecutor as Regulatory Agency

RACHEL E. BARKOW

We live in an age when prosecutors are a significant source of corporate regulation. The terms of NPAs, DPAs, and state settlement agreements abound with regulations that go far beyond simple commands to companies to stop disobeying the law or to pay for prior violations. These agreements insist on new business models and practices, and they have contained regulations that have covered everything from personnel decisions to the rates companies charge customers. In many instances, prosecutors have not stopped with the regulation of single companies; they have commanded entire industries to comply with new terms. These prosecutorial commands have been imposed without legislative guidance, much less relatively clear rules or intelligible principles.

Public law scholars have long examined the legitimacy and efficacy of regulation by the judiciary and regulatory agencies, both of which pose a direct challenge to the Constitution's system of separated powers. In particular, judges and regulatory agencies have been closely scrutinized to determine whether they have the accountability, institutional competence, and procedural reliability to regulate.

When prosecutors regulate, they, too, challenge the separation of powers. Yet the prosecutor as a source of regulation has largely escaped the attention of legal commentators. This chapter aims to remedy that oversight by considering prosecutor-imposed regulations using the same metrics that have long been applied to judges and regulatory agencies. The most sweeping regulations have come from the NY AG, but federal prosecutors have also imposed significant regulatory requirements on companies as part of NPAs and DPAs. This chapter will therefore consider the capacity of both state AGs and federal prosecutors to act as regulators.[1]

Section I begins by explaining the forces that give prosecutors the ability to step into a regulatory role. Section II describes prosecutor regulation by chronicling some of the major regulations prosecutors have imposed. Section III then evaluates the prosecutor's office as a regulatory agency by considering its democratic accountability, institutional competence, and procedural reliability.

I. The Power to Regulate

Prosecutors today exercise a broad range of authority. Their power to enforce the law is uncontroversial. More worrisome from a separation-of-powers perspective are the adjudicative and lawmaking activities that are becoming increasingly common in prosecutors' offices around the country.

Prosecutors have taken on adjudicative powers due to several dynamics.[2] First, many criminal laws are written in broad terms, and often more than one law covers a defendant's conduct.[3] These laws typically authorize different sentences, so a prosecutor can select the sentence or sentencing range by choosing one law over another.[4] This gives the prosecutor significant bargaining power because he or she can threaten to charge a defendant with a more serious crime if the defendant opts to take his or her case to trial. Second, many jurisdictions have turned to mandatory minimum sentences or sentencing guidelines, both of which limit judicial sentencing authority. The result is that a prosecutor's charging decision is more likely to dictate a particular sentence or narrow sentencing range. Third, many jurisdictions, like the federal system, give defendants substantial sentencing discounts for cooperating with the government and accepting responsibility. Prosecutors typically control downward departures for cooperation, and acceptance of responsibility reductions are usually disallowed when defendants exercise their trial rights or are discounted when defendants wait until too close to the eve of trial before pleading guilty.

The final keys to this system of prosecutorial dominance are the reluctance of the judiciary to police it and legislative efforts to foster it. Prosecutors can threaten defendants with more severe charges if they exercise their trial rights, and courts have refused to analyze these threats under the traditional unconstitutional conditions framework.[5] For their part, legislators now pass laws with the goal of furthering this plea-bargaining framework. Instead of limiting prosecutorial discretion through narrower, more precise laws, legislatures continue to pass broadly worded statutes that increasingly include punishments that are more severe than the facts of the typical case in violation of the statute would justify.

The end result is a criminal justice system in which upwards of 95 percent of convictions result from pleas instead of trials, and prosecutors are the adjudicators. The exercise of the trial right is simply too costly for most defendants, leaving prosecutors to decide a defendant's liability and sentence.

Corporate criminal liability is no exception to this overall regime of prosecutorial leverage, as earlier chapters have indicated. If anything, it is a more extreme example. The standard for corporate liability is itself broad. Corporations are criminally liable if any employee in the scope of his or her employment commits a crime with the intent to benefit the company. This low threshold for liability makes it easier for prosecutors to obtain indictments and meet their burden at trial, which in turn makes it more likely that corporate defendants will plead guilty.

In addition to the broad legal standard, the reputational hit from a conviction or even just an indictment can be devastating or fatal, depending on the company's line of business. Some companies can survive an indictment and conviction. They pay their fine, and they move on. But for others, a conviction is equivalent to a death sentence because the company loses its eligibility to be licensed. Indeed, for some companies, even an indictment can be "a matter of life and death" because the damage to their reputations is irreparable.[6] In the financial services and accounting industries in particular, a reputation for integrity is critical to the success of a corporation. The story of Arthur Andersen, which opted to go to trial instead of reaching an agreement with the government, is a perfect illustration of this phenomenon. When Andersen was indicted, clients abandoned the company in droves. The conviction of the company was the fatal blow, with the company collapsing when it was debarred by the SEC.

This kind of leverage has allowed prosecutors, in the words of one Assistant U.S. Attorney ("AUSA"), to "get[] the sort of significant reforms you might not even get following a trial and conviction."[7]

II. The Practice of Regulating

Both federal and state prosecutors have used their leverage to impose regulations on companies.

A. Regulation by Federal Prosecutors

As the introduction explains, DPAs and NPAs have been used in a range of areas, from securities to health care fraud, from money laundering and tax fraud to Foreign Corrupt Practices Act violations. Indeed, since the beginning of 2003, when the DOJ provided guiding principles for prosecuting business organizations in the Thompson Memo, DPAs have gone hand in hand with the filing of federal criminal charges against any major corporation.[8] In addition, the federal Organizational Sentencing Guidelines expressly provide that companies may be required, as a condition of probation, to "eliminate or reduce the risk that the instant offense will cause future harm."[9] The guidelines also provide for sentence reductions for companies that adopt certain compliance and ethics regimes.[10]

As a result, federal prosecutors now operate within a legal culture that expressly acknowledges a role for prosecutors in corporate governance. When federal prosecutors follow the Guideline standards for compliance and ethics regimes, they are operating under a scheme approved by Congress, so it is not fair to label those terms "prosecutorial" regulations. Similarly, when agreements simply insist upon personnel changes to rid the company of individuals engaged in wrongdoing or those who failed to prevent it, prosecutors are imposing a remedy directly tied to the past violation.

But many DPAs and NPAs go further and directly regulate the company's operations going forward. These are the conditions that are fairly characterized as regulations. For example, after engaging in a fraudulent scheme to inflate its earnings, Bristol-Myers Squibb signed a DPA that required the company to submit specific financial disclosures that go beyond the requirements currently imposed by law, to establish a training and education program, and to adopt additional operational changes recommended by a monitor. Some agreements in the health care arena provide further illustrations of this kind of regulation. Stryker Orthopedics, a medical device manufacturer, entered into an NPA that restricted the company's ability to pay medical consultants. Zimmer Holdings, another device manufacturer, signed a DPA that similarly regulated its relationship with medical consultants, including setting caps on the number of consultants that could work on a product development team and setting hourly wage rates.

Other agreements have imposed restrictions on companies to prevent them from engaging in otherwise lawful business practices for fear that they will cross the line into illegality. For instance, the Canadian Imperial Bank agreement responded to the company's participation in the Enron fraud by prohibiting the bank from engaging in certain structured finance transactions. Agreements with KPMG and German bank HVB bar them from marketing or selling prepackaged tax products in response to their marketing of fraudulent tax shelters.

In each of these examples, the agreements go beyond bans on illegal conduct or the removal of negligent or criminal personnel and dictate affirmative changes in business practices and governance. As the chair of the Attorney General's White Collar Crime Subcommittee informed Congress, the express goal of these agreements is "to root out illegal and unethical conduct, prevent recidivism, and ensure that they are committed to business practices that meet *or exceed applicable legal and regulatory mandates*."[11] Or, to use the words of former U.S. Attorney for the Southern District of New York, Mary Jo White, these agreements effectively turn federal prosecutors into "super-regulators."[12]

B. Regulation by State Prosecutors

While federal prosecutors have engaged in the regulation of some companies through DPAs and NPAs, some state attorneys general have been even more ambitious and have sought to regulate whole industries.[13] State attorneys general have long played a major role in changing company business practices through their enforcement of state antitrust, environmental, and consumer laws and through novel multistate litigation efforts.[14] In recent years, some AGs have gone beyond this model and have used general criminal law enforcement power to achieve regulatory goals.

In particular, in the last decade, the NY AG's Office has been more active than any other prosecutor's office in regulating corporate behavior. One reason New York AGs are able to be particularly aggressive is that they have a powerful state law at their disposal, the Martin Act.[15] The Martin Act gives the state AG broad powers to address financial fraud. With just about every public company traded on the New York Stock Exchange or NASDAQ, almost all securities fall within the Martin Act's jurisdiction. The act allows the AG to bring civil or criminal charges for securities fraud, and even in criminal cases it does not require showing either that the defendant intended to defraud or that anyone was actually defrauded.[16] The AG has the discretion to conduct a confidential investigation or a public one. Once the AG starts an investigation under the act, the act requires the company being investigated to provide the AG with "all the facts and circumstances concerning the subject matter" of the investigation and "such other data and information" as the AG deems relevant. The act gives the AG broad subpoena power, and failure to comply with the subpoena without reasonable cause is a misdemeanor and prima facie evidence of fraudulent conduct.[17] This subpoena power includes the authority to bring witnesses to the AG's office for so-called Martin Act hearings. Courts have held that witnesses have no right to counsel at Martin Act hearings, nor are they entitled to a transcript of the proceedings.[18] As one commentator has observed, "[T]he act's powers exceed those given any regulator in any other state."[19]

Eliot Spitzer was the first AG to make expansive use of the Martin Act to impose regulations on companies,[20] using it to reform abusive practices in the securities, mutual fund, and insurance industries. Spitzer used his investigative powers under the Martin Act to uncover a conflict of interest between research analysts and investment bankers at the nation's top investment firms. Through the Martin Act's subpoena power, Spitzer obtained emails sent by Merrill Lynch stock analysts, which led him to the discovery that stock recommendations by Merrill's analysts were influenced by whether the company issuing the stock had promised to give its banking business to Merrill. When Spitzer made his investigation of the company and his findings public, the market value of Merrill's stock decreased by $5 billion within a week. Spitzer quickly brought a similar case against Salomon Smith Barney and eventually targeted the rest of the top ten investment banking firms.

The SEC later joined Spitzer's efforts, and together they reached settlement agreements with the ten largest investment firms. To avoid prosecution, those firms agreed to "dramatically reform their future practices."[21] Specifically, they agreed, among other things, to physically separate their research analysts from their investment bankers, to stop their practice of having analysts accompany investment bankers on pitches and road shows, to create firewalls restricting interaction between the two departments, and to cease basing analyst compensation in any way on investment banking revenue. The agreement also included a five-year commitment by the investment companies to "contract with no fewer than three independent research firms that will make available independent research to the firm's customers." The firms further promised to pay for investor education and to restrict their practice of "spinning," whereby the firms would allocate securities in particularly hot initial public offerings to certain executive officers and directors who could influence investment banking decisions.[22] The firms additionally agreed to make publicly available their ratings and price target forecasts.[23] As Spitzer put it, the agreement's goal was to "permanently change the way Wall Street operates."[24]

Spitzer followed a similar path with respect to his regulation of mutual funds. In the course of investigating Morgan Stanley because brokers there were promoting in-house funds without disclosing that they received higher commissions for selling those funds, Spitzer discovered that mutual fund managers were allowing some clients to trade after hours and to engage in other market-timing transactions.[25] The clients who were permitted to perform these transactions profited at the expense of other shareholders. Mutual fund managers engaged in this preferential treatment because they received profit-sharing and other fees.[26] Spitzer eventually expanded the scope of his inquiry to target a number of the largest investment companies. Faced with criminal prosecution, they reached agreements with the AG's office to modify their business practices.[27] For example, in the AG's agreement with Alliance Capital Management, the company agreed to new disclosure requirements about its expenses and fees and to hire a full-time senior officer to ensure that mutual fund fees would be negotiated at arm's length. The SEC eventually joined the effort, and together the AG's office and the SEC reached settlements with the targeted firms, and the SEC later imposed industry-wide rules to address the issue.[28] Spitzer went further than the SEC was willing to go by additionally insisting that the mutual funds reduce their fund fees by 20 percent and maintain that reduced rate for a five-year period.[29]

The insurance industry was another Spitzer target. His office investigated Marsh & McLennan, AIG, and other large insurance brokers for accepting kickbacks from insurers and setting up a bid-rigging scheme.[30] After Marsh was indicted, its stock fell by 24 percent.[31] Seeking to avoid a further decline, the company agreed to the AG's terms for settling the case, which involved sweeping reforms in its business practices. In particular, the company agreed to discontinue receiving contingent compensation from insurance carriers, to provide clients with more comprehensive disclosures about the compensation it receives from insurers, to adopt a company-wide written standard for the placement of insurance, and to establish a compliance committee.[32] AIG and other insurance brokerage companies agreed to similar changes to their business practices.

Andrew Cuomo succeeded Spitzer as NY AG in 2007 and picked up where Spitzer left off, negotiating similarly sweeping settlements with the health care and student loan industries. Early in his tenure, Cuomo's office began an investigation into the health care industry's in-network doctor ranking programs, an increasingly widespread practice where insurers rank doctors according to certain metrics of quality and cost efficiency. Cuomo concluded that insurers have a potential conflict of interest when recommending doctors to consumers because the insurer pays for the care given by the doctor it recommends, giving it an incentive to recommend the cheapest, not necessarily the best, doctors.[33] Cuomo looked to the state's business laws against deceptive practices instead of the Martin Act to pursue the companies, and he reached his first settlement agreement with CIGNA in October 2007. That agreement established a new code of conduct for ranking doctors. The agreement requires health care companies to disclose how doctors are ranked, to employ separate categories of "quality of performance" and "cost efficiency," to identify the extent to which any ranking is based on cost, to use more accurate measures to compare physicians, including the use of nationally recognized evidence-based and/or consensus-based clinical recommendations or guidelines, to allow consumers to register complaints about the system, and to provide a process by which physicians can appeal the rankings. In addition, the agreement specifies that CIGNA will be monitored by a ratings examiner that will oversee compliance with the code of conduct. Cuomo has used the CIGNA agreement as a model for subsequent agreements with the industry's largest insurers, and it has become the industry standard.[34]

Cuomo has also reformed the health insurance industry's methods for reimbursing patients for out-of-network health care. Prior to reaching settlements with the AG's office, many of the nation's largest health insurance companies set the rates at which they would reimburse out-of-network care based on a schedule compiled by a data company called Ingenix. Cuomo's office found several problems with the practice. First, Ingenix is a wholly owned subsidiary of UnitedHealth, one of the health insurers. Second, Ingenix set the rates on the basis of data submitted by the insurers, all of whom had the incentive to manipulate the data to lower the reimbursement rates calculated in the schedule. Finally, the companies did not inform consumers of the reimbursement rates, putting customers in the situation of choosing doctors without knowing what costs would be covered by their insurer.[35]

As with the doctor-ranking system, Cuomo used the state's laws against deceptive business practices to reach settlements with some of the industry's largest companies imposing new regulations.[36] The centerpiece of all the agreements is the companies' commitment to select a qualified school of public health to establish a new, independent database that will create reimbursement rates for at least five years.[37] The information in the database will be available on a website available to the public, and the companies agreed to provide data, assistance, and money to help create the database.

Cuomo has also reformed the student loan industry by using the threat of prosecution. In 2007, his office uncovered various deceptive and illegal practices in the industry. For instance, his office found evidence that lenders were paying kickbacks to schools and giving school officials other benefits in exchange for being placed on the schools' preferred lender lists and otherwise getting preferential treatment. In response to these abuses, Cuomo drafted a College Loan Code of Conduct that specified new practices to govern lenders and schools.[38] The code prohibited lenders from giving anything of value to schools in exchange for being placed on a preferred lender list or otherwise gaining an advantage. The code also required a school using a preferred lender list to disclose the criteria used to establish such a list and to make clear to students their right to select from any lender, including those not on the list. The code further required lenders to disclose information to allow consumers to easily compare the lender's terms with others, including federal loans. In the course of the investigation, Cuomo wrote letters to more than 400 colleges and universities demanding disclosure of any conflicts of interest. Many schools and lenders adopted the code by reaching settlement agreements with Cuomo's office.[39] Ultimately, the code made its way into federal and state legislation.[40]

Cuomo also tackled the subprime mortgage crisis. He reached a settlement agreement with Freddie Mac and Fannie Mae that requires lenders who work with the agencies to reform their appraisal practices by adopting what Cuomo calls a "New Home Valuation Protection Code." In addition, the agreement also creates an independent agency to implement and monitor the new standards.[41]

The last two NY AGs have taken the prosecutor-as-regulatory-agency model to new heights. Spitzer explicitly noted he was a "prosecutor-slash-regulator," and the agreements that have emerged from his office and his successor's more than back up his claim.

III. Assessing the Prosecutor as Policymaker

The model of the "prosecutor-slash-regulator" is in tension with a government based on a strict separation of powers because that prosecutor is stepping into the role of policymaker by using his or her power to indict as leverage. Under a formalist account, to describe this lawmaking activity is to condemn it. Prosecutors are supposed to execute the law, not make it.

But courts and commentators increasingly dismiss a formalist approach to the separation of powers. Ours is now a government of blended powers across a range of areas, from administrative agencies to special prosecutors. The weak nondelegation doctrine that applies to administrative agencies rejects the notion that all policy judgments must rest with the legislative branch. How does regulation by prosecutors fit within this flexible modern order? Are the potential dangers sufficiently limited by checks and balances so that regulation by prosecutors is a social good?

These are difficult questions that will ultimately require more detailed empirical studies of how prosecutors are using this power. But one way to get a handle on these questions is to consider how regulation by prosecutors measures up when one applies the same institutional metrics that have guided analyses of judicial and agency policymaking. The key benchmarks in those contexts are accountability, institutional competence, and procedural reliability.

A. Accountability

When critics attack judges for their remedial decrees or their recognition of certain rights, they inevitably make the argument that judges should not make policy because they are not democratically accountable. Debates about the administrative state similarly focus on accountability, with those skeptical of agencies focusing on the fact that they are run by unelected bureaucrats and those defending agencies emphasizing that they must answer to political overseers.

Where do prosecutors sit on the accountability continuum? The answer differs depending on whether the prosecutor is a state or federal actor.

1. State Prosecutors

The vast majority of state AGs (including New York's) are directly elected by the people. In the handful of states where they are not, they are appointed by someone who is.[42] Moreover, while the public may not pay attention to much of what state AGs do, they are more likely to pay attention when the state AG brings an action that results in sweeping corporate changes because those cases are likely to receive significant media attention. Eliot Spitzer and Andrew Cuomo earned sky-high favorability ratings as the NY AG precisely because of their activism in pursuing corporate regulations.[43] On the surface, then, there appears to be no accountability concern with state-level prosecutors.

Nevertheless, there are some reasons to doubt that prosecutors are being held accountable for their regulatory decisions even when they face direct election by the people. First, it is unclear that the public notices when prosecutors opt not to seek sweeping changes from companies. Unless the corporate fraud has already been investigated and well publicized, an AG's failure to pursue a company is unlikely to garner much, if any, attention.[44] State AGs benefit from just about any media coverage that shows they are fighting crime or pursuing consumer interests. Because that can be satisfied with civil suits that obtain damages or criminal suits against individuals, it is not necessary for them to seek sweeping regulatory changes by threatening criminal prosecution. Just about every other AG, for example, has decided not to regulate corporations as aggressively as the NY AG, yet AGs everywhere, not just in New York, typically win reelection.[45] These AGs are not being penalized for failing to pursue regulation, which means that accountability is more of a one-way ratchet where only affirmative pursuits against companies get noticed and a failure to go after corporate wrongdoers is likely to escape public attention.

Second, even when the AG does act affirmatively to obtain new regulations against a company, there is little reason to believe that the public pays any attention to the details. The level of public knowledge about the terms of corporate regulations is not very deep. Andrew Cuomo has received as much attention—indeed, a great deal more—for his subpoena requests of AIG regarding its distribution of bonuses as he has for his entire reregulation of the insurance industry.

To put the matter another way, the worry with elected prosecutor accountability is that voters might easily be misled to believe any action is good action. This can lead to two dangers. Most likely, elected prosecutors will tend to underregulate because they have competing concerns that favor industry. As the former AG in Massachusetts has observed, "[y]ou rarely run for attorney general successfully by prosecuting the biggest corporations in your state, represented by the best law firms, with the best PR firms spinning it."[46] There is a political risk in alienating such a powerful, wealthy group. Thus, some prosecutors will resist pursuing companies, and others will reach settlement agreements that are largely favorable to industry given the conduct at issue because most prosecutors do not want to anger such a wealthy and powerful constituency. To be sure, voters may share this interest because if a statewide prosecutor is too aggressive, companies may opt to cease doing business in the state. But there is likely to be some distance between the AG's interests and those of the voters. Thus, in most states, prosecutors will not take on the role of regulatory agency.

To the extent that the NY AG office has departed from this trend, it is because of unique legal and economic factors in the state. As noted, the Martin Act is part of the story. The law is unusually broad, so it gives an AG who wants to use it aggressively a big stick with which to go after companies. New York's economic and political environment has given the last two state AGs the incentives to take that approach.

Consider first the economics of the state. While some state AGs may reasonably worry that businesses will opt to leave their state if they make the regulatory environment too unfriendly, New York is the commercial and financial center of the country; thus it is highly unlikely that companies will exit because of an aggressive stance by the AG.

New York is also unique in terms of the possible donor bases for an AG who seeks reelection or a higher office. NY AGs can raise campaign funds from a huge base of wealthy individual donors and companies across a broad range of industries. If the AG targets a few companies or even industries to regulate, there are still many others to which he can turn for donations, not to mention thousands upon thousands of individuals. In many other states, just a handful of industries dominate the state's economic landscape, and those industries and the people who work in them are likely to make up a significant share of possible campaign support.

The danger in a state like New York, then, is not so much underregulation but ill-conceived regulation that targets particular companies or industries that are politically unpopular at the moment. The NY AG may seek regulations that go too far or do not directly address the criminal behavior at issue in an effort to give the AG short-term political goodwill as opposed to long-term benefits for the state or a sensible regime for an entire industry.

There is not much the targets of the AG's regulatory efforts can do to overcome this. While some companies can turn to the adversary system as a check on prosecutors, others (particularly public companies in the financial services industry) cannot because the reputational hit is simply too great. The staggering losses many of these companies incurred when the AG's investigations became public give an indication of prosecutorial leverage. Companies do not want to risk additional reputational damage and the resulting financial losses by going to trial and having more damaging facts come out. And because the standard for liability is so low, particularly with a law like the Martin Act, trial is likely to be unsuccessful in any event.

The problem for these companies is that they have employees who have engaged in conduct that is criminal or close enough to the line of legality that the company is unlikely to get public sympathy when it comes to the penalty phase. The public has little incentive to scrutinize closely the regulatory demands made on the companies to ensure that they are rational and proportional to the offense. As with so much of criminal law today, there is unlikely to be much, if any, attention paid to the reasonableness of the sentence because the public does not pay attention to the individual facts of cases to determine if the punishment is proportional. Instead, judgments are formed based on aggregate information or paradigm cases. In the case of corporate misconduct, that means a public highly unlikely to consider whether a corporation is being regulated too much. Given this negative public sentiment, other elected officials are unlikely to step in to the company's defense if a regulation goes too far.

2. Federal Prosecutors

Federal prosecutors are not elected. Each U.S. Attorney is appointed by the president and confirmed by the Senate, and they are removable by the president. New administrations typically replace the previous administration's U.S. Attorneys as a matter of course so that their policies reflect those of the incoming administration.

But despite being subject to removal by the president, federal prosecutors retain a degree of independence. Although U.S. Attorneys are subject to DOJ oversight in various respects,[47] they have a great deal of latitude in which cases to bring and how to handle them.

This degree of de facto independence may help explain why different U.S. Attorney's Offices take different approaches to DPAs and NPAs. There is no evidence that DOJ is issuing centralized commands—other than broadly worded corporate charging memos—for U.S. Attorneys to follow. As a result, U.S. Attorneys are charting their own courses. Some districts seek DPAs and NPAs relatively frequently, whereas others have yet to enter into such an agreement at all. Even those districts that use these agreements diverge. The District of New Jersey has often imposed a requirement of an independent monitor, whereas the Southern District of New York did not make that a condition of any of its 2007 agreements.[48]

Moreover, to the extent that federal prosecutors are subject to centralized oversight, the law enforcement official who is ultimately accountable to the people is the president. And it is unlikely that corporate charging and regulatory decisions factor in to any single voter's choice of president in light of more salient and important national issues. The link between federal prosecutors and the voting public is therefore tenuous at best.

Nor does the career path of the average U.S. Attorney make them any more attentive to public opinion. Most U.S. Attorneys have no interest in seeking an elected office. After their government service, they typically want to obtain a lucrative job in the private sector or get appointed to the federal bench or to an even higher position in the executive branch.[49] For those that want a political appointment, they will aim to please their political benefactors, typically powerful senators or the president.

The biggest accountability danger in the federal context, then, is the same one that exists for most state AGs: the risk of underregulation relative to public preference. Neither the president nor a senator is likely to want prosecutors to regulate corporations too aggressively because they are powerful lobbyists and campaign contributors, and politicians might also be concerned about job losses and a decline in shareholder value.

It is more the exception than the rule when prosecutors opt for regulation. And although U.S. Attorneys operate with a great deal of independence, a sufficiently powerful corporate defendant can likely appeal the U.S. Attorney's decisions to someone at Main Justice if a U.S. Attorney's regulatory demands go too far. This, too, is likely to keep a federal prosecutor's regulatory demands in check.

3. Prosecutors Versus Agencies

So far, the discussion has considered prosecutorial accountability to the public. But the real question of accountability is a relative one. Under our traditional separation of powers governing structure, the responsibility for regulating rests with the legislature. Legislative elections are likely to get more public attention than elections for state AGs, and legislators are certainly more accountable than appointed prosecutors.

But in modern American government, the reality is that legislators are not the basis for comparison. In most areas, legislators do not regulate but instead pass broadly worded statutes that delegate regulatory authority to administrative agencies. The critical accountability question, then, is not how prosecutors stack up against legislators in responding to the public but how they compare with agency regulators.

In general, when it comes to accountability, elected prosecutors have an edge over their agency counterparts. Agency heads are not typically elected but appointed. In the few instances where they are elected—as they are in the case of some state agencies—voter turnout is abysmally low, and the public knows almost nothing about the people who are running. And although agency heads are accountable in other ways—through congressional hearings or budget decisions, by presidential appointment and (for some agencies) removal decisions, through oversight by the Office of Management and Budget ("OMB")—these forms of oversight aim to place agencies under greater control of elected officials so that, in turn, agencies are more directly responsive to voters. But there is no evidence that these indirect measures are superior substitutes for direct voting by the people, particularly when the political officials who oversee agencies are going to be elected based on their performance across a range of issues (international relations, the economy, cultural issues, etc.).

Elected prosecutors, in contrast, are judged by the public on the cases they pursue, including those against corporations. And while it is true that voters are unlikely to hold elected prosecutors accountable for failing to regulate or for underregulating, accountability for inaction or underregulation is a problem for regulatory agencies as well.[50] Overall, then, the accountability of elected state AGs is therefore likely to be stronger than or at least as strong as it is for administrative agencies.

The comparison between appointed federal prosecutors and agency heads reveals many similarities as far as accountability is concerned. Consider first how federal prosecutors compare with the heads of executive agencies. Both face similar presidential oversight. They are appointed and removable by the president. Although executive agencies submit proposed regulations to OMB, they do not need to get OMB approval for policies announced in adjudications. Thus, prosecutors and executive regulatory agencies alike evade OMB review when they regulate through their adjudicative powers. Congressional oversight is also comparable. Although congressional hearings of executive regulatory agencies are more common than hearings involving prosecutorial policies, Congress has noticed the trend of regulation by federal prosecutors and stepped in when it viewed it as going too far. For example, Congress held hearings on the use of monitors in DPAs and NPAs, and DOJ responded with a set of guidelines. Similarly, when prosecutors were demanding that companies cease paying attorney fees for individuals under investigation and asking for attorney-client waivers as proof of cooperation, Congress proposed legislation that prompted DOJ to make changes to its policies. Federal prosecutors are therefore roughly on par with executive agencies when it comes to accountability to the president and Congress and, through them, the voting public.

And federal prosecutors are arguably more accountable than the heads of independent agencies. Although appointed federal prosecutors have some independence as a practical matter, the heads of independent agencies have insulation as a legal matter. They are removable only for cause, stripping the president of one of his strongest mechanisms for exercising control over regulatory policy.

Thus, to the extent we accept the democratic accountability of agencies, we should be comfortable with the accountability of prosecutors.

B. Institutional Competence/Expertise

Many of the "regulations" imposed in prosecution agreements go the heart of how these companies should operate. How should late trading be reformed? What should be in the code of conduct for health insurance physician referrals? Are contingent commissions in the insurance industry harmful or beneficial? These questions go well beyond the question of whether a company committed a crime or even what punishment is appropriate. A key issue is whether prosecutors have the institutional competence to decide these substantive issues.

An initial question is whether prosecutors have the necessary resources to regulate. It is not surprising that most NPAs, DPAs, and settlement agreements come from a handful of offices. They are among the largest offices, with a bevy of prosecutors who have experience with sophisticated white-collar crime. But many federal offices and most state AG offices are smaller and lack the resources to properly investigate these cases and devise settlements that make sense. To the extent offices with fewer resources are taking on these cases, there is reason to be concerned that they may not have the time and staff necessary to think through an appropriate remedy.

Even in well-resourced offices, one can worry about expertise. Much turns on whether prosecutors are deciding these issues on their own or in consultation with relevant subject-matter experts, typically those at an expert agency like the SEC. Although it is hard to get concrete data on all federal and state prosecutions involving corporate regulation, it seems that consultation with expert agencies is fairly commonplace even if it is not formally institutionalized.

At the federal level, the ties between experts and prosecutors are stronger than in the states because there are long-standing institutional relationships between federal prosecutors and expert agencies. For starters, many, if not most, instances of corporate wrongdoing are likely to come to the attention of federal prosecutors as a result of a regulatory investigation. Federal regulatory agencies cannot bring criminal prosecutions on their own; they must persuade the DOJ to bring criminal charges.[51] As a result, in most cases, regulatory agencies will already be in contact with federal prosecutors about how the case should proceed, and their views are likely to be considered. This may explain why regulatory agencies are explicitly mentioned in two-thirds of deferred prosecution agreements—a figure that likely understates agency involvement because interactions undoubtedly occur that do not get mentioned in the agreements themselves.[52]

In addition, the president's Financial Fraud Enforcement Task Force creates an institutional framework specifically designed to foster cooperation between experts and prosecutors in corporate criminal matters. Created in 2002, the task force is an interagency group that includes among its membership the chairman of the SEC, the chairman of the Commodity Futures Trading Commission, the secretary of the Treasury, the secretary of Labor, and the chairman of the Federal Reserve. This working group allows the expert agencies and federal prosecutors to cooperate in investigating and prosecuting corporate crime.[53] The task force also addresses institutional questions, such as how to allocate DOJ resources in fighting corporate crime and how to promote cooperation among government agencies.

These institutional ties may help explain why federal DPAs and NPAs have been more measured in the regulatory obligations they have imposed on companies than those imposed by the NY AG. Federal prosecutors may be more reluctant to usurp the power of expert agencies and insist on broader regulatory reforms when they are in a long-term institutional dialogue and need to work together with these agencies on these types of cases in the future.

There is no similar institutional relationship between state prosecutors and the relevant governing agencies, so the influence of these agencies is likely to be less significant. To be sure, sometimes, maybe often, state prosecutors will make the effort to reach out to the relevant experts for guidance. In New York, for example, Eliot Spitzer began his investigations into investment firms without much consultation with the SEC.[54] As time went by, however, he began to consult the SEC about settlements.[55] Andrew Cuomo consulted with the American Medical Association and the Medical Society of the State of New York as well as numerous consumer groups before developing the code of conduct that governs how health care companies rank doctors.[56]

Nevertheless, the NY AG has hardly deferred to the SEC's judgment in all cases. The starkest example is the divergent response of each regulator to the mutual fund abuses of market timing and late trading. As noted, Spitzer's office insisted that mutual funds lower their fees by 20 percent for a five-year period as part of their settlement agreement with the AG's office. The SEC disagreed and even issued a press release explicitly disavowing the fee reduction. The SEC unanimously concluded that there was "no legitimate basis for the Commission to act as a 'rate-setter' and determine how much mutual fund customers should pay." In the commission's view, "[t]his decision is better left to informed consumers, independent and vigorous mutual fund boards, and the free market."[57] So, while state prosecutors can seek out expert advice, they do not necessarily take it.

But that raises the further question of whether the expert agency does, in fact, deserve deference. Regulatory agencies, despite their substantive knowledge, may not be in the best position to offer advice because their guidance could be driven by capture as much as expertise. If agencies are captured by the very groups they are charged with regulating and therefore less aggressive than they should be, it may be in the public interest for prosecutors to make an independent judgment whether and how to proceed. For instance, whether or not one agrees with the specific requirement of imposing a fee reduction, it does seem obvious that something needed to be done to address abuses in the mutual fund industry. Yet the SEC failed initially to address in *any* manner the problems of late trading and market timing in the mutual fund industry until Spitzer started putting pressure on the industry. Similarly, it was only after Spitzer exposed in detail the conflicts of interests between firms' securities analysts and underwriters that the SEC joined with him to create new rules for underwriters as part of a global settlement.[58]

Many have observed that the SEC's reluctance was not the result of an expert decision but was instead the product of powerful lobbying that opposed SEC interference,[59] and of a general sense at the SEC that, given the "rapidly revolving door between the SEC and private legal practice, . . . unless an issue has become high profile, it is best not to rock the boat."[60] The SEC had become "fully acclimated to existing market practices" and had staff members who "identified with the market participants they were ostensibly regulating."[61] Arthur Levitt, the chair of the SEC from 1993 to 2001, describes the SEC during his tenure as being constantly threatened by budget cuts if it pursued aggressive regulations because of corporate lobbying of the SEC's congressional overseers.[62] The result was an agency prone to lax enforcement—leaving a void that the NY AG's office filled.[63]

In assessing the institutional competence of a prosecutor to regulate corporations, one must therefore balance competing concerns. On the one hand, substantive expertise is critical. On the other, even experts might end up with tainted views because of regulatory capture.

The fact, then, that prosecutors do not always defer to the judgment of experts is not necessarily a reason to condemn regulation by prosecutors. In some instances, prosecutors might be the ones with the necessary institutional competence because they have not been captured by industry. Because of the dynamics discussed earlier, this is unlikely to happen often because prosecutors may also find themselves concerned with placating powerful corporate interests. But there will be instances where prosecutors—either because they are federal prosecutors who are not beholden to a particular regulated entity or because they are in a state like New York and have a broad base of public support—can make regulatory decisions free of the biases of capture. In those instances, prosecutors might be serving as a valuable corrective to some of the accountability failures of agencies.

But it is worrisome if prosecutors are not seeking expert opinion as at least an input in their decision making or if they are failing to give expert opinions sufficient deference when they are based on data and expertise. Instead of correcting problems with capture, prosecutors might in some cases make unwise and inefficient decisions because they are not properly trained to develop the right remedies.

C. Procedural Reliability

Accountability and expertise are not the only metrics for assessing regulatory policies. The methods used to reach decisions are also important. Prosecutors necessarily come to their regulatory policy decisions in the course of individual adjudications. Although a few agencies make policy decisions through that mechanism,[64] most agencies prefer to set policy through notice-and-comment rulemaking. That process is specifically designed for creating new rules of behavior. It allows input by all interested parties, not just those the prosecutor happens to charge or consult.

Indeed, even if a prosecutor consults with the relevant expert agency before reaching a decision, that agency will be operating at an informational disadvantage if it has not solicited and received comments on the issue. Regulators need detailed information about companies and their operation before crafting regulatory solutions, and the best way to obtain that information is to seek input from a variety of sources. So, for example, even if an attorney general's office were to contact the SEC before fashioning a new rule for investment banks, the SEC itself may not know how best to proceed without feedback from the industry and other interested groups. The SEC recognized the value of notice-and-comment procedures when it criticized Spitzer's fee reduction agreements with mutual funds, noting that it possessed "broad and unique rulemaking powers" and that "rules uniformly applicable to the entire industry are more desirable than a piecemeal approach that fragments the marketplace." In the SEC's view, any resolution of the fee issue should take place as part of a rulemaking process because that "is a better way to address fee issues than the imposition of arbitrary discounts in individual enforcement actions about market timing."[65]

When agencies or prosecutors make policies in adjudications instead of rulemakings, there is also the danger of insufficient oversight. The use of notice-and-comment rulemaking to change policies puts everyone on notice, including political overseers. This allows interested government officials the opportunity to weigh in before a regulatory shift occurs. Policymaking by adjudication takes place without advance warning to anyone other than the parties involved; by the time an agreement is reached, it is too late for others to weigh in.[66]

Policymaking through prosecution is subject to even less oversight because it also evades judicial review. When an agency adopts new rules of conduct for a company or an industry—whether in adjudications or rulemakings—it faces judicial oversight to ensure the agency's decision is consistent with its statutory mandate and is not otherwise arbitrary and capricious. The regulations in DPAs, NPAs, and other settlement agreements reached with prosecutors are generally not subject to judicial review.[67] Prosecutors, unlike agencies, are therefore setting policies through procedures that make it difficult for interested parties to intervene and for political and judicial overseers to check abuses.

Policymaking through adjudication raises other procedural concerns as well. There is a real danger that this approach to regulation will lead to disparate treatment of similarly situated companies because whether a new regulation applies to a corporation depends entirely on whom the prosecutor decides to target. Even if other companies have committed similar crimes, there is no guarantee that prosecutors will pursue them or, if they do, will seek the same terms for all violators. While agency adjudications suffer from the same shortcomings, agency rulemakings avoid these concerns with equity because these rules necessarily define the class of those affected, and judicial review ensures that the targeted group is based on a rational policy.

In recent years, the federal government has made an effort to make corporate regulation by prosecutors more uniform. In a series of memos circulated by deputy attorneys general, DOJ laid out standards for AUSAs to follow when investigating companies and their employees for wrongdoing. But these memos fail to solve the fundamental equity problems because they are written in broad terms and there is no requirement that any particular company be charged or that the same regulations should be sought in all cases raising the same issues.

Moreover, another shortcoming of adopting regulations in settlement agreements is that the terms are not subject to the kind of cost-benefit analysis that applies to most proposed rules. When executive agencies propose rules, they typically must explain to the president's OMB that the benefits of the regulation outweigh the costs. Even independent agencies like the SEC often think about their proposed regulations in these terms because of statutory requirements.[68] Decisions made in prosecutors' offices, however, undergo neither cost-benefit analysis nor any other kind of systemic review.[69]

To be sure, there are some procedural advantages to setting regulatory policy in an adjudication. There is no concern with ossification or delay because the process is streamlined. The notice-and-comment process is notoriously time-consuming, and judicial and OMB review take even more time. In the case of companies that have engaged in criminal misconduct, delay in reforming their business practices could make recidivism more likely. Regulation by prosecutors can avoid this delay and also allow prosecutors to change practices easily in future cases if it turns out that a particular strategy is not working well.

But efficiency is not a sufficient reason by itself to accept regulation by prosecutors. There must be some assurance that prosecutors are producing quality substantive regulations and evaluating them properly to ensure that they are appropriate. There is little in the existing procedures followed by prosecutors to give one much confidence on this score.

IV. Conclusion

The prosecutor as policymaker is not the Framers' vision, but it is increasingly the reality in many jurisdictions. This new role for the prosecutor sits uncomfortably with the institutional design of the prosecutor's office. To be sure, prosecutors are relatively accountable for their decisions, but their procedures and structure are not ideally suited to make the complex judgments they are now making, particularly when entire industries are being reformed. There is no mechanism in place to seek out comment from a range of interested parties, nor are prosecutors subject-matter experts in the areas in which they are regulating. To ensure that prosecutorial activism succeeds at improving public policy, then, greater attention must be paid to updating the prosecutor's office to better fulfill its new regulatory function. If prosecutors are going to behave like regulators, they should borrow from the best regulatory law has to offer.

NOTES

1. There are federalism and balkanization issues raised when any state actor, including a prosecutor, regulates a field that is also addressed by a federal body, but those issues are beyond the scope of this chapter. Sara Sun Beale tackles some of these questions in her chapter. *See infra* Sara Sun Beale, *What Are the Rules If Everybody Wants to Play? Multiple Federal and State Prosecutors (Acting) as Regulators*.

2. Rachel E. Barkow, *Institutional Design and the Policing of Prosecutors*, 61 Stan. L. Rev. 869 (2009).

3. William J. Stuntz, *The Pathological Politics of Criminal Law*, 100 Mich. L. Rev. 505, 512 (2001).

4. *Id.* at 552.

5. Bordenkircher v. Hayes, 434 U.S. 357 (1978).

6. United States v. Stein, 435 F. Supp. 2d 330, 381–82 (S.D.N.Y. 2006).

7. Brandon L. Garrett, *Structural Reform Prosecution*, 93 Va. L. Rev. 853, 861 (2007).

8. Peter Spivack & Sujit Raman, *Regulating the 'New Regulators': Current Trends in Deferred Prosecution Agreements*, 45 Am. Crim. L. Rev. 159, 167 (2008).

9. U.S.S.G. §8B1.2(a).

10. *Id.* at §8B2.1.

11. *Deferred Prosecution: Should Corporate Settlement Agreements Be Without Guidelines: Hearing Before the Subcomm. on Commercial and Admin. Law, Comm. of the H. Comm. on the Judiciary*, 110th Cong. (2008) (statement of David E. Nahmias, U.S. Attorney, Northern District of Georgia, and Chairman, White Collar Crime Subcommittee, Attorney General's Advisory Committee of United States Attorneys, U.S. Dep't of Justice) (emphasis added).

12. Mary Jo White, *Corporate Criminal Liability: What Has Gone Wrong?*, PLI Order No. 6063 (Nov. 2005).

13. In rare cases, DAs have imposed regulations on companies. For example, after eager post–Thanksgiving Day shoppers trampled a man to death at a Wal-Mart store in Long Island, the Nassau County district attorney reached a settlement agreement with Wal-Mart that required the company to implement a statewide crowd-control plan, make $1.5 million in donations to the community, and provide fifty jobs every year to teenagers in Nassau County. *Wal-Mart, DA Reach Settlement in Fatal Trampling*, North Country Gazette (May 6, 2009), http://www.northcountrygazette.org/2009/05/06/trampling_settlement/.

14. *See infra* Sara Sun Beale, *What Are the Rules If Everybody Wants to Play? Multiple Federal and State Prosecutors (Acting) as Regulators.*

15. N.Y. Gen. Bus. Law Art. 23-A, §352 et seq.

16. Frank C. Razzano, *The Martin Act: An Overview*, 1 J. Bus & Tech. Law 125, 126 (2006).

17. Louis Loss, Joel Seligman & Troy Paredes, 1 Securities Regulation 167–68 (4th ed. 2006).

18. Carey S. Dunne, *Role of the States Attorneys General in Policing the Securities Markets*, 1344 PLI/Corp 1079, 1087–92 (2002).

19. Nicholas Thompson, *The Sword of Spitzer*, Legal Affairs 50 (June 2004).

20. Previous NY AGs used the law mainly for small-time frauds and scams.

21. Joint Press Release, Ten of Nation's Top Investment Firms Settle Enforcement Actions Involving Conflicts of Interest Between Research and Investment Banking (Apr. 28, 2003), *available at* http://www.sec.gov/news/press/2003-54.htm.

22. *Id.*

23. Press Release, N.Y. Att'y Gen., SEC, NY Attorney General, NASD, NASAA, NYSE, and State Regulators Announce Historic Agreement to Reform Investment Practices (Dec. 20, 2002), *available at* http://www.oag.state.ny.us/media_center/2002/dec/dec20b_02.html.

24. *Id.*

25. "Market timing is the practice of short-term buying and selling of mutual fund shares in order to exploit inefficiencies in mutual fund pricing." Harold S. Bloomenthal, Securities Law Handbook § 20:18.10 (Dec. 2008).

26. *Id.*

27. Other states also pursued mutual fund fraud. *See, e.g.*, Press Release, Cal. Att'y Gen. Bill Lockyer, Attorney General Lockyer Launches Investigation of Fraudulent Sales Practices by Mutual Funds (Jan. 2, 2004), *available at* http://www.ag.ca.gov/newsalerts/2004/04-001.htm; News Release, Cal. Att'y Gen. Lockyer Announces $9 Million Settlement with PA Distributors in PIMCO Fund Case (Sept. 15, 2004), *available at* http://ag.ca.gov/newsalerts/release.php?id=796.

28. Compliance Programs of Investment Companies and Investment Advisers, 68 Fed. Reg. 74714 (Dec. 24, 2003) (codified at 17 C.F.R. §§ 270.38–1, 275.206(4)-7, 275.204–2 & 279.1).

29. *See* Press Release, N.Y. Att'y Gen., Alliance Agreement Includes New Form of Relief for Shareholders, *available at* http://www.oag.state.ny.us/media_center/2003/dec/dec18c_03.html.

30. *Spitzer Sues Marsh & McLennan*, Associated Press, Oct. 14, 2004 (listing Marsh, AIG, Ace Insurance Company, The Hartford, and Munich American Risk Partners as targets).

31. Kulbir Walha & Edward E. Filusch, *Eliot Spitzer: A Crusader Against Corporate Malfeasance or a Politically Ambitious Spotlight Hound? A Case Study of Eliot Spitzer and Marsh & McLennan*, 18 Geo. J. Legal Ethics 1111, 1127 (2005).

32. *Marsh Reaches $850 Million Deal with N.Y. AG Spitzer and Insurance Department*, Ins. J., Jan. 31, 2005, *available at* http://www.insurancejournal.com/news/national/2005/01/31/50470.htm?print=1.

33. *See* N.Y. Att'y Gen., UnitedHealthcare Agreement Concerning Physician Performance Measurement, Reporting and Tiering Programs 1 (Nov. 15, 2007), *available at* http://www.oag.state.ny.us/media_center/2007/nov/United%20Final%20Executed.pdf.

34. *See* Consumer-Purchaser Disclosure Project, Patient Charter for Physician Performance Measurement, Reporting and Tiering Programs: Ensuring Transparency, Fairness and Independent Review (Apr. 1, 2008), *available at* http://healthcaredisclosure.org/docs/files/PatientCharter.pdf.

35. *See generally* N.Y. Att'y Gen., Healthcare Industry Taskforce, Health Care Report: The Consumer Reimbursement System Is Code Blue (Jan. 13, 2009), *available at* http://www.oag.state.ny.us/bureaus/health_care/HIT2/pdfs/FINALHITIngenixReportJan.13,%202009.pdf.

36. Cuomo reached agreements with AETNA, CIGNA, HealthNow, Independent Health, MVP Health Care, UnitedHealth, and WellPoint.

37. *See, e.g.*, N.Y. Att'y Gen., AETNA Assurance of Discontinuance Under Executive Law § 63(15), Investigation No. 09–005, at 9–11 (Jan. 2009), *available at* http://www.oag.state.ny.us/bureaus/health_care/HIT2/pdfs/Aetna%20AOD%20Final.pdf.

38. N.Y. Att'y Gen., New York University Agreement on Code of Conduct 1–4 (Apr. 2, 2007), *available at* http://www.oag.state.ny.us/bureaus/student_loan/PDFs/NYU%20AOD.pdf.

39. Press Release, N.Y. Att'y Gen., Attorney General Cuomo Announces Groundbreaking Settlements with 8 Companies That Market Student Loans Directly to Students and Their Families (Sept. 9, 2008), *available at* http://www.oag.state.ny.us/media_center/2008/sep/sep9a_08.html.

40. Higher Education Opportunity Act of 2008, Pub. L. No. 110–315, 122 Stat. 3078 (codified in scattered sections of 20 U.S.C.); Student Lending Accountability, Transparency, and Enforcement Act, N.Y. Education Law §§ 620–632 (McKinney 2007).

41. Press Release, N.Y. Att'y Gen., New York Attorney General Cuomo Announces Agreement with Fannie Mae, Freddie Mac, and OFHEO, *available at* http://www.oag.state.ny.us/media_center/2008/mar/mar3a_08.html.

42. In five states—Alaska, Hawaii, New Hampshire, New Jersey, and Wyoming—they are appointed by the governor. In Maine, the AG is selected by a secret ballot of the legislature. In Tennessee, the state's supreme court (which is itself elected) selects the attorney general. State Attorneys General: Powers and Responsibilities 15 (Lynne M. Ross ed., 1990).

43. In 2003, Spitzer had the highest job approval rating of any New York state official. News Release, Quinnipiac University, Pataki Approval Inches Up, But Spitzer's Is Better (Oct. 2, 2003), *available at* http://www.quinnipiac.edu/x1318.xml?ReleaseID=349. Cuomo's approval rating as of February 2009 was 71 percent (http://www.maristpoll.marist.edu/nyspolls/NY090303.htm).

44. Rachel E. Barkow, *The Ascent of the Administrative State and the Demise of Mercy*, 121 Harv. L. Rev. 1332, 1353 (2008).

45. Stephen Ansolabehere and James M. Snyder, Jr., *The Incumbency Advantage in U.S. Elections: An Analysis of State and Federal Offices*, 1942–2000, 1 Election L.J. 315, 326 (2002).

46. Thompson, *supra* note 19 (quoting Scott Harshbarger, former attorney general of Massachusetts).

47. There is centralized review by Main Justice, for example, in RICO cases, for wiretaps, and in capital cases.

48. Spivack & Raman, *supra* note 8, at 173.

49. *See* Richard T. Boylan, *What Do Prosecutors Maximize? Evidence from the Careers of U.S. Attorneys*, 7 Am. L. & Econ. Rev. 379, 383 (2005).

50. Nicholas Bagley & Richard L. Revesz, *Centralized Oversight of the Regulatory State*, 106 Colum. L. Rev. 1260 (2006).

51. Michael Herz, *Structures of Environmental Criminal Enforcement*, 7 Fordham Envtl. L.J. 679, 706 (1996).

52. Daniel Richman, *Institutional Competence and Organizational Prosecutions*, 93 Va. L. Rev. In Brief 115, 116 (2007).

53. *See* Exec. Order No. 13,271, 67 Fed. Reg. 46,091, 46,091–92 (July 9, 2002), *available at* http://www.usdoj.gov/dag/cftf/execorder.htm.

54. Robert B. Ahdieh, *Dialectical Regulation*, 38 Conn. L. Rev. 863, 875 (2006).

55. *Id.*

56. Press Release, N.Y. Att'y Gen., Attorney General Cuomo Announces Doctor Ranking Agreement with Third Largest Health Insurer in U.S. (Nov. 13, 2007), *available at* http://www.oag.state.ny.us/media_center/2007/nov/nov13c_07.html.

57. Press Release, U.S. Sec. & Exch. Comm'n, Alliance Capital Management Will Pay Record $250 Million and Make Significant Governance and Compliance Reforms to Settle SEC Charges (Dec. 12, 2003), *available at* http://sec.gov/news/press/2003-176.htm.

58. John C. Coffee, Jr., *Corporate Securities*, N.Y. L. J., Mar. 20, 2008.

59. John C. Coffee, Jr., *A Course of Inaction*, Legal Affairs 46 (Apr. 2004).

60. *Id.*

61. Jonathan R. Macey, *State-Federal Relations Post–Eliot Spitzer*, 70 Brook. L. Rev. 117, 128 (2004).

62. Arthur Levitt, Take on the Street 123, 132 (2002).

63. Even when the SEC did get involved in enforcement, it was not as aggressive as the NY AG in obtaining restitution for harmed shareholders. Eric W. Zitzewitz, *Prosecutorial Discretion in Mutual Fund Settlement Negotiations*, 2003–7, B.E. J. Econ. Analysis & Pol'y: Vol. 9: Iss. 1 (Contributions), Article 24, abstract, *available at* http://www.bepress.com/bejeap/vol9/iss1/art24/ ("settlement negotiations that involved New York as well as the Securities and Exchange Commission (SEC) resulted in restitution ratios that were higher by a factor of 5–10").

64. Joan Flynn, *The Costs and Benefits of "Hiding the Ball": NLRB Policymaking and the Failure of Judicial Review*, 75 B.U. L. Rev. 387 (1995).

65. SEC Press Release, *supra* note 57.

66. Rachel E. Barkow & Peter W. Huber, *A Tale of Two Agencies: A Comparative Analysis of FCC and DOJ Review of Telecommunications Mergers*, 2000 U. Chi. Legal Forum 29, 77 (2000).

67. Garrett, *supra* note 7, at 922–29.

68. James J. Park, *The Competing Paradigms of Securities Regulation*, 57 Duke L.J. 625, 667 (2007).

69. Miriam Hechler Baer, *Governing Corporate Compliance*, 50 B.C. L. Rev. 949, 977 (2009).

9

What Are the Rules If Everybody Wants to Play?

Multiple Federal and State Prosecutors (Acting) as Regulators

SARA SUN BEALE

This chapter describes the multiple layers of overlapping jurisdiction involving prosecutors at the federal, state, and local level and explores the issues this multiplicity of actors raises. The federal structure has long created the possibility that the various federal, state, and local actors might all seek to open investigations or bring charges against the same defendants. The potential for multijurisdictional prosecutorial activity is particularly high when prosecutors are acting in a regulatory capacity because those cases typically involve multistate activity. For purposes of this chapter, activity is "prosecutorial" not only when formal criminal charges are filed but also when a prosecutor pursues an investigation to determine whether criminal charges are warranted or when the potential for criminal liability becomes a factor affecting negotiations concerning civil charges.

Multijurisdictional prosecutorial activity takes many forms. The number of jurisdictions can vary from two to many more. There may be close cooperation between the jurisdictions or conflict regarding which jurisdiction's case should take precedence, how to proceed, or what terms to include in a negotiated agreement or sentence. Often there are closely related civil proceedings, and such civil cases frequently involve additional jurisdictions that are not formally parties to the criminal case(s). There is, of course, some variation in the procedural course of multijurisdictional prosecutions, but trials are extremely rare, and many cases are concluded during the investigative phase or shortly after formal charges are filed. This is especially true in cases involving corporations or other entities. As discussed throughout this volume, prosecutors have so much leverage over corporations facing a criminal prosecution that they are often able to negotiate quick settlements with wide-ranging regulatory effects. These agreements are often global settlements disposing of both criminal and civil liability, and many agreements provide for payments to jurisdictions that would not have been parties to the formal prosecution. Other multijurisdictional civil charges are settled with no formal reference to criminal liability. To the degree that prosecutors negotiate such facially "civil" agreements in the shadow of criminal liability, those cases are encompassed in this discussion. It will often be difficult, however, for external observers to determine with certainty which facially civil cases fall within this category, though press reports and insider accounts sometimes indicate that the potential for criminal liability was a major factor in particular negotiations.

The first section of this chapter describes a variety of examples in which prosecutors from more than one jurisdiction initiated criminal investigations or brought formal prosecutions concerning the same conduct, and it analyzes the factors that determine whether more than one prosecutor will become involved. Access to shared resources and enhanced negotiating power serve as powerful incentives favoring cooperative multijurisdictional prosecutions; most of the cases to date exhibit significant (and often complete) cooperation among the various prosecutors. There are, however, multijurisdictional cases in which prosecutors from different jurisdictions do not act cooperatively. The state and federal prosecutions of telecommunications giant WorldCom and its executives demonstrate some of the complexities that can arise in the absence of voluntary cooperation among the prosecutors who are targeting the same defendants.

The second section of this chapter considers the issues raised if prosecutors in multijurisdictional cases do not cooperate voluntarily. There is no single principle or mechanism that regulates or coordinates all of the actors. Federal law does not, in general, preempt state and local laws, and the federal Double Jeopardy Clause does not preclude multiple convictions by different jurisdictions. Although there are laws in many states barring conviction for conduct that has been the basis for a conviction or acquittal in another state or in federal court, the effect of these laws is quite limited. They prohibit additional trials and the imposition of multiple penalties once a first prosecution has concluded, but they do nothing to relieve the burdens created by multiple investigations and charges before there has been a conviction or acquittal in another jurisdiction. No other coordinating device currently exists. Courts in one jurisdiction cannot generally order a stay of criminal proceedings in another jurisdiction, and no mechanisms are in place that would permit the consolidation of criminal cases from multiple jurisdictions in a single court.

I. Concurrent Criminal Jurisdiction and the Potential for Multijurisdictional Prosecutions

National and international corporations like WorldCom are subject to two forms of concurrent jurisdiction that give rise to the potential for regulatory activity by multiple prosecutors: concurrent federal/state jurisdiction and concurrent state/state jurisdiction. Indeed, concurrent criminal jurisdiction of both forms is now ubiquitous, raising the question whether and when prosecutors from more than one jurisdiction will elect to prosecute the same defendants.

Most federal criminal laws govern conduct also addressed by state law, creating concurrent federal/state jurisdiction. Very few subjects are delegated exclusively to the federal government, and the Constitution allows states to retain concurrent authority unless their laws have been preempted.[1] Express preemption provisions are rarely included in federal criminal laws, and absent an express provision courts seldom find state criminal laws preempted. The Supreme Court has made it clear that preemption is the exception rather than the rule,[2] and it has found preemption in the absence of an express provision in only three situations: (1) federal law completely occupies the field, leaving no room for state law; (2) compliance with both federal and state law is impossible; or (3) state law is an obstacle to a federal statute's purposes.[3] Although implied preemption has been found in the case of some state regulatory laws, in the criminal context there is a clear understanding that Congress ordinarily intends federal laws to supplement state law rather than to regulate comprehensively and occupy the field. Concurrent state/state jurisdiction arises because any person or entity that conducts business or has a significant presence in more than one state is subject to prosecution in each state (and perhaps in multiple subdivisions within states) for conduct that occurs or causes consequences in those states. For example, because its securities were sold nationwide, WorldCom's quarterly and annual financial statements were subject not only to the federal securities laws but also to each state's securities laws. States' so-called blue-sky laws, which are intended to protect investors, generally include prohibitions against making false statements in the sale of securities.[4] Thus, fraudulent accounting practices could simultaneously violate federal and state law. For businesses of any size, conduct that spans or affects more than one state is now the norm. Indeed, the availability of the Internet and other forms of technology has increased the ease with which entities (and individuals) now conduct multistate or national transactions. Those transactions subject them to prosecution in multiple states under a wide variety of laws governing matters such as consumer protection, the environment, and business competition, as well as the sale of securities.

A. Examples of Multijurisdictional Prosecutions

Most high-profile multijurisdictional prosecutions involve both federal and state prosecutors. The relationships between the federal and state prosecutors in these cases have varied widely.

The Barkow and Garrett chapters describe several prominent examples of multijurisdictional regulatory actions initiated by NY AGs Eliot Spitzer and Andrew Cuomo. Although these cases ended in civil settlements, they fall within the ambit of this chapter's analysis because Spitzer and Cuomo employed the criminal investigative process and the potential for criminal liability appears to have been a significant factor in the negotiations. For example, in cases involving investment banks and mutual funds, Spitzer initiated the investigations and federal regulators from the SEC eventually joined, either eagerly or reluctantly, in global settlements with far-reaching regulatory effects.[5] Behind the scenes, it appears that other states were also involved in the investment banking investigation when it widened beyond Merrill Lynch, and these states informally coordinated their efforts with one another and with federal regulators so that each investment bank found itself facing both federal and state investigators.[6] The cases initiated by Spitzer and Cuomo, though nominally civil, are generally regarded as prime examples of prosecutors acting as regulators.

In many other multijurisdictional cases, federal prosecutors have taken the lead, with states participating and joining in the settlement. For example, federal prosecutors in three districts, working with a host of federal agencies and the Civil Division of the DOJ, concluded an investigation of pharmaceutical giant Pfizer's drug marketing practices with a civil and criminal settlement that included a record-setting package of $2.3 billion in criminal fines and forfeitures plus civil damages to be paid to both the federal government and the states.[7] The agreement also required Pfizer to enter into an extensive corporate integrity program. There was state participation coordinated by a team from the National Association of State Medicaid Fraud Units, which played a role in the investigation and then represented the settling states in the negotiations.[8]

In the Spitzer prosecutions and the Pfizer case there was sufficient cooperation among the different jurisdictions to allow the negotiation of joint federal/state settlements, though there may also have been some areas of disagreement. Indeed, in the settlement with the mutual fund companies, the

SEC publicly noted its disagreement with Spitzer's insistence that the funds reduce their fees by 20 percent and maintain this reduced rate for five years.[9] Occasionally federal and state officials agree to share a regulatory investigation and prosecution. For example, federal and state officials jointly raided the offices of WellCare Health Plans, and both the Florida attorney general and the U.S. Attorney's Office for the Middle District of Florida were parties to a DPA (in which they were described as "the Offices").[10] The agreement, filed in federal court, states that "in lieu of the Offices' pursuit of a criminal conviction of WellCare," the Offices accepted WellCare's agreement to undertake corporate reforms under the supervision of an independent monitor and pay a civil forfeiture of $40 million to the United States and restitution of $40 million to Florida.[11] In another matter, the press reported that the U.S. Attorney for the Southern District of New York and New York Attorney General Andrew Cuomo met and agreed to share the investigation of companies engaging in credit-default swaps.[12] In a third matter, the Enron Task Force sought unsuccessfully to recruit state regulators to take over a discrete part of the case they could not handle, and also gave the go-ahead to a state attorney general who indicated an interest in investigating part of the case.[13]

In some cases, it appears that federal and state investigations have simply been pursued independently, with neither cooperation nor interference. For example, seven states are cooperating in an investigation of Financial Securities Assurance and seeking discovery in state court of hundreds of hours of audio recordings that have already been provided to the DOJ and the SEC.[14] The states are investigating possible antitrust violations, and the federal investigations reportedly focus on allegations that brokers and providers steered business in return for kickbacks, retainers, or other financial incentives.

Finally, in some multijurisdictional cases there have been turf battles rather than cooperation. For example, the U.S. Attorney's Office in the Southern District of New York accepted the guilty plea of a defendant in a federal securities fraud case despite the protests of Manhattan District Attorney Robert Morgenthau, effectively terminating the ongoing state proceeding.[15] Press accounts have noted the perception that the "'Sovereign District of New York' . . . doesn't necessar[il]y play well with others."[16]

B. WorldCom: A Case Study

The state and federal prosecutions of communications giant WorldCom provide a well-documented case study of a complex multijurisdictional prosecution involving a federal regulatory agency, multiple civil actions, both state and federal criminal charges, and a degree of competition and conflict between the federal and state prosecutors. Operating as MCI, WorldCom was the nation's number-two long-distance carrier. WorldCom's restatement of its financial statements reduced its earnings by $11 billion, touching off extended proceedings in the bankruptcy court, an SEC investigation, multiple shareholder suits, and both state and federal criminal investigations. The gist of the charges was that WorldCom falsely portrayed itself as a profitable business by capitalizing (and deferring) rather than expensing (and immediately recognizing) billions of costs in violation of established generally accepted accounting principles. The civil proceedings began quickly and moved very rapidly. The SEC filed a civil case in the Southern District of New York charging WorldCom with multiple counts of securities fraud;[17] shortly thereafter WorldCom filed what was, at the time, the largest ever Chapter 11 bankruptcy case. Just over twelve months later, the district court approved a settlement agreement, stating that it was "aware of no large company accused of fraud that has so rapidly and so completely divorced itself from the misdeeds of the immediate past and undertaken such extraordinary steps to prevent such misdeeds in the future."[18] Under the supervision of a court-appointed monitor, WorldCom had cleaned house, replacing its entire board of directors, hiring a new chief executive officer, recruiting other senior managers, and firing or accepting the resignation of every employee accused of having participated in the fraud or having been insufficiently attentive in preventing the fraud. The company consented to a permanent injunction authorizing the monitor to undertake a complete overhaul of its corporate governance after a comprehensive review by new outside auditors. It also agreed to provide employees with specialized training in accounting, reporting, and ethics in programs to be developed for the company by experts from two universities, and the new CEO and other employees executed a sworn ethics pledge requiring a degree of transparency that went well beyond SEC requirements. Thus the SEC achieved its regulatory objectives through civil litigation. Finally, WorldCom agreed to pay a penalty of $2.25 billion (reduced to $750 million by the bankruptcy proceedings), which was more than 15 percent of the estimated value of the company following bankruptcy reorganization and seventy-five times greater than any prior penalty imposed by the SEC.

While the SEC's civil case was proceeding, federal prosecutors in the Southern District of New York conducted a criminal investigation, focusing initially on the lower-level corporate actors directly involved in preparing the financial statements (such as the director of accounting). The cooperation of these first defendants was necessary to determine whether a case could be made against the senior officers who were more insulated from the fraudulent filings. Federal prosecutors had obtained guilty pleas and cooperation from four individual defendants (though no charges had yet been filed against CEO Bernard Ebbers, and no final decision had been made on whether to charge WorldCom itself) when the intervention of the Oklahoma AG threw the federal investigation into what one press report described as "chaos."[19]

Two months after the district court accepted the settlement in the SEC action, Oklahoma filed state criminal charges against WorldCom itself, the four executives who had already pled guilty to the federal charges and were cooperating, CFO Scott Sullivan (who had been indicted on federal charges but not yet pled or gone to trial), and CEO Bernard Ebbers (who was still under investigation but had not yet been charged). The fifteen-count Oklahoma indictment charged violations of the Oklahoma Securities Act that tracked the allegations of federal securities fraud, alleging that the documents filed with the SEC overstated the value of the company.[20] The individual defendants faced possible penalties of fines plus ten years' imprisonment on each count (consecutively or concurrently), and WorldCom faced a maximum fine of $150,000. Oklahoma Attorney General Drew Edmondson informed the press that attorneys general in four other states were also considering whether to file criminal charges, but no other state did so.

The Oklahoma charges had the potential to throw the federal criminal cases completely off track. Indeed, the U.S. Attorney's Office issued a statement saying it was "disappointed" that the state failed to consult federal prosecutors before filing and expressing hope that Oklahoma's actions would not interfere with the federal prosecutions.[21] Attorney General Edmondson responded that in the past the state had delayed action in deference to federal prosecutors and had been left with no options when the federal proceedings dragged on so long that the state statute of limitations expired; he also stated that he viewed the SEC's civil settlement as "painfully inadequate" and "fundamentally unjust."[22]

The state charges injected a major new factor into the equation. The defendants who had already pled guilty to the federal charges and were cooperating with the federal investigation in the hopes of reducing their own sentences now faced the risk that a federal conviction would establish most or all of the elements of a state crime and that their cooperation with federal authorities could further incriminate them in the state proceedings. In the case of CFO Sullivan, who had been indicted but had not pled guilty, there were immediate conflicts in sequencing the procedures in state and federal proceedings. Sullivan asked the federal judge to stay the state proceedings, contending that the state case would compromise his ability to defend himself in the federal proceeding. The judge declined, adding that she hoped federal and state prosecutors could work out the issue.[23] The prosecutors attempted to resolve these problems by a gentlemen's agreement, with the state agreeing not to call any witnesses until after Sullivan's trial, but that plan was frustrated by the state court, which refused to delay Sullivan's preliminary hearing. To avoid a direct conflict, the Oklahoma AG then dismissed the state charges for what he described as "tactical" reasons, stating that he would refile after the federal trial. This allowed federal prosecutors to continue the investigation against Ebbers, but the specter of the state charges still hung over the heads of the cooperating witnesses whose testimony was essential to bringing successful charges against Sullivan and Ebbers. Equally important, it derailed WorldCom's efforts to resolve all charges against it. Finally, it raised the possibility that regulators from other states might impose additional demands on WorldCom, notwithstanding the fact that the corporation was already making what the federal district court found were unprecedented efforts to reform itself and paying record-setting penalties within the constraints of what was, at that point, the largest-ever U.S. bankruptcy proceeding. Critics expressed concern that the state's charges against the corporation were influenced by MCI's competitors, some of which were close to the Oklahoma AG, and warned that the charges could punish innocent people working to reestablish the corporation while benefiting its competitors.[24]

How was the potential conflict or impasse between state and federal officials resolved? WorldCom settled the Oklahoma criminal charges with a DPA that gave the state an estimated financial benefit of more than $100 million,[25] and the state refiled but ultimately dismissed charges against the former WorldCom officials after the conclusion of the federal prosecutions. The Oklahoma DPA included an economic development agreement requiring WorldCom to create 1,600 jobs in Oklahoma over the next ten years or, failing that, to pay the state a percentage of the salaries.[26] The AG explained his decision to forgo criminal charges against the corporation on several grounds. A conviction would mean that WorldCom would lose its license to operate in Oklahoma, precluding MCI from providing a nationwide calling plan. This would hurt not only WorldCom but also the state's pension funds, which held stock in the corporation. He also acknowledged the steps WorldCom had taken to purge itself (though of course those had been taken before the state charges were filed). Noting that if the state took the case to trial it could put the company out of business, he characterized the economic development agreement as restitution for the state's losses in a different form.

The DPA also required WorldCom to assist Oklahoma in efforts to prosecute its former executives, and the state filed new charges against the individual defendants. Federal and state prosecutors eventually forged a working relationship in which the federal prosecutors took the lead and the AG monitored the federal proceedings, reserving the right to proceed against the individuals if the federal proceedings did not culminate in what the state viewed as sufficient punishment. Apparently the individual defendants who cooperated with the federal prosecutors cooperated with state authorities as well.[27] When the federal proceedings culminated in the conviction of all the defendants charged by the state, including a twenty-five-year sentence for CEO Ebbers, the AG dismissed all the state charges because the federal sentences were sufficient to serve the state's interests.[28]

What purpose, if any, did the Oklahoma charges serve? The value of WorldCom's commitment to create new jobs in Oklahoma partially offset the state's pension fund loss of about $63 million, and the Oklahoma AG speculated that the filing of the state charges spurred on federal prosecutors.[29] The prosecution also provided substantial publicity for the AG, who subsequently announced his candidacy for governor.

One other state filed a criminal charge arising out of the WorldCom case, but its actions seem to have been coordinated with the federal prosecution. After CFO Scott Sullivan pled guilty to the federal charges and agreed to testify at the trial of his boss, Bernard Ebbers, Mississippi quietly accepted Sullivan's guilty plea to one count of conspiracy to violate the state's securities laws.[30] There was no interference with the federal proceedings, but it is not clear why Mississippi pursued the case. It was not designed to increase Sullivan's punishment or provide any revenue to the state, and perhaps for that reason the Mississippi AG did not do much to draw attention to the charges.

C. Prosecutorial Incentives and Barriers to Multijurisdictional Prosecutions

Multijurisdictional prosecutions require not only concurrent jurisdiction but also a discretionary commitment of significant prosecutorial resources. The question is whether and when conditions will be conducive to the commitment of such resources, particularly in the case of state prosecutors. Federal prosecutors have many incentives to participate in cases involving conduct or effects spanning multiple states—which by definition exceed the investigative abilities of any single state—and conduct of this nature is frequently subject to national regulatory schemes.[31] Additionally, federal prosecutors generally have more investigative and prosecutorial resources than those available to state authorities (though some federal investigative resources have shifted from white-collar cases to terrorism). These factors make federal prosecutors likely players in cases in which concurrent jurisdiction exists. The factors affecting state prosecutors are more complex and vary greatly from state to state. Although there are significant incentives for states to initiate or participate in multistate litigation, those incentives vary depending on the subject matter of the controversy, and historically the states have been more active in civil (or facially civil) actions than in prosecuting multistate activity.

1. Incentives for Multistate Regulatory Litigation

There are significant incentives for states to pursue regulatory goals through multistate litigation. The experience of the past three decades suggests that state AGs are the best positioned and most likely to bring such regulatory prosecutions, though a few district attorneys (most notably Manhattan District Attorney Robert Morgenthau) also developed the requisite resources and expertise. State attorneys general became a powerful regulatory force in the 1980s and 1990s. During this period they tripled the size of their staffs and exponentially increased their budgets.[32] Seeking to fill the gap created by federal deregulation, state attorneys general developed and institutionalized the practice of coordinated multistate civil litigation. Developing the necessary cooperation was initially a difficult task that required significant entrepreneurship on the part of some individual attorneys general and private lawyers who assisted them.[33] The National Association of Attorneys General ("NAAG") also played a role, promoting close ties among attorneys general and helping to coordinate litigation in different policy areas.[34]

The multistate approach has been "strikingly effective" in a wide range of cases, including most notably the tobacco litigation.[35] Multistate litigation allowed the states to reach critical mass in terms of both resources and the threat of potential sanctions. By coordinating their strategy, pooling their resources, and bringing parallel actions, states were able to force major corporations and entire industries to change their business practices and pay significant settlements in cases involving consumer protection, antitrust, environmental, and securities regulation.[36] This practice is now well established, and groups of two to fifty states routinely bring mirror-image lawsuits in their own state courts.[37]

State attorneys general are now seen increasingly as policy entrepreneurs with strong incentives to pursue innovative litigation. Forty-three state attorneys general are elected, and many use the position as a stepping-stone to higher office. Many notable political figures, including Bill Clinton, Joe Lieberman, and John Ashcroft, once served as state attorney general. Of those who served as attorneys general from 1980 to 1999, more than 40 percent ran for the office of governor or senator, and others pursued judicial office.[38] An attorney general who intends to seek higher office has an incentive to innovate and to take high-profile actions that may appeal to voters interested in a wide range of issues.[39] Multistate litigation has provided states with a means to obtain both substantial financial settlements (for the state and/or for individuals) and beneficial regulatory or structural changes. Despite the comparatively greater resources available to federal investigators, states working cooperatively have shown the capacity to act more quickly and aggressively than federal authorities. Indeed, many attribute the increased activism of state attorneys general to the void created by federal deregulation in the 1980s. More recently, states have taken the lead in seeking relief on behalf of homeowners during the mortgage crisis. In October 2008 an initial group of eleven states hammered out what was hailed as the "most comprehensive, mandatory loan workout program since the mortgage crisis began" with Countrywide, the nation's largest lender and loan servicer.[40] Countrywide agreed to provide an estimated $8.4 billion in direct loan relief, waive certain fees, and set aside additional funds to help people cope with foreclosures and relocations, and it signed a "Multistate Settlement Term Sheet" that ultimately provided a basis for twenty-nine additional states to join the settlement by July 2009.[41] By contrast, the federal response has been much slower. More than a year after the initial state settlement, the SEC had filed but not resolved civil charges against Countrywide executives, and a federal grand jury was reportedly investigating Countrywide.[42] But not everyone thinks the federal investigation is moving too slowly. Some observers familiar with similar investigations think the slower pace of the federal investigation reflects greater care in evaluating evidence and less willingness to use leverage to press for a quick settlement.

The incentives for state participation in multistate litigation vary, and several factors have been found to influence whether particular states will participate in multistate litigation. One study found that elected state attorneys general participate more frequently, as do those heading larger offices with more resources.[43] And states with liberal electorates were more frequent participants in multistate litigation.[44] Some factors influence participation in particular cases. For example, some state attorneys general have reported that they are less likely to cooperate with another attorney general who has sued their state or who has a different party affiliation.[45] Attorneys general also consider the impact of particular litigation on their own state. Not surprisingly, states in which tobacco was an important part of the economy were reluctant to participate in the multistate tobacco litigation.

2. Barriers or Factors Limiting Multistate Regulatory Prosecutions

Despite these incentives, states have been much more active in initiating multijurisdictional civil rather than criminal litigation. With the exception of the cases involving Eliot Spitzer and Andrew Cuomo,[46] the federal/state prosecutorial activity noted earlier was initiated by federal authorities or jointly by federal and state authorities. There are no criminal parallels to the multistate tobacco litigation or the multistate Countrywide settlement (though in the case of the Countrywide settlement one press report suggested that Countrywide entered the settlement to avoid prosecution).[47] Why, then, have states (other than New York) been so much more aggressive in pursuing multijurisdictional civil rather than criminal litigation, even when criminal litigation is broadly defined to encompass settlements designed to avoid criminal prosecutions? Although there is no clear answer to this question, several factors seem to have played a role.

There are differences in the legal tools available (though there are many variations from state to state). The powers that NY AGs Eliot Spitzer and Andrew Cuomo have wielded so effectively are not shared by their counterparts in other states. The authority of the attorneys general varies widely, from states in which they have no prosecutorial authority to other states in which they hold the sole prosecutorial authority.[48] In many states the attorney general's prosecutorial authority is limited to certain classes of cases. In cases that fall outside the state attorney general's authority, local district attorneys—who are less likely to have the resources and expertise to bring innovative regulatory prosecutions—have the exclusive prosecutorial authority.

Even state attorneys general who have prosecutorial authority still may not have a full complement of the procedural and substantive tools that would facilitate criminal charges in multistate litigation. At the investigative stage, no other state gives the attorney general the powerful investigative authority provided by New York's Martin Act. And states contemplating multistate litigation may have a common framework for bringing parallel civil actions in each state but not for parallel criminal charges. For example, the multistate Countrywide settlement resolved consumer protection claims that have no clear counterpart in the criminal laws of many states. The same may be true of other established common-law and statutory causes of action, though the details will vary from state to state. The gap between criminal and civil authority will be even greater if states seek to establish new theories of civil liability because it is generally agreed that courts have no authority to create common-law crimes.

Resources are also an issue. In the tobacco litigation, the states brought in experienced and aggressive private lawyers who worked on a contingency fee basis, and that assistance was very significant in bringing the states' resources up to par with those of the tobacco companies.[49] But contingency fees cannot be used to finance prosecutions, and resource constraints are being felt especially keenly as most or all states experience budget shortfalls.

Perhaps equally important, there are some structural and cultural features that distinguish the state attorneys general (though their roles do vary from state to state) from the federal prosecutors who are in many respects their counterparts. States have plenary authority rather than the limited powers granted to the federal government, and the role of the state attorneys general is far broader than that of the prosecutors in the U.S. Attorneys' offices (where most DOJ attorneys are located). The ability of state attorneys general to bring suit to protect the health, comfort, and welfare of state citizens under a *parens patriae* theory[50] is just one reflection of the broad responsibility delegated to them.[51] The broad responsibilities of the state attorneys general may affect their choice between civil and criminal theories when both are available. Indeed, the ordinary sanctions for criminal conduct—imprisonment for individuals and fines for corporations—are not designed to achieve wide-ranging regulatory reform, and a criminal conviction (or even the filing of criminal charges) may cripple or even destroy a corporation, leading to catastrophic losses to shareholders, employees, and other third parties.[52] An attorney general seeking regulatory change to benefit the public (or appeal to voters) would not ordinarily want to risk putting a major corporation out of business.

In the case of multistate frauds perpetrated by large corporations, for example, federal and state prosecutors are likely to weigh the trade-offs of enforcement differently. Neither prosecutors in the state in which a corporation has its principal activities nor prosecutors in other states where only victims are found may have the necessary incentives and resources to prosecute large, complex frauds. Prosecutors from the state in which a large corporation has its main activities will assess the costs and benefits of prosecution differently than federal prosecutors, typically giving more weight to the costs of prosecution.[53] When many of the victims live out of state, the benefits of the prosecution will go outside the state, but the costs in terms of lost employment, loss of the tax base, and the costs of enforcement will be borne within the state. Additionally, state officials are likely to have ties to the corporation and its leadership. Other states where victims reside may also be unlikely to prosecute, though for a different reason: in those states, enforcement may be too costly.[54]

In the future, however, multistate criminal investigations and prosecutions could become more common. To the degree that states have seen criminal litigation as ill-suited to achieving regulatory reforms, the federal practice of negotiating DPAs and NPAs provides a template for states seeking to preserve yet reform corporations or entire industries. Indeed, the WellCare case shows that it is possible for both the federal government and one or more states to be parties to a single agreement that would defer prosecutions by all the signatories. Although one sovereign cannot be a party to a criminal case brought by another sovereign, DPAs are contracts that can bind any parties who agree to them. Additionally, there is a trend toward granting state attorneys general prosecutorial authority in some cases of statewide importance, including those involving white-collar crime.[55] The adoption of new state laws giving whistle-blowers a financial incentive to come forward with evidence of corporate fraud may also help put state prosecutors more on a par with federal prosecutors, who have relied heavily on the information provided by corporate insiders.[56]

D. Incentives for Cooperation or Conflict in Multijurisdictional Prosecutions

Although most of the multistate prosecutions described here appear to have been characterized by cooperation (and many were concluded by a global settlement), the involvement of multiple jurisdictions also raises the possibility of conflict that might delay, impede, or even preclude or terminate the prosecutorial efforts of other jurisdictions. The potential for conflict was clearly present in the WorldCom case, but Oklahoma's DPA with the corporate defendant and its temporary dismissal of the charges against the individual defendants were sufficient to address the concerns of the federal prosecutors and the defense.[57]

Several factors encourage cooperative behavior in multijurisdictional prosecutions. From the state perspective, past experience in civil multijurisdictional litigation has demonstrated the power of cooperative behavior and sharing of resources and legal theories. That experience creates a powerful precedent, and it is particularly important when, as now, state attorneys general are facing severe budgetary pressures. Going it alone is more costly. Indeed, when federal authorities are actively pursuing civil and/or criminal proceedings, it may be most efficient for states to allow the federal authorities to pull the laboring oar, thereby capturing the tangible and political benefits of a global settlement with little or no outlay of state resources. This model provides substantial benefits to the states—and to the attorneys general both personally and institutionally—at little or no cost.

The Oklahoma prosecution in the WorldCom case, however, suggests that with relatively little effort any (or all) of the state attorneys general who have prosecuting authority could file state criminal charges during the pendency of federal proceedings and by so doing extract unique and favorable benefits for their states. Oklahoma's actions did not require a major commitment of resources. The state indictment largely tracked the federal charges filed against the individual defendants, and the guilty pleas of four of the defendants meant that their state convictions would be a virtually foregone conclusion. More important, in order to reach a global settlement, it was essential for WorldCom to dispose of the criminal charge against it. The intriguing question is why other states did not pursue a similar course of action in the WorldCom case (and in others like it) given the benefits it provided to Oklahoma. There was criticism of the state charges, but it came largely from sources outside Oklahoma. Why would the citizens (and voters) in Oklahoma disapprove of an agreement that brought them a guarantee of either well-paid jobs or millions of dollars to their state treasury? One partial answer specific to the WorldCom case is that many state attorneys general have only limited authority in securities cases. The general regulation of securities is housed within the attorney general's office in only five states, and only about half of the attorneys general have the authority to file criminal charges in securities cases.[58]

More generally, it seems likely that a variety of informal factors have restrained state attorneys general from bringing independent criminal charges that could interfere with an ongoing federal prosecution or multistate civil litigation. The state attorneys general generally know one another and work closely together on a variety of issues of common interest.[59] These working relationships promote cooperative behavior. Additionally, since many states are repeat players in multistate litigation, they may be reluctant to incur the disapproval of their traditional partners in this litigation. If these jurisdictions were sufficiently displeased, they could refuse to cooperate and share resources in other cases. States that went it alone might also face pressure from within the NAAG, which has developed a significant role in encouraging and coordinating multistate litigation. Federal prosecutors might also have access to additional carrots and sticks, since there are many different avenues of cooperation between the state attorneys general and the DOJ and other federal agencies.[60] Finally, state attorneys general might take the view that adopting an especially aggressive litigation strategy might be disadvantageous. It might create an unfavorable business climate within the state or increase the risk of undesirable regulatory or statutory preemption,[61] consequences that state attorneys general wish to avoid.

Shared party affiliations may provide an additional incentive for cooperative behavior. Attorneys general from different states but the same political party have one more incentive not to interfere with one another's investigations and prosecutions. Similarly, an attorney general from the same party as the president (and thus the U.S. Attorney) has a heightened incentive to be cooperative and not to cause problems for the administration. In this situation a state attorney general would be much less likely to proceed in any fashion that would interfere with an ongoing federal investigation or prosecution. A state attorney general from the president's party might also be reluctant to earn the displeasure of her party's leadership by taking aggressive action in a case that federal authorities had declined to prosecute, since her action might be interpreted as criticism of the administration.

II. Formal Mechanisms for Coordinating Multijurisdictional Prosecutions

Although there are many informal mechanisms that promote coordination and cooperation in multijurisdictional prosecutions, they may not always be sufficient. Thus it is germane to ask what formal mechanisms, if any, are available to preclude multiple prosecutions for the same conduct or to require some sort of coordination among simultaneous multijurisdictional prosecutions when conflicts occur. The answer is that present law offers few tools either to preclude multiple prosecutions or to require coordination.

A. Constitutional and Statutory Limitations on Multiple Prosecutions

Although both federal and state law preclude double jeopardy or successive prosecutions, these laws do little or nothing to solve the problems posed by multiple prosecutors seeking to act as regulators.

The Double Jeopardy Clause of the Fifth Amendment is limited by the dual sovereignty doctrine, which holds that prosecutions under federal and state law (or under the laws of different states) are not prosecutions for the same offense.[62] Accordingly, one state may prosecute a defendant who has already been prosecuted by the federal government or another state for the same conduct.[63]

Many states impose limitations on successive prosecutions, and some of the state provisions are broader than the Double Jeopardy Clause. Twenty-three states have generally applicable statutes that restrict successive prosecutions.[64] Although the statutory language and judicial interpretations of these statutes vary considerably, they generally bar prosecution or provide an affirmative defense after acquittal or conviction in federal court or in another state's court for the same "conduct," "act," or "offense."[65] In addition, some states have enacted legislation that restricts successive prosecution for particular offenses.[66] For example, New York's statutory bar on successive prosecutions explains Manhattan District Attorney Robert Morgenthau's protest when federal prosecutors accepted a guilty plea from a defendant who was also facing state charges: the federal conviction barred a conviction under state law.[67]

But the existing patchwork of state laws restricting successive intersovereign prosecution provides little more than nominal protection for corporations with a significant presence throughout the United States. State statutory and constitutional provisions cannot prevent a federal prosecution after a state has taken action. More important, more than half of the states have no general limits on successive prosecutions. Facing the possibility of twenty-seven prosecutions (including a federal prosecution) may make it difficult for a business to appreciate the limitations that do exist. Finally, restrictions on successive prosecutions do not ordinarily apply until there has been a final judgment—either an acquittal or a conviction.[68] Thus these provisions have no effect before trial, and they provide no basis for objecting to simultaneous federal and state investigations.

It should be noted, however, that the DOJ has adopted an internal policy that imposes a significant degree of restraint on successive federal prosecutions for substantially the same act(s) or transaction(s) that have been prosecuted in another jurisdiction. Under what is called the "Petite Policy," federal prosecutors are permitted to bring a prosecution after a prior state or federal prosecution concerning substantially the same acts or transactions only with the approval of an assistant attorney general based upon, among other things, a showing that the prior prosecution left a substantial federal interest demonstrably unvindicated.[69]

B. Injunctive Relief and Sequencing Cases

If dueling prosecutions occur in more than one jurisdiction, the defendants may wish that the cases not proceed simultaneously, and each of the prosecutors may also wish to move her case ahead without any interference arising from another prosecution. For example, in the WorldCom case CFO Scott Sullivan asked the federal court to stay the state proceedings so that he would not be whipsawed between them, and the federal prosecutors who were dismayed by the state charges may have been sympathetic to this request.

Neither the federal nor the state courts ordinarily have the authority to issue such orders coordinating multiple cases by staying prosecutions in other jurisdictions. The federal structure explains why state courts cannot issue such injunctions or stays. One state court cannot enjoin a prosecution in another state because they are coequal independent sovereigns. Nor do state courts have the authority to enjoin federal prosecutions.

And despite the fact that federal law is supreme, with only a few narrow exceptions the federal courts are barred from enjoining ongoing state criminal proceedings.[70] Though exceptions have been recognized for state prosecutions brought in bad faith or under patently unconstitutional laws, in general considerations of both equity and comity preclude the federal courts from interfering with ongoing state criminal proceedings.[71] This doctrine is grounded in respect for state sovereignty, and it promotes harmonious relations between federal and state courts. The long-standing policy against federal interference with the judicial proceedings of the sovereign states is also reflected in the Anti-Injunction Act, which bars federal courts from granting injunctions to stay proceedings in state courts, subject to certain statutory exceptions.[72] Except as otherwise authorized by statute, the Anti Injunction Act permits the federal courts to enjoin state courts only when necessary in aid of the federal court's jurisdiction or to protect or effectuate its judgment. Neither the common law nor the statutory exceptions would ordinarily apply to multijurisdictional criminal prosecutions.

When state criminal proceedings are threatened but not yet pending, the federal courts may enter declaratory relief and, according to the prevailing view in lower courts, even a permanent injunction.[73] But declaratory or injunctive relief of this nature would be appropriate only when necessary to protect the plaintiff's constitutional or statutory rights. In most multijurisdictional cases the potential defendants would lack even a colorable claim that such rights were at issue.

III. Conclusion

To date, most multijurisdictional prosecutions have involved the federal government as well as one or more states and have been resolved by precharge negotiations concluded by an agreement to defer or not to bring formal criminal charges. Agreements of this nature provide an opportunity for prosecutors to achieve regulatory objectives. In the future it is possible that multiple states will coordinate similar litigation without a federal presence, particularly if they believe federal regulators and prosecutors are dragging their feet and the states in question have the substantive and procedural tools to deal with the specific subject matter.

Relatively few problems or full-blown conflicts have emerged in multijurisdictional prosecutions, but this appears to be a product of resource constraints and informal norms and incentives favoring cooperation and coordination. At present there are no formal mechanisms to preclude duplicative or dueling prosecutions in different jurisdictions, require prosecutors in such cases to cooperate, or sequence the cases to avoid conflicts.

NOTES

1. Pennsylvania v. Nelson, 350 U.S. 497 (1956), is a rare exception. The Court held that a federal criminal statute preempted the Pennsylvania Sedition Act. *Id.* at 509. But it has been nearly half a century since this case, and the decision has not been read broadly. To the contrary, lower courts routinely reject preemption claims in criminal cases. Norman Abrams et al., Federal Criminal Law and Its Enforcement 98–100 (5th ed. 2009).

2. There is a general presumption against preemption. *See, e.g.*, Riegel v. Medtronic, Inc., 128 S. Ct. 999, 1013 (2008) (Ginsburg, J., dissenting).

3. Caleb Nelson, *Preemption*, 86 Va. L. Rev. 225, 225–29 (2000); Christopher H. Schroeder, *Supreme Court Preemption Doctrine, in* Preemption Choice: The Theory, Law, and Reality of Federalism's Core Question 119, 120–35 (William W. Buzbee ed., 2009).

4. Most state blue-sky provisions are modeled after some version of the Uniform Securities Act. *See* Unif. Sec. Act (2002).

5. *See supra* Brandon L. Garrett, *Collaborative Organizational Prosecution.*

6. John Cassidy, *The Investigation*, New Yorker, Apr. 7, 2003, at 54, 65 (reporting that as the investigation widened beyond Merrill Lynch, New York and California each undertook to investigate two firms, and Alabama, Arizona, Illinois, Massachusetts, New Jersey, Texas, Washington, and Utah each took one firm). Each firm thus faced one regulator and one of the states. Goldman Sachs, for example, was dealing with the N.Y. Stock Exchange and the Utah securities commissioner. *Id.*

7. Press Release, U.S. Dep't of Justice, Justice Department Announces Largest Health Care Fraud Settlement in Its History (Sept. 9, 2009), *available at* http://www.justice.gov/opa/pr/2009/September/09-civ-900.html.

8. Press Release, Douglas F. Gansler, Md. Att'y Gen., Pfizer Inc. to Pay $2.3 Billion in Historic Settlement (Sept. 2, 2009), *available at* http://www.oag.state.md.us/Press/2009/090209a.htm (describing negotiating team made up of representatives from seven states).

9. *See supra* Rachel E. Barkow, *The Prosecutor as Regulatory Agency*.

10. U.S. Dep't of Justice, U.S. Attorney, Middle District of Florida, WellCare Health Plans, Inc.—Deferred Prosecution Agreement (May 5, 2009); United States v. WellCare Health Plans, Inc., No. 8:09-cr-00203-T-27EAJ (M.D. Fla. May 5, 2009); *see* Press Release, U.S. Dep't of Justice, Charges Filed Against WellCare Health Plans, Inc.; WellCare Enters into Deferred Prosecution Agreement, Agrees to Pay $80 Million in Restitution and Forfeiture (May 5, 2009), *available at* http://tampa.fbi.gov/dojpressrel/2009/ta050409.htm (stating that more than 200 Special Agents and investigators from the FBI, the OIG, and the State of Florida Medicaid Fraud Control Unit, Office of the Attorney General ("MFCU"), raided WellCare's offices).

11. Press Release, *supra* note 10 (obligating WellCare to pay forfeiture and restitution for funds it had received from Florida Medicare and the Florida Healthy Kids program).

12. Benjamin Weiser & Ben White, *In Crisis, Prosecutors Put Aside Turf Wars*, N.Y. Times, Oct. 31, 2008, at B1.

13. John R. Kroger, *Remarks: Enron and Multi-jurisdictional Fraud*, 28 Cardozo L. Rev. 1657, 1661 (2007).

14. Andrew Ackerman, *Connecticut Attorney General Fights for FSA Recordings*, Bond Buyer, Aug. 26, 2009, http://www.bondbuyer.com/article.html?id=20090825LKV34XO7.

15. Weiser & White, *supra* note 12 (describing Morgenthau's protest and reply by U.S. Attorney Mary Jo White that prosecuting the securities law offenses under state law would have diminished their seriousness). New York law generally bars separate prosecutions for two offenses based upon the same act or transaction. Adam Harris Kurland, Successive Criminal Prosecutions: The Dual Sovereignty Exception to Double Jeopardy in State and Federal Courts 217–27 (2001).

16. Weiser & White, *supra* note 12.

17. Complaint, SEC v. WorldCom, Inc., 273 F. Supp. 2d 431 (S.D.N.Y. 2003) (No. 02-CV-4963), *available at* http://www.sec.gov/litigation/complaints/complr17588.htm.

18. SEC v. WorldCom, 273 F. Supp. 2d at 433. The remainder of the description of WordCom's remedial actions is drawn from the court's opinion.

19. Russell Gold et al., *Leading the News: MCI and Ebbers Are Charged in Oklahoma*, Wall St. J., Aug. 28, 2003, at A3.

20. Felony Information, State v. WorldCom, Inc., CF 2003–4689 (Dist. Ct. Okla. Aug. 27, 2003), *available at* http://news.findlaw.com/wsj/docs/worldcom/okwrldcm82703cmp.pdf; Press Release, W. A. Drew Edmondson, Okla. Att'y Gen., Oklahoma Files Criminal Charges Against WorldCom, Six Former Employees (Aug. 27, 2003), *available at* http://www.oag.state.ok.us/oagweb.nsf/0/3F64034E4C94A3EE862572B4006F608C!OpenDocument.

21. Don Mecoy, *Edmondson Defends Charges*, Daily Oklahoman, Aug. 29, 2003, at 1-A (internal quotation marks omitted).

22. *Id.* (internal quotation marks omitted).

23. *Federal Judge Won't Grant Stay to Halt State's WorldCom Case*, Daily Oklahoman, Sept. 5, 2003, at 1-B.

24. Mecoy, *supra* note 21; Gold, *supra* note 19 (noting that a major Democratic fund-raiser and friend of the attorney general who served as outside counsel for SBI Communications had pressed for more punishment for MCI).

25. Okla. Att'y Gen., WorldCom, Inc.—Deferred Prosecution Agreement (Mar. 12, 2004), *available at* http://www.corporatecrimereporter.com/documents/mciok_000.pdf; Press Release, W. A. Drew Edmondson, Okla. Att'y Gen., State to Gain 1,600 Jobs from WorldCom Agreement (Mar. 12, 2004), *available at* http://www.oag.state.ok.us/oagweb.nsf/0/600964B1B71BD51B862572B4006F60AA!OpenDocument.

26. Economic Development Agreement by and Between the Oklahoma Department of Commerce and WorldCom, Inc. (Mar. 11, 2004), *available at* http://www.corporatecrimereporter.com/documents/mcijobs_000.pdf. The agreement provided a formula for the "financial commitment" of 5 percent of the number of new jobs not added each year at a rate of $35,000 per job. *Id.* at 2 (internal quotation marks omitted).

27. *See* Don Mecoy, *State Drops WorldCom Fraud Charges: Former Executives Received Sentences in Federal Court*, Daily Oklahoman, Aug. 17, 2005, at 6-B.

28. *Id.*

29. Barbara Hoberock, *AG Won't Pursue WorldCom Counts*, Tulsa World, Aug. 17, 2005, at A8.

30. Al Jones, *Ex-CFO of WorldCom Pleads Guilty*, Sun Herald, June 8, 2004, at D5.

31. The United States Attorneys' Manual ("USAM") states in general terms the factors to be considered by federal prosecutors. *See* U.S. Dep't of Justice, U.S. Attorneys' Manual § 9-27.000 (2005). Federal prosecutors are influenced by factors including the priorities of the presidential administration and the local U.S. Attorney, the perceived strength of the federal interest, the strength of the evidence, and a host of other factors. *Id.* For a discussion of federal prosecutors' decision making in cases involving federal agencies, see *supra* Brandon L. Garrett, *Collaborative Organizational Prosecution*.

32. Cornell W. Clayton & Jack McGuire, *State Litigation Strategies and Policymaking in the U.S. Supreme Court*, 11 Kan. J.L. & Pub. Pol'y 17, 18 (2001) (indicating that from 1970 to 1990 the average state attorney general's office increased its staff from 51 to more than 148 and its budget from $612,089 to $9.9 million).

33. *See, e.g.*, Thomas A. Schmeling, *Stag Hunting with the State AG: Anti-tobacco Litigation and the Emergence of Cooperation Among State Attorneys General*, 25 L. & Pol'y 429 (2003) (analyzing the causes of cooperation of state attorneys general in tobacco litigation).

34. *See* Nat. Ass'n of Attorneys Gen., State Att'ys General: Powers and Responsibilities 415–18 (Emily Myers & Lynn Ross eds., 2d ed. 2007) [hereinafter State Attorneys General] (describing role of NAAG); Jason Lynch, Note, *Federalism, Separation of Powers, and the Role of State Attorneys General in Multistate Litigation*, 101 Colum L. Rev. 1998, 2008 (2001) (describing NAAG working groups).

35. Lynch, *supra* note 34, at 1998.

36. *See id.* at 2003–07 (describing rise of litigation by state attorneys general and noting significant cases, including multistate agreements negotiated between 1995 and 1997 involving America Online, American Cyanamid, Bausch & Lomb, General Motors, Mazda, Packard Bell, and Sears, Roebuck); Timothy Meyer, Comment, *Federalism and Accountability: State Attorneys General, Regulatory Litigation, and the New Federalism*, 95 Cal. L. Rev. 885, 887 nn.8–9 (2007) (multistate litigation concerning environmental and securities laws).

37. *See id.* at 2003–09 (describing development of cooperation among state attorneys general).

38. Colin Provost, *State Attorneys General, Entrepreneurship, and Consumer Protection in the New Federalism*, Publius, Spring 2003, at 37, 40; *see also* Cornell W. Clayton, *Law, Politics and the New Federalism: State Attorneys Generals as National Policymakers*, 56 Rev. Pol. 525, 537–38 (1994) (describing the transformation of "placid and reactive" state attorney general offices to "aggressive, activist" offices and noting the emergence of a "new breed" of younger, better educated state attorneys general who "'increasingly exploited the political advantages of their offices'" (quoting Thomas R. Morris, *States Before the U.S. Supreme Court: State Attorneys General as* Amicus Curiae, 70 Judicature 298, 299 (1987))).

39. Meyer, *supra* note 36, at 895–96.

40. Gretchen Morgenson, *Countrywide to Set Aside $8.4 Billion in Loan Aid*, N.Y. Times, Oct. 6, 2008, at B1 (describing settlement).

41. *See* Multistate Settlement Term Sheet (Oct. 6, 2008), *available at* http://www.oag.state.tx.us/newspubs/releases/2008/100908bac_cfc_settlement.pdf; Press Release, James D. Caldwell, La. Att'y Gen., Attorney General Buddy Caldwell Announces Multi-state Settlement to Benefit Louisiana Homeowners (July 31, 2009), *available at* http://wwwprd.doa.louisiana.gov/LaNews/PublicPages/Dsp_PressRelease_Display.cfm?PressReleaseID=2150&Rec_ID=2.

42. A federal grand jury reportedly issued subpoenas to Countrywide in the summer of 2008, but observers described this as an early stage of the investigation, and the U.S. Attorney cautioned that such investigations "take years." Richard B. Schmitt, *3 Big Southland Lenders Under Federal Investigation*, L.A. Times, July 24, 2008, at A1 (describing subpoenas and scope of investigation). The SEC filed suit against Countrywide's former CEO, COO, and CFO in June 2009. Complaint, SEC v. Mozilo, No. CV09–03994 (C.D. Cal. June 4, 2009).

43. Provost, *supra* note 38, at 51–53.

44. *Id.* at 51.

45. Joseph F. Zimmerman, *Interstate Cooperation: The Roles of the State Attorneys General*, 28 Publius, Winter 1998, at 71, 86.

46. *See supra* Rachel E. Barkow, *The Prosecutor as Regulatory Agency*; *supra* Brandon L. Garrett, *Collaborative Organizational Prosecution*.

47. Monica Hatcher, *Countrywide Mortgage Not Living Up to Deal, Critics Say*, Miami Herald, July 28, 2009 (noting that the agreement "allowed Countrywide to avoid prosecution for allegedly using deceptive sales and marketing practices to sell borrowers risky, high-cost mortgages").

48. State Attorneys General, *supra* note 34, at 310–12.

49. Schmeling, *supra* note 33, at 444.

50. *See generally* State Attorneys General, *supra* note 34, at 102–04 (summarizing authority to bring *parens patriae* litigation). For a critique of the state attorneys general role as "superplaintiff" in *parens patriae* litigation, see Donald G. Gifford, *Impersonating the Legislature: State Attorneys General and* Parens Patriae *Product Litigation*, 49 B.C. L. Rev. 913 (2008).

51. *See* State Attorneys General, *supra* note 34, at 42–48 (summarizing powers and duties, including right to intervene in legal proceedings on behalf of the public interest, the power to determine the state's legal policy, the duty to appear for and defend the state and its agencies, the right to control state litigation and appeals).

52. Eliot Spitzer was reportedly reluctant to charge Merrill Lynch criminally rather than civilly because he did not want to put it out of business for behavior that was common on Wall Street. Cassidy, *supra* note 6, at 62. Spitzer was aware that Drexel Burnham Lambert and Arthur Andersen went bankrupt after they were indicted, and he thought the indictment of Andersen was a mistake. *Id.*

53. *See* Darryl K. Brown, *The Distribution of Fraud Enforcement*, 28 Cardozo L. Rev. 1593, 1595–97 (2007).

54. *Id.*

55. State Attorneys General, *supra* note 34, at 311–12.

56. *See* Pamela H. Bucy, *Federalism and False Claims*, 28 Cardozo L. Rev. 1599, 1603 (2007). Between 2000 and 2007, nineteen states passed false claim statutes, and legislation enacted in 2005 encouraged the remaining states to follow suit. *Id.* at 1599, 1604. There was considerable variety among the initial nineteen statutes. *Id.* at 1604–05.

57. If a defendant pleads guilty and cooperates in one jurisdiction, he may be providing evidence that would convict him in another jurisdiction. This makes it difficult for prosecutors to obtain the assistance of would-be cooperators and greatly increases the problems faced by the defense.

58. State Attorneys General, *supra* note 34, at 249–50, 265–68.

59. *See* Nat. Ass'n of Att'ys Gen., State Attorneys General: Powers and Responsibilities 412 (Lynn Ross ed., 1990) (stating that the NAAG "is a closely knit professional organization, the hallmark of which is the warm collegiality of its members," and that Democratic or Republican members do not caucus separately within it).

60. *See* Zimmerman, *supra* note 45, at 87.

61. *See* Johnathan Mathiesen, *Dr. Spitzlove or: How I Learned to Stop Worrying and Love "Balkanization,"* 2006 Colum. Bus. L. Rev. 311, 350–52 (2006).

62. Abbate v. United States, 359 U.S. 187 (1959); Bartkus v. Illinois, 359 U.S. 121 (1959).

63. *See, e.g.*, Heath v. Alabama, 474 U.S. 82 (1985).

64. Adam Kurland conducted a comprehensive survey of the state laws that limited successive intrasovereign prosecutions in 2001. States with generally applicable (i.e., not subject-matter-specific) statutory limits are Arkansas, California, Colorado, Delaware, Georgia, Hawaii, Idaho, Illinois, Indiana, Kansas, Kentucky, Minnesota, Mississippi, Montana, Nevada, New Jersey, New York, North Dakota, Pennsylvania, Utah, Virginia, Washington, and Wisconsin. *See* Kurland, *supra* note 15, at 87–289. In 2008 Alaska repealed its generally applicable limit on successive prosecutions. 2008 Alaska Sess. Laws, ch. 75, § 40 (repealing Alaska Stat. § 12.20.010).

65. Kurland, *supra* note 15, at 49–57. Many of these provisions hew closely to Model Penal Code § 1.10, which provided a model for restricting successive prosecutions. *See id.* at 47–48; Model Penal Code § 1.10 (1985). Even among these generally applicable statutes, at least one state restricts prosecution following attachment of jeopardy in other states but not in the federal system, while another state applies the statute only after federal conviction or acquittal. Mississippi Code Annotated § 99-11-27 bars successive prosecution following the conviction or acquittal of the defendant for the same offense in another state, country or territory, but the Mississippi Supreme Court has held that the statute does not apply to prior federal prosecutions. Evans v. State, 725 So.2d 613, 659 (Miss. 1997). In two other states, Wisconsin and North Dakota, similar statutory language has not been fully interpreted. *See* Kurland, *supra* note 15, at 231, 284. Va. Code Ann. § 19.2-294 (2008) explicitly applies only to prior federal prosecutions.

66. Twenty-eight states, some of which do not also have general statutes, specifically restrict state prosecutions for controlled substances offenses following an acquittal or conviction under the Federal Controlled Substances Act. *See* Kurland, *supra* note 15, at 87–289. Drug-specific statutes are in place in Alaska, Connecticut, Delaware, District of Columbia, Hawaii, Idaho, Illinois, Iowa, Michigan, Mississippi, Nebraska, Nevada, New Hampshire, New Jersey, New Mexico, New York, North Carolina, North Dakota, Oklahoma, Oregon, Pennsylvania, Rhode Island, South Carolina, Vermont, Washington, West Virginia, Wisconsin, and Wyoming. *See id.* Arkansas revised Ark. Stat. Ann § 5–64–405 in 2005, removing the statutory limit on successive state prosecution in drug cases.

67. *See* Weiser & White, *supra* at 12 (describing Morgenthau's protest and reply by U.S. Attorney Mary Jo White that prosecuting the securities law offenses under state law would have diminished their seriousness).

68. Although one of the principal purposes of the Double Jeopardy Clause is protecting the finality or integrity of judgments, the Supreme Court has also recognized that the protection of the finality of verdicts can be subverted by actions that terminate a trial prior to verdict and deprive the defendant of the opportunity to gain an acquittal. Accordingly, the Double Jeopardy Clause also protects the defendant's right to have his trial completed by a particular tribunal. *See generally* Wayne R. LaFave et al., Criminal Procedure 1176–78 (4th ed. 2000).

69. U.S. Attorneys' Manual, *supra* note 31, at § 9–2.031.

70. *See generally* Erwin Chemerinsky, Federal Jurisdiction § 13.2 (5th ed. 2007); *see also* U.S. Attorneys' Manual, *supra* note 31, at § 13.4 (describing exceptions for bad faith prosecutions, suits under patently unconstitutional statutes, where an adequate state forum is not available in which to raise constitutional issues, and waiver).

71. Younger v. Harris, 401 U.S. 37, 43–44 (1971).

72. 28 U.S.C. § 2283 (2006).

73. Chemerinsky, *supra* note 70, at 843.

10

Reforming the Corporate Monitor?

VIKRAMADITYA KHANNA

Over the last decade enforcement authorities have increasingly relied on the appointment of corporate monitors as part of DPAs and NPAs. However, this growth has not been without criticism or controversy. In the last few years a great deal of attention has been focused on the conditions for obtaining a DPA or NPA, how monitors are selected, how they are paid, and what kinds of powers and obligations they have.[1] This increased attention has been accompanied by a series of legislative and enforcement developments leading to discussions on how to reform and regulate corporate monitors. This chapter explores what steps may prove beneficial in reforming and regulating the corporate monitor.

Section I begins by defining some key terms in the debate and examining the growth of corporate monitors until the advent of the so-called Morford Memo in early 2008. During this period, monitoring assignments were subject to little scrutiny outside of the DOJ; thus this time frame represents a period of "organic" growth for monitors. Further, this section also lays out an analytical framework for examining when monitors may be desirable, what powers and obligations they should have, and what steps may facilitate the development of a market for monitor services. Section II explores the most recent developments, including the Morford Memo and recent bills put forward by the U.S. House of Representatives. These developments arose in response to concerns about the appointment and pay of monitors, among other issues, and can be seen as the first steps toward formalizing the process of appointing monitors and creating a market for monitor services.[2] This section critically analyzes these developments and proposes further reforms to enhance the benefits of using corporate monitors, recognizing that monitors do have an impact on the governance of firms and what implications arise from that. In particular, this section will explore some measures that might help to enhance the development of a market for monitor services. Section III concludes the chapter.

I. The Initial, and Largely Unregulated, Growth of Corporate Monitors

Before discussing how to reform corporate monitors, it is important to define the key terms used in this area and to sketch out the initial growth of monitors. A corporate monitor is an individual or entity appointed before judgment and as per agreement (i.e., a DPA or NPA) between enforcement authorities and the firm to monitor a firm's compliance activities. Sometimes the monitor's powers exceed simple oversight of compliance efforts and bleed into other aspects of the firm's operations. For ease of exposition I will use the term DPA to refer to both DPAs and NPAs unless otherwise specified.

Although the terms of DPAs were not regulated prior to the Morford Memo or required to follow a set pattern, some common terms developed fairly quickly. In exchange for the DOJ's deferring and later dismissing charges, firms would often agree to pay fines and restitution, comply with ongoing investigations, accept responsibility for the wrongdoing, and agree to take remedial steps, as well as agreeing to the appointment of a monitor. Further, if a monitor was appointed, its powers could be quite wide-ranging and varied greatly with each DPA, as could the terms of the monitor's appointment (e.g., duration, postmonitoring obligations).[3] This is perhaps not surprising given that DPAs and monitors were largely the result of negotiation on a case-by-case basis by the DOJ, or other enforcement authority, and the firm.

A. Overview of Process of Appointing Monitors and Their Scope

Initially, DPAs and monitors were a relatively limited phenomenon. The first modern instance of a monitor is found in the 1994 *Prudential Securities* case, where an independent expert was appointed to monitor Prudential's compliance as part of a DPA.[4] However, monitors made only a handful of appearances in the 1990s, and their real growth began in the early part of the new millennium.[5]

The Enron series of scandals and the increasing attention to corporate wrongdoing brought the issue of DPAs and monitors to the fore. In particular, the indictment of Arthur Andersen in connection with the Enron scandal and the fairly large collateral consequences propelled interest in considering alternatives to the full criminal process.[6] Further, the increasing number of cases of alleged criminal wrongdoing over a short period and the government's relatively fixed enforcement budget may have made the value of an alternative even more attractive.[7] Indeed, the true growth in DPAs and monitors began right after Enron, with some commentators finding that monitoring assignments rose from six in 2003 to fourteen in 2006 to a high of thirty-seven in 2007.[8] Although the number of monitoring assignments dropped in 2008, they are more in line with the numbers in years before the somewhat unusual 2007 result.[9]

The increasing use of DPAs and monitors coincided with the 2003 revisions to the DOJ's *Principles of Federal Prosecution of Business Organizations* by the Thompson Memo, which laid out the factors in which corporations would be criminally charged with wrongdoing.[10] Following the Thompson Memo, the use of DPAs and monitors increased, and commentators consider it likely that their use will continue and probably increase.[11]

Indeed, if we step back and look at the incentives of both the government and the firm, it would appear they both have strong incentives to settle with something like a DPA. From the government's perspective, prosecuting a corporate crime case is not an easy task. Cases tend to be complex, time-consuming, and expensive to conduct.[12] Moreover, corporate defendants (especially larger ones) may have more resources with which to contest the prosecution than other defendants.[13] From the government's perspective, getting a settlement may be quite desirable in this context, especially if it involves changes to the firm that might reduce future wrongdoing (e.g., compliance measures). For the firm, such cases are also expensive, subject the firm and its executives to significant liability risks, and can visit large reputational penalties on the firm and its executives.[14] Settling may then prove attractive for the firm and its executives as well, especially if it occurs before too much publicity attaches (e.g., before an indictment). In this context, the incentives to settle are strong on both sides. It is perhaps not surprising, then, that DPAs and monitors have grown as they have in the last few years.

Although monitors are of relatively recent vintage, they have been applied to an impressive array of areas ranging from securities fraud to tax fraud to health care fraud to violations of the FCPA.[15] It is noteworthy that so far monitors have been appointed only for publicly traded firms.[16] This is not especially surprising because publicly traded firms may suffer larger collateral consequences than smaller privately held firms, and the larger firms may benefit more from developed compliance programs. For example, a small grocery store may not benefit from an elaborate compliance program supervised by a monitor, but a large retail grocery chain might.[17]

The breadth of where monitors were used stands in contrast to the relatively informal process for their appointment and the delineation of their powers and duties. First, the appointment of the monitor seemed to vary considerably—sometimes the firm might put forward names from which the DOJ selected, or it could run the other way, with the DOJ putting forward names and the firm selecting from that list.[18] How the lists were arrived at was also something that was not formalized, but the perception was that the government had the final say on whom the monitor would be.[19] Although the process for appointing a monitor contained considerable flexibility, the backgrounds of the monitors were fairly uniform, with most being former government enforcement officials or former judges.

Once the monitor was identified, the process tended to be even more contextualized. For example:

1. Compensation for the monitor was determined on a case-by-case basis by individual negotiation between the monitor and the firm with some government oversight. The firm paid the monitor's fees.
2. The duration of the monitoring assignment could vary usually somewhere between one and three years, though it could reach up to five years as well.
3. The monitor's powers varied considerably, from being limited to a compliance adviser to someone having greater say in the day-to-day operations of the firm across multiple units. Although the broad contours of these powers were usually determined by negotiation, the more day-to-day operational matters were often determined after the monitoring process was under way.
4. It was unclear how, if at all, a monitor could be replaced or removed (e.g., if the firm was acquired by an otherwise compliant firm).
5. Monitors were often expected to submit reports, but their frequency and content tended to vary.
6. After the monitoring assignment was completed, the monitor may still have an influence on the firm through whatever legacy is left by the monitor (e.g., changes to the firm's governance structure). The extent of this also varied from firm to firm.[20]

There was little guidance provided on how these items were to be addressed, and they ended up being addressed in a case-by-case manner before the assignment started, during the assignment, or sometimes not at all. This level of flexibility does have some advantages (i.e., things can be crafted for each individual firm's situation), but it can raise concerns about uniformity of practice, as well as whether there is sufficient focus on the key goals of the monitoring assignment.

Such a broad ranging and relatively unfettered process raises questions about whether it is desirable and whether there are reforms that can enhance its desirability. I begin to address these questions in the next section, but before that, it is important to recognize that monitors bear some similarities to other kinds of supervisors that have been appointed in matters related to judicial proceedings.

Although monitors are relatively new, they find their roots in the Special Masters of yore which date back to the early sixteenth century in England.[21] Since then the courts have relied on a variety of supervisors, including trustees in bankruptcy, corporate probation officers and special masters. The monitor is unique in that it combines elements from these various supervisors, but maintains sufficient flexibility to adapt to different circumstances.[22] The key attributes that monitors combine are that they are appointed before a judgment is rendered, they have frequent on-going contact with the firm over years (at times), and they can have quite wide-ranging and highly varied powers. [23] This combination (especially on-going contact) places monitors in a good position from which to detect and address wrongdoing that would require near continuous oversight to discover.[24] Further, the greater information monitors are likely to have (due to their frequent contact and expertise) may help them to advise more accurately than other supervisors, which is particularly important if the costs of errors are very high (i.e., it is important to "get it right" the first time).[25] With this comparative perspective in mind, let us begin to examine when, as a conceptual matter, it is desirable to appoint monitors and what kinds of powers and duties they should have.

B. Analysis of Corporate Monitor as a Sanction

In prior research, a coauthor and I explored in some depth the issue of when monitors should be appointed and the optimal scope of their authority.[26] The starting point for our analysis was to ask: When is it desirable to require a monitor as a condition of settling? To answer this question we need to explore when it might be desirable to move away from simple cash fines as penalties and toward supervisory or other noncash penalties, like monitors. If the threat of a cash fine alone would trigger a firm to undertake remedial and compliance measures (including hiring its own compliance experts) to avoid wrongdoing in the future, then there seems little need to *impose* a monitor on the firm and go through the process described earlier.

Generally, we should rely on the least costly sanctions to garner deterrence and then explore the more costly sanctions if we desire greater deterrence and if the gains from increased deterrence outweigh the incremental costs of relying on the more costly sanctions.[27] This helps to achieve the desired level of deterrence at the lowest cost. Cash fines are usually treated as the socially lowest-cost sanction because they involve the costs associated with transferring cash from one party to the other. Other sanctions are considered more expensive because they normally impose additional costs. For example, prison is seen as more costly than cash fines because the costs of imposing prison involve not only the costs of adjudication but the costs of depriving someone of his liberty, the costs of maintaining prisons, and so forth. Thus, if a compensatory cash fine of $X and a prison term of one year both generate similar levels of deterrence, we should prefer the cash fine because it imposes lower social costs.

In the context of corporate wrongdoing the specter of costly prison time is attenuated when the defendant is the corporation. However, there are other costly sanctions that can be imposed on the corporation, including the denial of a license to do business, punitive damages, or requiring a supervisor to be appointed to chaperone the corporation in some manner. These sanctions can impose larger costs than a simple compensatory cash fine in terms of overdeterrence costs (e.g., punitive damages), the costs associated with calculating the exact impact of the sanction on a firm (e.g., how much loss is suffered for a one-year denial of license to do business), and the costs associated with being subject to outside supervision (e.g., the costs of having a nonmanagement person with more limited expertise in your business essentially making/strongly recommending some decisions for the firm).[28]

Thus, relying on a monitor as a sanction may prove desirable when the deterrent effects of cash fines are exhausted and we desire more deterrence. Generally the deterrent effect of cash fines is tapped out when the firm has no further assets to attach or when the size or effect of the desired fine has become so large that it is not politically or socially acceptable (e.g., the collateral consequences become unpalatable).[29] Here a monitor sanction may prove desirable if the incremental gain in deterrence exceeds the incremental costs of appointing a monitor. When might this happen?

First, as the amount of harm caused by the wrongdoing increases, it becomes more likely that the total cash fine needed for deterrence will exceed the firm's assets or pass the unacceptable threshold. Second, sometimes recidivist corporations might merit the imposition of supervisory sanctions. Although not always a justification for the imposition of monitors, it appears that when the firm repeatedly engages in wrongdoing because it receives large socially unacceptable gains from doing so, then a monitor sanction would be more appropriate.[30] Yet another justification for monitors may be that they help to save government enforcement resources that can then be used in other cases while the firm pays for its monitor.[31] Finally, some may suggest that the imposition of monitors has more to do with incapacitation (i.e., restraining this firm from future violations) rather than deterrence. Perhaps, but it seems incapacitation matters most when one thinks that a particular defendant (in this case a corporation) is unlikely to be deterred from engaging in wrongdoing in the future by the threat of a cash fine.[32] This seems consistent with the notion that monitors and other supervisory sanctions make the most sense when deterrence—albeit specific deterrence here—via a cash fine is likely to fail. In light of this there are some instances where the imposition of a monitor is likely to be desirable:

1. The likely harm caused is so large that an appropriate cash fine for deterrence exceeds a firm's assets (or a firm is insolvent) or some politically acceptable threshold (e.g., concerns for collateral consequences).
2. The defendant firm appears to be receiving large gains that are socially unacceptable (although this may urge one toward sanctioning top management directly).
3. The costs of appointing a monitor are less than the gains received by redirecting enforcement resources to other ends.

In this mix one should also note that the powers granted to the monitor will influence when monitors will be desirable. The grander the monitor's powers, the potentially greater its social costs and perhaps its benefits. The more limited the monitor's powers, the lower its social costs and perhaps its benefits.[33]

Ultimately, one may wonder why we need to *impose* a monitor on a firm. If a monitor is desirable and provides benefits to firms, then why would firms not voluntarily hire a monitor or compliance expert?[34] One explanation is that the firms are not receiving the full social benefits associated with having a monitor. This might happen when the harm avoided by having a monitor is greater than the fine a firm may suffer. This situation could arise because fines have been set too low relative to the harm caused (in which case the response is to increase fines) or because fines cannot be set any higher (i.e., the firm's assets are limited or we have reached a sanction ceiling). In the latter case we may need to contemplate a monitor sanction. Another explanation could be that firms are ignorant of the advantages of a monitor, in which case we should inform them of the advantages. Yet another explanation is that a firm's managers may not want to hire a monitor that benefits the firm because that monitor may reduce the manager's private benefits. In other words, agency costs prevent a firm from hiring a monitor. Again here, the normal response would be to increase the cash fine until it overpowered the effect of agency costs (or perhaps sanction the agent directly). If a cash fine cannot do this (or the cash fine that would do it is unacceptable), then we are back to an insufficiency in cash fines explaining the need for a monitor.[35]

One additional wrinkle to this analysis is that it is plausible that firms are willing to agree to a DPA and a monitor because that evades liability for certain corporate agents (e.g., the CEO).[36] Such an agency cost story is possible (albeit the opposite of the agency costs discussed earlier) but is perhaps unlikely. The reason is that prosecutors often opt for a DPA when the firm provides information on other culpable individuals (usually higher-up individuals).[37] In any case, there may still remain some risk that firms opt for DPAs to avoid liability for corporate agents, in which case some degree of judicial approval before a DPA is entered may prove valuable. I discuss the role for judicial supervision in more detail in section II.

C. Analysis of What Duties, If Any, Should Apply to Monitors

After making the decision to appoint a monitor, the next question is what duties should she have? Khanna and Dickinson examine this question and recast it as being one of whether and what kind of fiduciary duties monitors should owe to shareholders. Monitors' decisions can influence the fortunes of shareholders, and that may place them in a position analogous to that of a fiduciary (e.g., a director or top corporate officer). Thus, it becomes important to understand why fiduciary duties are important in the corporate sphere and how they serve to fill gaps left by market forces and necessarily incomplete contracts. We utilize this to develop an analytical framework for addressing these issues in the context of corporate monitors.

The starting point is how market forces and fiduciary duties interact to restrain managers from diverting assets from firms and from slacking off on the job (i.e., reducing agency costs). For example, if the market for managerial services is competitive, then managers have little incentive to slack on the job or divert assets because they may be removed, denied a promotion, or otherwise penalized for such behavior. Similarly, competitive product markets force managers to engage in less slack and diversion because, if they did engage in such activities, the firm's product quality would likely suffer, and so would firm profits.[38] They would then face the real risk of being removed or suffering other adverse consequences. These market forces constrain some measure of managerial misbehavior, but when these markets do not register certain slack or where slack is quite common, one cannot expect much constraint from these forces.[39] Further, sometimes the gains to managers from misbehavior are so great that they are willing to forgo future opportunities or bear the adverse consequences from market forces.[40] In these circumstances the market forces will not be able to effectively contain behavior. One might try to adjust managerial incentives via contract, but this is not a costless or perfect endeavor. After all, one cannot foresee and contract for every possible contingency. Thus, some gaps will remain, and these may get filled by fiduciary duties like the duty of loyalty and duty of care.

In the context of monitors, market forces may have somewhat limited effect. First, the product and monitor services markets may have limited effect because it is difficult to remove monitors. The primary serious constraint is the reputational market for monitors' services, which, given their small numbers, may be quite strong. However, if all monitors are selected from a small set of former enforcement officials, then prior connections to enforcement may carry greater weight than such reputational constraints. In light of these potential limits on market forces, one might consider fiduciary-like duties for monitors that run to the firm's shareholders. One could, of course, provide for the possibility of insurance and indemnification so that monitors do not face crushing liability risks.

The exact nature and content of these fiduciary duties would vary based on the degree of influence a monitor has at a firm and the correlative degree of vulnerability shareholders have to the monitor's decisions. Thus, if the monitor's powers are quite circumscribed, then the extent of those fiduciary duties may be fairly attenuated. Further, one could have more limited fiduciary duties if there were other methods of addressing the concerns with monitors. For example, oversight of the monitor by the appointing agency or a court that could lead to removal of the monitor may also serve to further assuage concerns with the limits of market forces for monitors (who currently cannot be removed without great difficulty).

Indeed, this last point suggests that one way in which one might improve the desirability and efficiency of relying on corporate monitors is to facilitate the development of a market in monitor services. This would serve multiple purposes. First, a well-functioning market would enhance competition in the provision of monitor services, which has obvious benefits. Second, a well-functioning market may serve to strengthen the market forces on monitor behavior, thereby lessening the need to rely on fiduciary duties to fill in gaps. Third, a well-functioning market, combined with good information,

TABLE 10.1

Decision to Make	*Factors to Consider*
How to Appoint a Monitor	1. The creation of a "market" of sorts of monitors with the government serving as an informational intermediary. 2. Monitors owe some duties to shareholders or are subject to increased agency or judicial oversight.
Powers of a Monitor	1. Monitor's powers should vary depending on what is necessary for the task at hand. 2. Greater specificity at the beginning (when negotiating the DPA) seems desirable especially as it relates to: (a) the scope of the monitor's powers, (b) the reporting chain between the monitor, firm, firm's internal players, and government, (c) termination of monitoring assignment upon triggering events (e.g., acquisition), and (d) third-party liability. 3. Referral back to appointing agency or court to resolve critical issues that arise.
Duties of a Monitor	1. The greater the monitor's powers, the greater the extent of fiduciary duties or oversight by the appointing agency or the judiciary (especially with the power to remove the monitor). 2. Presence of insurance for monitors.

would help assuage concerns about who is selected as a monitor and whether the amount she is being paid is reasonable or excessive.

In light of this, Khanna and Dickinson explore what features can facilitate the growth of a market in monitor services by examining arguments made in the literature to encourage the growth of a market for independent directors.[41] Monitors and independent directors serve some analogous purposes—both can monitor management (one for compliance matters and the other for general business), and both involve selection from a market of professionals. That literature suggests that such a market may be facilitated if independent directors were elected by a firm's institutional investors from a pool of qualified directors (whose detailed background information was contained in a central clearinghouse).[42] This would ensure that these directors were competent, somewhat dependent on shareholders, and subject to an organized market for their services, which would generate some pressure to perform well.[43]

Monitors, on the other hand, are not really selected by shareholders, are not subject to a formal market, and are not required to meet some minimum level of qualification. Based on this, the system of appointing monitors could be improved in some ways. First, if monitors owed some fiduciary duties to shareholders, as suggested, then monitors would be somewhat more accountable to them.[44] Further, as the market for monitors grows, the government could serve as the clearinghouse on monitors' backgrounds so that there is a central place where one can obtain information on them. If the systems of appointing monitors begin to reflect these suggestions, then a well-functioning market for monitor services may develop.

In light of this analysis, Table 10.1 summarizes some recommendations for the better functioning of monitors. Some of these were soon adopted in prosecution practice.

II. The First Steps Toward Regulating the Corporate Monitor

The growth in the appointment of corporate monitors continued at a steady and increasing pace through 2007. In that year, however, a number of events brought the issue of DPAs and appointment of monitors to the media's attention. In particular, the practice of requiring firms to waive attorney-client privilege as a condition precedent to obtaining a DPA, the appointment of former U.S. Attorney General John Ashcroft as a monitor for what some claimed was a princely sum, and the sense that DPAs (and implicitly monitors) might be used as ways to let corporations "get off" with lighter penalties led to a flurry of media attention.[45] The increased attention led to the House of Representatives putting forward two bills, one in 2008 and one in 2009, that began the process of regulating monitor assignments.[46] This was accompanied by steps at the DOJ to provide guidance (via the Morford Memo) on how and when monitors would be appointed and what kinds of powers they might have.[47] These developments can be divided into three categories that affect monitors:

1. Guidelines on when corporate monitors should be appointed and how they should be selected.
2. Judicial oversight of monitoring assignments.
3. Disclosure obligations of monitors.

A. When Should We Appoint Corporate Monitors and How Should They Be Selected?

If a DPA is desirable, when should it provide for a corporate monitor? The Morford Memo lays down some general thoughts on the appointment of monitors and nine more specific principles. First, the decision to appoint a monitor should depend on an overall assessment of the benefits of appointing a monitor compared with its costs and impact on the firm's business operations.[48] Second, the nine additional specific factors should be applied flexibly given the heterogeneity of cases before the DOJ. Third, the monitor's primary task should be to ensure compliance and reduce the chances of future wrongdoing. Thus, "it may be appropriate to use a monitor where a company does not have an effective internal compliance program . . . [but a monitor may not be necessary] where a company has ceased operations in the area where the criminal misconduct occurred."[49] With these general thoughts in mind, the specific factors laid out by the Morford Memo are as follows:

1. Before selecting a monitor, the firm and the government should discuss the qualifications of the monitor, avoid conflicts of interest, and select someone on the basis of merits only. To avoid conflicts the DOJ will set up ad hoc committees to consider candidates. The Office of the Deputy Attorney must approve the selection, and the monitor must be impartial.
2. A monitor is not considered an agent for either the firm or the government.
3. A monitor should focus on assessing and monitoring a firm's compliance with the DPA as it relates to reducing future wrongdoing (i.e., its compliance programs).
4. The monitor's obligations should be no more than necessary to reduce the risk of future offending.
5. In some situations it may be desirable to have the monitor make periodic reports to both the government and the firm.
6. If a firm declines to follow a monitor's recommendations, then it should provide reasons for that choice, which the government can rely on to decide whether the firm has met its obligations under the DPA.
7. The DPA should identify "any types of previously undisclosed or new misconduct that the monitor will be required to report directly to the Government."[50] The monitor should have discretion as to what to report to the government.
8. The duration of the DPA should be targeted to the concerns that exist at the firm and to remedial measures being taken.
9. Finally, the DPA "should provide for an extension of the monitor provision(s) at the discretion of the Government in the event that the corporation has not successfully satisfied its obligations under the agreement. Conversely, in most cases, an agreement should provide for early termination if the corporation can demonstrate to the Government that there exists a change in circumstances sufficient to eliminate the need for a monitor."[51]

The selection process for the monitor is becoming more formalized, with a greater focus on ensuring independence. In addition, it appears the focus for monitors is increasingly on enhancing compliance and internal controls rather than some of the responsibilities that earlier monitors may have had. Consequently, the DOJ finds that the monitor is not responsible to the firm's shareholders and that the overall responsibility for the firm's compliance programs rests with the firm, subject to the monitor's evaluations and recommendations.[52]

Further, the DOJ pushes firms and the government to discuss and detail the powers and tasks of the monitor in the DPA itself rather than waiting to do it during the assignment or not at all. The DOJ encourages discussion on the duration, reporting obligations, and other matters that in the past may have been less formalized. Two particular issues raise interesting questions. First, early termination of the monitor's assignment open up the possibility for removal of the monitor. Although the memo envisages termination on grounds akin to the firm being acquired, perhaps there is some room for other kinds of termination as well.[53] Second, the DOJ expects monitors to disclose evidence of credible and significant wrongdoing to the government but seems to stop short of public disclosure.[54]

In addition to the Morford Memo, which makes important strides in regulating the use of monitors, Congress has become active in this area. Two proposed House bills also add some flesh to the process of monitor selection.[55] They require that monitors be selected from a public national pool of prequalified candidates and that the final selection be approved by a judge.[56] Further, the process should be an open and competitive one where the monitor's powers should extend no further than the compliance concerns at the firm. An interesting aspect of the House bills is that they require potential monitors to have experience in criminal and civil litigation.[57] This does not match the Morford Memo (where individuals with specialist compliance work are also potential candidates even if not attorneys).[58] The House bills also expect monitors to be compensated based on a predetermined fee table rather than in a market-based negotiation.[59] This differs from the Morford Memo, which makes no mention of how the monitor's compensation should be determined.

Taken together, the House bills and the Morford Memo add some further substance to the process of deciding when to have a monitor, how the monitor should be selected, and what powers she should have. These steps bear considerable similarity to the suggestions listed in Table 10.1—in particular, how a market for monitor services may be created, and that greater effort needs to be focused on defining the terms of the monitoring assignment at the DPA stage. There are, however, important differences as well (the method of compensating monitors and the apparent absence of any duties monitors owe to shareholders). Let us critically examine the steps taken so far.

First, the Morford Memo states that monitors should be appointed only when their benefits exceed their costs. There is not much information given on how to calibrate this, but some statements may prove to be illustrative. For example, included in the measure of costs is the impact on the firm's business. This seems like a good proxy for the costs associated with supervisor-type sanctions (e.g., disruption to firm business) discussed earlier, and in this sense, this development is positive. However, there is little explicit reference to attempting to squeeze out the deterrence potential of cash fines before imposing a monitor. Perhaps a useful reform would be to have the DOJ or other enforcement authority state why it thinks the maximum imposable cash fine on this firm would not be enough for deterrence purposes. Such a statement serves two functions. First, it narrows the use of monitors to where they are likely to be desirable. Second, it helps to reduce concerns that the monitor has been appointed in order for firms to avoid hefty fines. This is because if the firm could have paid the desired fine, then a monitor would not have been appointed.

Second, the Morford Memo states that if the firm does not have an internal control/compliance program in place, that pushes us toward appointing a monitor. If the focus of DPAs (and hence monitors) is only on publicly traded firms, then this approach appears sensible. For some time now Delaware jurisprudence has required directors to make efforts toward compliance, so an absence of compliance efforts suggests that the firm has a fairly cavalier attitude toward compliance and may well be a likely repeat offender.[60]

Third, the Morford Memo provides an example of when a monitor is unnecessary: a firm sells off an offending division. Presumably the logic behind this is that noncompliance can be isolated to the division that was sold off. This may be a questionable assumption for many firms where managers move between divisions or where members of top management may be using a particular division to engage in illegal activities (corruption in particular raises such concerns). Selling off the violating unit may be a reason not to appoint a monitor if there is some proof that the wrongdoing was really isolated to that one unit. Perhaps requiring proof of this before deciding against a monitor would be a useful supplement.

Once the parties have agreed in principle to the DPA and appointment of a monitor, then more detailed inquiries begin—who should be the monitor, how should she be paid, and what powers and duties does she have? The House bills envisage a competitive selection process where a monitor is selected from a national pool of qualified candidates with final approval by the court. This seems designed to address concerns about selecting only former enforcement officials and having some court oversight. This bears some similarity to the suggestion in Khanna and Dickinson that the government could serve as a clearinghouse (or informational intermediary) to help in the formation of a monitor market.[61] Creating this pool of candidates seems like quite a good development because it may help to further the development of a market for monitor services.

However, the method of compensating monitors seems like it might raise concerns. The House bills require that monitors receive payments based on a flat and fixed fee structure.[62] Such a structure may be motivated by concerns that some monitors are getting paid an excessive amount, but addressing this concern with a flat fee structure may undermine the development of a market for monitor services. The core problem with a flat fee structure is that it treats each expert's time as if it is fungible. This does not seem likely to be generally true. For example, if someone is ill and needs the services of a neurosurgeon, then offering to pay neurosurgeons the average going hourly rate for all physicians is unlikely to attract many neurosurgeons to the task. Similarly, the skills required to be a compliance expert on issue X may be different (and more expensive to obtain) than a compliance expert on issue Y. These experts are likely to charge different rates per hour. Flattening out the differences may hurt the development of a market for monitor services especially for more expensive expertise.

Nonetheless, avoiding a flat fee does not mean we have no ways to limit excessive compensation. One might consider having open competitive bidding for monitoring assignments from people of similar expertise. Alternatively, one might explore the idea of having some review for certain fees. For example, we could allow monitors, firms, and the government to negotiate an hourly fee (which would be disclosed publicly), but if the fee exceeds some threshold amount (e.g., $3,000 per hour), then we could require a court to approve the rate before the start of the monitoring assignment where the monitor and firm bear the burden of proving why this rate is appropriate.[63] Although not perfect, it would allow the development of a market with some oversight for hourly rates that might seem excessive.

Once a monitor is selected, the powers and duties of the monitoring assignment merit greater discussion. Here the DOJ takes important steps. The overarching theme is that monitoring assignments should capture impartiality along with a fairly narrow compliance perspective. In other words, the days of broad-ranging monitor powers seem finished at the federal level, and the more limited role for monitors as compliance advisers (with a little extra bite) is the direction the DOJ wishes to pursue. Indeed, one might anticipate that, with time, the DOJ may be able to provide industry-specific (or wrongdoing-specific) guidelines on a monitor's tasks. The corollary of this is that monitors are not expected to have duties to the firm or its shareholders. This appears troubling at first blush because the analysis in this chapter suggests that some fiduciary duties should apply (even limited duties for limited powers). However, that was in the context of great difficulty in removing monitors, which makes it harder for market forces to constrain monitors. If a market for monitors develops (with clearinghouses and the like) along with some prospect of removing monitors for weak performance, then the absence of fiduciary duties may not be as problematic.[64] However, absent that, some degree of fiduciary duty should apply to monitors—perhaps not the full panoply of fiduciary duties but more limited duties such as those for advising counsel.

B. What Role Should the Judiciary Play in the Monitoring Process?

The House bills indicate a strong preference for judicial approval of the monitor and the terms of the DPA along with the provision of ongoing judicial oversight.[65] Judicial oversight may indeed be valuable, but it is a question of degree. Having a requirement for judicial approval before a DPA is finalized (e.g., on monitor compensation, monitor selection) may serve to avoid many problems at relatively little additional cost, as prosecutors and firms have already done the work for the DPA and it will be fresh in their memories. However, judicial oversight once the monitoring assignment has started may be more costly because the parties (and the court) would be required to get "up to speed" all over again along with gathering further information. Indeed, frequent judicial oversight during the monitoring assignment may undermine one of the benefits of having monitors—to economize on enforcement resources. For these midstream incursions it may prove useful to have them triggered by certain limited events (e.g., an acquisition, repeated instances of wrongdoing).

C. Should the Reports of Monitors Be Made Available to the Public?

Finally, an important issue is whether the reports of the monitor should be made public. After all, a criminal prosecution (a matter of public interest) was averted through the DPA, and it seems that the public has an interest in knowing what the monitor found.

TABLE 10.2

Decision to Make	*Factors from Analysis*	*Factors from DOJ and House Bills*	*Comments and Suggestions*
Whether to Opt for a DPA That Includes a Monitor	1. Harm caused is very large so that cash fines to deter it are considered too large to be imposed (i.e., the firm's assets are insufficient or there are other constraints on sanction size). 2. The firm's gains from wrongdoing are large and socially unacceptable. 3. Costs of appointing a monitor are less than the benefits of appointing a monitor. This is particularly important if there is a risk of managers using a DPA and monitor to evade liability for themselves.	1. Effect on stakeholders. 2. Costs of appointing a monitor are less than its benefits. 3. Absence of compliance program. 4. Selling off division where wrongdoing occurred. 5. Waiving attorney-client privilege is not required to obtain a DPA or monitor.	1. Some discussion of why a cash fine is insufficient for deterrence. 2. There should be some proof that wrongdoing was limited to the division sold off.
Appointing a Monitor	1. The creation of a "market" of sorts of monitors with the government serving as an informational intermediary. 2. Monitors owe some duties to shareholders or are subject to increased agency or judicial oversight.	1. Creation of national list of qualified monitors. 2. Selection of monitor through open process. 3. Impartiality of monitor. 4. Set fee schedule.	1. A flat fee schedule may limit the development of the market. An alternative to address concerns with excessive compensation is judicial oversight if compensation exceeds some threshold.

Decision to Make	*Factors from Analysis*	*Factors from DOJ and House Bills*	*Comments and Suggestions*
Monitor's Powers	1. Monitor's powers should vary depending on what is necessary for the task at hand. 2. Greater specificity at the beginning (when negotiating the DPA) seems desirable especially as it relates to: a. the scope of the monitor's powers, b. the reporting chain between the monitor, firm, firm's internal players, and government, c. termination of monitoring assignment upon triggering events (e.g., acquisition), and d. third-party liability. 3. Referral back to appointing agency or court to resolve critical issues that arise.	1. Monitor's powers should be tailored to situation. 2. Greater specificity at the beginning of the DPA is important. 3. Judicial oversight. 4. However, monitor's powers should be limited to addressing only compliance issues.	
Monitor's Duties	1. The greater the monitor's powers, the greater the extent of fiduciary duties or oversight by the appointing agency or the judiciary (especially with the power to remove the monitor). 2. Presence of insurance for monitors.	1. Monitors have no duties to the firm or its shareholders. 2. There is the possibility of terminating the monitoring assignment.	1. Monitors should have some limited duties if it is still difficult to remove a monitor and if the market for monitor services has limited functioning. Some residual judicial/agency oversight is useful.

The House bills presume that the monitors' reports would be made available at least to the court, but they are silent on public disclosure. Generally, disclosure of the monitors' reports is the preferred course of action because it serves to provide information both about firm wrongdoing (thereby alerting victims and potentially helping to reduce the severity of their losses) and also about ways to reduce this kind of wrongdoing. However, it is possible that certain parts of the monitors' reports may not be essential to enhance the chances of reducing wrongdoing or alerting victims, but rather may be more embarrassing to the firm as a whole or may undermine its competitive position. Such situations may call for some power (either with the court or with the DOJ) to redact parts of the monitors' reports for public dissemination. Of course, firms should not be permitted to take public positions that are inconsistent with the monitor's reports without clear explanation.[66]

Having traversed considerable ground in this chapter, it may prove useful to provide a summary of the analysis and where the current reform steps may merit consideration for further amendment and where those reforms should be applauded. Table 10.2 provides that summary. This table suggests that further steps to facilitate the development of a market for monitors (e.g., moving away from a set fee schedule) while holding monitors accountable in some manner to shareholders would be desirable. Coupling greater specification of monitor tasks in the DPA with some explanation for why a simple cash fine cannot generate the desired results will likely result in the better use of monitors and eventually in the growth of a well-functioning market in monitor services. One may also gain some important insights by looking to experiences with the development of other compliance-related markets.[67]

Finally, although outside the scope of this chapter, the development of a market for monitor services raises other issues that merit greater future thought and inquiry. For example, a market for monitor services could have important corporate governance consequences. If boards serve at least two functions—strategic advisers and watchdogs—then the presence of monitors could substitute or supplement the board as a watchdog. This may be beneficial because the board's two roles operate in some tension, and monitors may help to reduce that tension by taking more of the watchdog role from the board.[68] Thus, a market for monitors could help to clarify, streamline, and simplify the role of the board and thereby improve its functioning as well.

III. Conclusion

The development of corporate monitors as an institution for preventing wrongdoing and enhancing compliance has come upon us quite quickly. In just the last decade this new enforcement tool has grown rapidly and offers to revolutionize the prosecution of corporate crime. However, in the last year or so, the rather unregulated growth of corporate monitors has come in for criticism, leading to multiple attempts to regulate the use of this new enforcement tool. In this chapter, I examine whether the suggestions for reform would help ensure that monitors are appointed when they are desirable and in a manner that helps to reduce the likelihood of future wrongdoing by assisting in the development of a market for monitor services.

My analysis suggests that many of the proposed reforms may indeed be beneficial and facilitate the development of a market for monitors. However, certain reforms may impede the development of that market. In particular, set hourly fees for monitor services and the absence of duties on monitors running to shareholders seem like areas that warrant further thought and reform. The desire to obtain greater specificity for monitoring assignments in the DPA is laudable and should continue with perhaps further guidance from the DOJ as it develops experience with monitors in specific industries or areas of wrongdoing. Some additional discussion of when monitors are desirable also seems warranted, especially to identify why cash fines may not serve the deterrent purposes of the law as well. Further, greater openness in the monitor selection process and the government potentially serving as an informational intermediary or clearinghouse for monitors enhance confidence in the likely future growth of a market for monitors. Such reforms would enhance the value of appointing corporate monitors where they are desirable.

NOTES

1. *See* Brandon L. Garrett, *Structural Reform Prosecution*, 93 Va. L. Rev. 853 (2007); Vikramaditya Khanna & Timothy L. Dickinson, *The Corporate Monitor: The New Corporate Czar?*, 105 Mich. L. Rev. 1713 (2007).

2. *See* John C. Coffee Jr., *Deferred Prosecution: Has It Gone Too Far?*, Nat'l L.J., July 25, 2005, at 13; Eric Lichtblau, *In Justice Shift, Corporate Deals Replace Trials*, N.Y. Times, Apr. 9, 2008, at A1; Khanna & Dickinson, *supra* note 1, at 1720–27.

3. *See* Khanna & Dickinson, *supra* note 1, at 1720–27.

4. *See* U.S. Dep't of Justice, U.S. Attorney, Southern District of New York, Prudential Sec.—Deferred Prosecution Agreement (Oct. 27, 1994), *available at* http://www.corporatecrimereporter.com/documents/prudential.pdf; *see also* SEC v. Prudential Sec., Inc., No. 93 Civ. 2164, 1993 WL 473189, at *2–3 (D.D.C. Oct. 21, 1993).

5. *See* Khanna & Dickinson, *supra* note 1, at 1715–20.

6. *See* 2008 Year-End Update on Corporate Deferred Prosecution and Non-prosecution Agreements, Gibson, Dunn & Crutcher LLP Publications (Jan. 6, 2009) [*hereinafter* Gibson Dunn], *available at* http://www.gibsondunn.com/publications/pages/2008Year-EndUpdate-CorporateDPAs.aspx.

7. *See* Gibson Dunn, *supra* note 6; Lawrence D. Finder & Ryan D. McConnell, *Annual Corporate Pre-trial Agreement Update 2007* (Jan. 3, 2008) (unpublished paper), *available at* http://ssrn.com/abstract=1080263.

8. *See* Gibson Dunn, *supra* note 6.

9. *See id.*

10. *See* Memorandum from Larry D. Thompson, Deputy Attorney General, U.S. Dep't of Justice, to Heads of Department Components and United States Attorneys, *Principles of Federal Prosecution of Business Organizations* (Jan. 20, 2003), http://www.usdoj.gov/dag/cftf/corporate_guidelines.htm. The Thompson Memo was later followed by another revision to these principles, the McNulty Memo. *See* Memorandum from Paul J. McNulty, Deputy Attorney General, U.S. Dep't of Justice, to Heads of Department Components and United States Attorneys, *Principles of Federal Prosecution of Business Organizations* (Dec. 12, 2006), http://www.usdoj.gov/dag/speeches/2006/mcnulty_memo.pdf.

11. *See* Gibson Dunn, *supra* note 6.

12. *See* Khanna & Dickinson, *supra* note 1, at 1721; Benjamin M. Greenblum, Note, *What Happens to a Prosecution Deferred? Judicial Oversight of Corporate Deferred Prosecution Agreements*, 105 Colum. L. Rev. 1863 (2005).

13. *See* Khanna & Dickinson, *supra* note 1, at 1721.

14. *See* James K. Robinson, Philip E. Urofsky & Christopher R. Pantel, *Deferred Prosecutions and the Independent Monitor*, 2 Int'l J. Disclosure & Governance 325, 325–27 (2005).

15. *See, e.g.*, U.S. Dep't of Justice, U.S. Attorney, District of New Jersey, Bristol-Myers Squibb—Deferred Prosecution Agreement (June 13, 2005), *available at* http://www.usdoj.gov/usao/nj/press/files/pdffiles/deferredpros.pdf; U.S. Dep't of Justice, U.S. Attorney, District of Oregon, SSI Int'l Far East, LTD—Deferred Prosecution Agreement (Oct. 16, 2006), *available at* http://www.secinfo.com/d1znFa.v22t.d.htm#1stPage; Letter from David N. Kelly, U.S. Attorney for the S.D.N.Y., U.S. Dep't of Justice, to Robert S. Bennett, Skadden, Arps, Slate, Meagher & Flom LLP, Counsel to KPMG LLP (Aug. 25, 2005), *available at* http://www.corporatecrimereporter.com/documents/kpmgdeferred_000.pdf; Sue Reisinger, *Companies' Denial of Guilt Is New Twist in Prosecution Deals*, Corporate Counsel, Jan. 2, 2008, *available at* http://www.law.com/jsp/cc/PubArticleCC.jsp?id=1198836303636 (discussing instances of monitors being appointed in the context of health care firms).

16. Also, the first non-American monitor has been selected. *See Friend or Foe? Selecting a Compliance Monitor*, WrageBlog, Feb. 5, 2009, http://wrageblog.org/2009/02/05/friend-or-foe-selecting-a-compliance-monitor/.

17. Also, for smaller private corporations individual liability against the owners may be sufficient given who may own the bulk of the assets and who was probably culpable.

18. *See* Khanna & Dickinson, *supra* note 1, at 1722–23.

19. *See id.*

20. This list is based on Khanna & Dickinson, *supra* note 1, at 1723–27. Similar lists can be seen in Garrett, *supra* note 1.

21. *See* Khanna & Dickinson, *supra* note 1, at 1715–20.

22. *See id.*

23. *See id.*

24. *See id.*

25. *See id.*

26. *See id.*

27. *See id.* at 1727–32.

28. *See id.*

29. *See id.* at 1728–30.

30. *See id.* at 1730.

31. *See id.* at 1730–31.

32. *See id.* at 1731.

33. *See id.* at 1732–33.

34. *See id.* at 1729 n.67.

35. *See id.*

36. *See* Lichtblau, *supra* note 2.

37. It is possible the firm may provide "scapegoats" rather than the CEO, but how often this happens would probably be limited.

38. *See* Frank H. Easterbrook & Daniel R. Fischel, The Economic Structure of Corporate Law 90–92 (1991); Khanna & Dickinson, *supra* note 1, at 1733–35.

39. *See* Easterbrook & Fischel, *supra* note 38; Khanna & Dickinson, *supra* note 1, at 1733–35.

40. *See* Easterbrook & Fischel, *supra* note 38; Khanna & Dickinson, *supra* note 1, at 1733–35.

41. *See* Ronald J. Gilson & Reinier H. Kraakman, *Reinventing the Outside Director: An Agenda for Institutional Investors*, 43 Stan. L. Rev. 863, 883–92 (1991).

42. *See id.*

43. *See* Khanna & Dickinson, *supra* note 1, at 1742.

44. *See id.*

45. *See* Lichtblau, *supra* note 2.

46. *See* Accountability in Deferred Prosecution Act of 2009, H.R. 1947, 111th Cong. (1st Sess. 2009), *available at* http://frwebgate.access.gpo.gov/cgi-bin/getdoc.cgi?dbname=111_cong_bills&docid=f:h1947ih.txt.pdf; Accountability in Deferred Prosecution Act of 2008, H.R. 6492, 110th Cong. (2d Sess. 2008), *available at* http://www.govtrack.us/congress/billtext.xpd?bill=h110-6492.

47. Memorandum from Craig S. Morford, Deputy Attorney General, U.S. Dep't of Justice, to Heads of Department Components and United States Attorneys, *Selection and Use of Monitors in Deferred Prosecution Agreements and Non-prosecution Agreements with Corporations* (Mar. 7, 2008), http://www.usdoj.gov/dag/morford-useofmonitorsmemo-03072008.pdf.

48. *See id.*

49. *Id.*

50. *Id.*

51. *Id.*; *see also* Memorandum from Gary G. Grindler, Acting Deputy Attorney General, U.S. Dep't of Justice, to Heads of Department Components and United States Attorneys, *Additional Guidance on the Use of Monitors in Deferred Prosecution Agreements and Non-prosecution Agreements with Corporations* (May 25, 2010), http://www.justice.gov/dag/dag-memo-guidance-monitors.html. The Grindler Memo provides guidance to prosecutors crafting DPAs on how to address and explain the DOJ's role in resolving disputes between the firm and the monitor. The Memo states (1) DOJ's role is limited to whether the firm has complied with the DPA, and (2) DOJ's role depends on the enforcement interests at stake (i.e., the dispute should involve compliance or enforcement issues) rather than other issues as the DOJ is not a party to the monitor agreement and the DOJ is not a general arbitrator. The Memo provides suggestions on how firms should approach potential areas of disagreement and suggests regular meetings between the DOJ, the firm, and the monitor to discuss the progress of the monitorship.

52. *See* Morford Memo, *supra* note 47.

53. *See id.*

54. *See id.*

55. *See* H.R. 6492, *supra* note 46; H.R. 1947, *supra* note 46.

56. *See* H.R. 6492, *supra* note 46; H.R. 1947, *supra* note 46.

57. *See* H.R. 6492, *supra* note 46; H.R. 1947, *supra* note 46.

58. *See* Morford Memo, *supra* note 47.

59. *See* H.R. 6492, *supra* note 46; H.R. 1947, *supra* note 46.

60. *See* Stone ex rel. AmSouth Bancorporation v. Ritter, 911 A.2d 362 (Del. 2006) (en banc); In re Caremark Int'l Inc. Derivative Litig., 698 A.2d 959 (Del. Ch. 1996).

61. *See* Khanna & Dickinson, *supra* note 1, at 1741–42.

62. *See* H.R. 6492, *supra* note 46; H.R. 1947, *supra* note 46.

63. Such targeted review bears some similarity to discussions of the structure of appeals systems. *See* Maurits Barendrecht, Korine Bolt & Machteld W. De Hoon, *Appeal Procedures: Evaluation and Reform*, Tilburg L. & Econ. Center Discussion Paper No. 2006–031 (Nov. 2006), *available at* http://ssrn.com/abstract=942289; Steven Shavell, *On the Design of the Appeals Process: The Optimal Use of Discretionary Review Versus Direct Appeal*, Harv. L. & Econ. Discussion Paper No. 625 (Jan. 1, 2009), *available at* http://ssrn.com/abstract=1326563.

64. Even in this situation some fairly weak fiduciary duties or agency or court oversight may prove a useful "Sword of Damocles."

65. *See* H.R. 6492, *supra* note 46; H.R. 1947, *supra* note 46.

66. Indeed, doing so might trigger violations of the Federal Securities Laws.

67. *See* Ronald Goldstock & James B. Jacobs, *Monitors and IPSIGS: Emergence of a New Criminal Justice Role*, 43 Criminal Law Bulletin 217 (2007); Christie Ford & David Hess, *Can Corporate Monitorships Improve Corporate Compliance?*, 34 J. Corp. L. 679, 682–89 (2009).

68. Monitors with considerable expertise in compliance matters and frequent ongoing firm contact are probably better placed to be watchdogs than a board, with probably less compliance expertise, which meets only a dozen or less times a year.

Conclusion

ANTHONY S. BARKOW AND RACHEL E. BARKOW

The preceding chapters have shown that the increasingly broad policymaking role of prosecutors in corporate affairs raises a host of complex issues. Indeed, the question of regulation by prosecutors is as complicated as the question of regulation itself. Whether a regulatory regime makes sense requires a careful assessment of its costs and benefits; the same holds true for the regulatory system created through DPAs, NPAs, and settlement agreements. Thus, just as regulatory reform in general must rest on reliable empirical information, so, too, must regulatory reform in the context of prosecutors' offices. Accordingly, before suggesting a comprehensive set of reforms for the practice of prosecutorial regulation, we would need more empirical data about the effectiveness of settlement agreements in reducing misconduct, the costs of their use, the availability of alternatives, and the costs and benefits of particular terms within agreements. This empirical inquiry should be the primary aim of further research.[1]

But although some reform avenues will require further study, the previous chapters demonstrate that we actually do know quite a bit about these agreements already, as a matter of both theory and practice. And on the basis of this knowledge, the contributing authors have suggested several reforms.

Some of these reforms would require fundamental shifts in the way we currently approach not just DPAs, NPAs, and settlement agreements but corporate regulation in general. On many of these issues, our commentators are not in agreement. For instance, Richard Epstein would "junk corporate criminal liability" because in his view it leads to overdeterrence. Mariano-Florentino Cuéllar, in contrast, makes the case for criminal law enforcement as a key part of the regulatory enterprise of risk regulation. He notes, among other things, that the use of criminal prosecutions can shape public perceptions in a way that allows for more civil regulation. Samuel Buell would similarly retain corporate criminal liability, though he advocates for less criminal enforcement and more activity by the SEC in addressing corporate misconduct. He would have the SEC insist on DPA-like remedial terms when it settles with companies and abandon its practice of allowing firms to "neither admit nor deny" the charges against them. To accomplish that latter goal, he suggests giving the SEC the power to veto securities fraud class actions so that an admission of wrongdoing would not subject companies to a flood of collateral civil suits, barring the collateral use of SEC settlements, or perhaps ultimately even doing away with the private right of action under Rule 10b-5. Thus, Buell's proposal, as he admits, would require fundamental rethinking of private actions for securities fraud. Jennifer Arlen similarly would place greater responsibilities with regulatory agencies, giving them the authority over compliance programs. Lisa Kern Griffin, Cindy Alexander, and Mark Cohen argue for greater resources to prosecutors. Griffin wants more funding so that prosecutors and investigators are less reliant on private cooperators to detect crime. Alexander and Cohen argue that the greater the likelihood of detection, the greater the deterrence, thus law enforcement budgets should increase.

These proposals address the issues raised by regulation by prosecutors, but they touch on much broader topics of corporate regulation, securities regulation, and law enforcement resources. Thus, they should be considered as part of a much broader study of these issues. Scholars should thus take cues from the contributing authors and consider the ways in which these reforms could improve not just the use of settlement agreements in criminal law but corporate regulation more generally.

Not every path to reform requires further study. The analyses of the contributing authors also point to some improvements that could be made right now.

1. *Establishing Guidelines and Improving the Internal Review Process for When the Use of a DPA, NPA, or Settlement Agreement is Appropriate.* The preceding chapters make clear that that there is room for improving the internal process within prosecutors' offices before prosecutors set out to establish regulations that will govern a company.

As an initial matter, prosecutors should establish internal guidance describing what steps prosecutors should take before imposing regulations on companies.

The first step should involve consultation with someone not involved in the case before going forward with any DPA, NPA, or settlement agreement. The prosecutor or team of prosecutors investigating a company should not decide unilaterally whether or not to launch an indictment or accept a DPA, NPA, or settlement agreement in its place. In addition to the risk that those prosecutors may have biases from their involvement in the investigation, there is the additional equity concern that similarly situated companies will be treated differently depending on which prosecutor is assigned their case. To minimize those risks, prosecutors' offices that pursue settlement agreements with regulatory terms should set up some independent advisory board or committee to offer independent judgment on the proposal. This body should have the requisite independence to assess the facts of a case without the personal investment that comes from being part of the investigative team. And, it could help ensure uniformity by being the centralized point of reference for all cases involving the potential regulation of corporations through the threat of indictment.

This risk of inconsistent policymaking is greatest at the federal level because there are ninety-three U.S. Attorneys with a large degree of independence. High-level political appointees at the DOJ could provide independent oversight as a check on inconsistent policymaking, or that same function could be performed by the Financial Fraud Enforcement Task Force, which, as Brandon Garrett notes, contains representatives from ten federal agencies and federal prosecutors.

Although these agreements are rarer at the state and local levels, if they are going to be used, these offices should also set up an appropriate internal structure that provides the same checking mechanism to ensure that prosecutors make decisions about regulations on the merits and without a bias that could develop from being involved in the investigation of the case. And, as Sara Sun Beale notes, state AGs may wish to contact other state AGs to coordinate enforcement efforts.

In addition to seeking guidance from a source responsible for central oversight of all such agreements in a jurisdiction, prosecutors should also consult with any relevant administrative agency before instituting a criminal action or pursuing a DPA, NPA, or settlement. Several of the contributing authors note the advantages of prosecutors working in collaboration with agencies to create better substantive policies. For example, Cuéllar, Arlen, Buell, Garrett, and Rachel Barkow all note that agencies may be better positioned in many ways to make the assessment of what kind of regulations should govern the company. While these agencies may have their judgment clouded because they have been captured to some extent by the targets of their regulation, they remain a source of expertise. Thus, at the very least, prosecutors should make sure they know an agency's position on any proposed term and give it serious consideration. Garrett notes that the Financial Fraud Enforcement Task Force might be the best entity at the federal level to further this coordination between agencies and prosecutors, but whatever the mechanism for coordination and consultation, there is a consensus that greater efforts should be made to ensure that agency input is part of the prosecutorial decision-making calculus.

Agencies can and should be used at the initial charging decision stage in other ways. To the extent criminal behavior seems to span an industry, prosecutors should consider petitioning the relevant agency with authority over the industry to consider instituting notice-and-comment proceedings with an eye toward passing rules that would outlaw the practice across the board. This would help address some of the equity and competition concerns associated with having prosecutors regulate on a piecemeal basis only those companies for which they happen to have evidence of wrongdoing but where the problem is more systemic.

In addition to detailing the need for consultation with an independent overseer and the relevant experts in the field, guidelines on DPAs, NPAs, and settlement agreements should also explain when these agreements are desirable and the factors that should be taken into account in deciding whether to use them. The DOJ already has internal guidelines for organizational prosecutions, but these guidelines focus on factors that should inform a decision whether to charge a company at all; they do not offer guidance on what terms are appropriate for a DPA or NPA.[2]

2. *Setting Limits on the Types of Conditions That Can Be Imposed.* Because prosecutors need freedom to craft conditions that are specifically tailored to the violation at issue, the capacity and attributes of the company being pursued, and the characteristics and dynamics of the industry within which the company operates, it is not possible to specify in advance all available conditions that are appropriate or advisable for a settlement agreement. But whatever the specific term, at a minimum, that term should be related to the alleged violation and aimed at achieving future compliance with the law. In that regard, terms requiring audits and reports fall well within the law enforcement objectives of these agreements. What should not be allowed, as Epstein points out, are terms that would limit the ability of a company to participate in the political process or compromise constitutional rights.

If any penalty is imposed on the company, that money should be in the form of fines that are payable to the shareholders and those injured by the corporation's practices, or payable to the U.S. Treasury. No additional party should receive payment as a result of a DPA, NPA, or settlement agreement. The provision in the Bristol-Myers Squibb DPA that required the company to endow an ethics chair at Seton Hall (the alma mater of the U.S. Attorney who oversaw the negotiation of the agreement) is an example of a term that is inappropriate as part of a settlement agreement and that raises an appearance of (if not an actual example of) impropriety that undermines the validity of the use of DPAs, NPAs, or settlement agreements as regulatory devices. Just as regulations must bear a rational relationship to the harm they are addressing, so, too, must the regulations in these agreements. On the heels of the Bristol-Myers Squibb DPA and the congressional reaction to it, DOJ appropriately adopted such a restriction.[3]

Whether there should be other restrictions on the content of the terms in DPAs, NPAs, and settlement agreements is less clear. Arlen argues that agreements with publicly held firms generally should not contain structural reforms and that structural regulation and compliance should be left to expert agencies whenever possible. On the other hand, because these agreements have almost uniformly contained terms regulating the firm's compliance, it does seem appropriate for a guidance document to spell out what type of compliance programs should be considered as long as they are going to remain in use. The Organizational Sentencing Guidelines already provide detail on what compliance programs are appropriate at the federal level, but states that pursue regulatory settlement agreements in lieu of prosecution should adopt similar guidelines on what kind of compliance terms are appropriate. Moreover, guidance documents should specify when, if ever, either line of business restrictions or prosecutorial control over personnel decisions is appropriate.

3. *Improving the Process for Formulating Regulatory Conditions.* As several of the chapters make clear, once a decision has been made to proceed with a DPA, NPA, or settlement agreement, prosecutors should take care to devise the soundest substantive regulations possible. Several steps can be taken to improve the content of the terms in these agreements.

First, as noted earlier, prosecutors should make every effort to get feedback from relevant experts in the field. So, for instance, if the term being considered involves the regulation of a player in the securities industry, the SEC would be a natural point of contact. Prosecutors are already doing this to some degree, of course, but this should become standard practice.

Second, Barkow's analysis of prosecutorial procedures suggests that prosecutors should implement procedures for soliciting comments and consulting with other subject matter experts before proceeding on what will, in effect, become new codes and regulations for industry. For example, if DOJ or an individual U.S. Attorney's office wants to seek a certain compliance arrangement or monitoring structure that goes beyond what is in the Sentencing Guidelines, it should seek comments before imposing those conditions in agreements to make sure they are substantively wise. Similarly, before an AG like Cuomo or Spitzer wants to impose a new industry code for health care providers or mutual funds, it should seek comments not just from the targets of their investigations but from anyone interested in the issue. This could be done on an expedited timetable, and it need not be subject to judicial review. The important point would be to get feedback institutionalized.

Third, Barkow's analysis also suggests that prosecutors should assess in some measure the costs and benefits of proposed reforms and consider alternative measures as a matter of good internal governance. For instance, when Spitzer considered a fee reduction requirement for all mutual fund providers, he should have considered whether the benefits to consumers would outweigh costs to competition in the industry and whether less costly alternatives would address the criminal behavior just as well. This does not have to be as elaborate as the cost-benefit analysis that takes place within the Office of Information and Regulatory Affairs at the federal level, but at the very least it should entail someone on the case drafting a memo that explains the costs and benefits of the requirement and discusses why alternative regulations were rejected. There should be someone in the prosecutor's office designated to review these proposals. At the federal level, this could be done within the Office of Information and Regulatory Affairs or somewhere in Main Justice. A state AG could have this review conducted internally by someone who was not involved in pursuing the case.

4. *Evaluating Agreements after They Are in Place.* Prosecutors cannot know whether their use of these agreements is effective without conducting an evaluation of them after they have been put into place. The GAO recently made this point with respect to federal DPAs and NPAs, observing that currently "DOJ cannot evaluate and demonstrate the extent to which DPAs and NPAs . . . contribute to the department's efforts to combat corporate crime because it has no measures to assess their effectiveness" and urging DOJ to establish performance measures.[4] In response to the GAO report, DOJ committed itself to continuing to develop performance measures evaluating the effectiveness of DPAs, NPAs, and, indeed, its overall effectiveness in combating corporate crime. But DOJ agreed with only one of GAO's suggested metrics—a company's success at complying with the terms of an agreement, which DOJ previously began to measure in part in response to an earlier GAO report—and rejected GAO's suggestion to use recidivism as a metric.[5]

Obviously prosecutors will be paying attention to whether a company reoffends or fails to comply with an agreement. But evaluation should be more systemic than that to ensure that the regulations imposed on companies are not simply deterring the commission of future crimes but also improving public welfare. Agencies that regulate typically revisit their regulatory decisions and conduct evaluations to make sure they make sense. Prosecutors are not set up for this kind of review, but they should set up some kind of reviewing structure if they are going to get in the business of regulation. Even though DPAs, NPAs, and settlement agreements have relatively short life spans, terms should be reviewed on a biennial basis to ensure that they have not led to unintended consequences that undermine their utility. The reviewing body could be the same one discussed earlier that conducts the initial cost-benefit analysis of the regulations, or it could be done within the office itself. But some actor should be revisiting these agreements overall so that prosecutors are learning what is working and what is not on a systemic basis.

5. *Reforming the Role of Monitors and Private Actors*. Monitoring compliance with these agreements is critical to their success. Vikramaditya Khanna's chapter explains that DOJ took steps in the Morford Memo to provide guidance on when monitors should be used, how they should be selected, and the scope of their authority. This memo is a positive step toward improving the use of monitors, but additional steps should also be taken. Khanna's chapter provides greater detail, but a few key points are emphasized here.

First, the selection of monitors could be improved. As the GAO points out, although the Morford Memo establishes guidance on the selection process, it "does not require documentation of the process used and the reasons for selecting a specific monitor."[6] Thus the GAO recommends better documentation and more transparency, and we concur. Moreover, although the Morford Memo requires that monitors be selected solely based on merit and that any particular monitor must be approved by the Office of the Deputy Attorney General, there is still the potential for improper conflicts of interest. For example, although current law prohibits former DOJ employees from litigating the same matters in which they personally and substantially participated while in government service, it does not expressly prohibit a former prosecutor from serving as a monitor for a company that he himself investigated and prosecuted. Nor does it clearly prohibit a former prosecutor from serving in a monitorship that arose out of a DPA or NPA that she herself negotiated. The proposed Transparency and Integrity in Corporate Monitoring Act of 2009[7] would take steps toward remedying these gaps. Although it does not appear that any monitors have been appointed who previously worked on the same matter they later monitored, such an appointment, if it were to occur, would foster public cynicism about government by feeding the public's belief that government actors are engaged in self-dealing. Thus, prophylactic measures to eliminate the possibility of such appointments are wise.[8] States that employ monitors should pass similar internal guidance to avoid conflicts of interest and any appearance of impropriety.

Selection could be improved in other ways as well. Khanna recommends that the government seek to encourage the development of a market for monitors. Griffin recommends using a model along the lines of the one used for Supplemental Environmental Projects ("SEPs"). SEPs are agreements between the Environmental Protection Agency and industry as part of enforcement of the Clean Air Act in which violators can undertake certain obligations to receive decreased penalties. They therefore mirror DPAs and NPAs in many respects. The EPA, however, leaves it to the regulated entity to contact any third parties for implementation of the agreement to avoid being entangled with the management of SEP funds.

The analysis of both Khanna and Griffin thus lends support to the approach proposed in the Accountability in Deferred Prosecutions Acts of 2008 and 2009, which would promote the creation of a national list of organizations and individuals who could serve as monitors. This would go a long way toward developing a market for monitors and away from having prosecutors handpicking monitors in an uncompetitive process.

Second, monitor fees should be set either through a competitive bidding process or with judicial oversight. Khanna and Griffin both point out the dangers posed when prosecutors unilaterally set or approve monitor fees.

Third, Khanna and Griffin agree that any agreement making use of a monitor should clearly state the monitor's responsibilities and duties. The Morford Memo is a step in the right direction, for it clarifies that monitors are agents of neither the company nor the government. But the memo should go further in requiring that DPAs and NPAs state the scope of the monitor's powers; the triggering events for the termination of a monitor; and the reporting chain between the monitor, the firm, and the government. Khanna also recommends having the government state why a monitor was selected instead of a cash fine. In addition, to the extent that a market for monitors does not develop, Khanna recommends including a provision in the DPA or NPA that would impose some fiduciary-like duties on monitors to shareholders.

These proposals address the most pressing problems posed today by regulation by prosecutors. As prosecutors continue to step into boardrooms and the role of substantive regulator, undoubtedly more issues will arise. The analyses provided in this book provide a framework not only for addressing current problems but also for thinking about the future issues that will inevitably arise.

NOTES

1. The Government Accountability Office, at congressional request, has collected data regarding these agreements. *See, e.g.*, *Accountability, Transparency, and Uniformity in Corporate Deferred and Non-prosecution Agreements: Hearing Before the Subcomm. on Commercial and Admin. Law of the H. Comm. on the Judiciary*, 111th Cong. (2009) (statement of Eileen R. Larence, Director, Homeland Sec. and Justice, U.S. Gen. Accountability Office) [hereinafter *GAO Testimony*]. Brandon Garrett collects federal organizational prosecution agreements and makes them publicly available. *See* Brandon Garrett & Jon Ashley, Prosecution Agreements (Sorted by Company), http://www.law.virginia.edu/html/librarysite/garrett_bycompany.htm. This website is a valuable source of empirical data that scholars and policymakers could use to track and analyze such agreements.

2. The GAO reported that prosecutors say that they base their decision on whether to enter into a DPA or NPA rather than prosecute a company or decline to do so on DOJ's Principles of Federal Prosecution of Business Organizations, *see* Memorandum from Mark Filip, Deputy Attorney General, U.S. Dep't of Justice, to Heads of Department Components and United States Attorneys, *Principles of Federal Prosecution of Business Organizations* (Aug. 28, 2008), http://www.usdoj.gov/dag/readingroom/dag-memo-08282008.pdf, placing the most significance on whether the company cooperated with the investigation. The GAO reported that companies involved in DPAs and NPAs perceived the prosecutors' decisions to be based on these guidelines. *See GAO Testimony*, *supra* note 1, at 9–10.

3. U.S. Dep't of Justice, U.S. Attorneys' Manual, § 9–16.325.

4. *See* U.S. Gen. Accountability Office, GAO 10–110, DOJ Has Taken Steps to Better Track Its Use of Deferred and Non-Prosecution Agreements, but Should Evaluate Effectiveness 20–24 (2009), *available at* http://www.gao.gov/new.items/d10110.pdf [hereinafter GAO Report].

5. *See* Letter from Edward N. Siskel, Assoc. Deputy Gen. Counsel, Office of the Deputy Attorney Gen., U.S. Dep't of Justice, to Eileen Larence, Director, Homeland Sec. and Justice, U.S. Gen. Accountability Office 3–5 (Dec. 15, 2009), *in* GAO Report, *supra* note 4, at 36. It is notable how DOJ has changed its guidelines and policies regarding DPAs and NPAs in response to criticism, including earlier GAO reports, see id. at 3–4, especially in light of the significant lobbying power wielded by corporations.

6. *GAO Testimony*, *supra* note 1, at 26.

7. Transparency and Integrity in Corporate Monitoring Act of 2009, H.R. 4283, 111th Cong. (2009).

8. *Transparency and Integrity in Corporate Monitoring: Hearing Before the Subcomm. on Commercial and Admin. Law of the H. Comm. on the Judiciary*, 111th Cong. (2009) (statement of Anthony S. Barkow, Executive Director, Center on the Administration of Criminal Law).

About the Contributors

CINDY R. ALEXANDER is Assistant Chief Economist at the Securities and Exchange Commission, and previously worked as Senior Economist, Council of Economic Advisers, specializing in corporate governance reform, and at the U.S. Department of Justice (Antitrust Division) and Vanderbilt University (OGSM), in addition to appointments at University of Chicago Law School and Yale Law School. Her published work on corporations and crime appears in academic journals on finance, economics, and law. She received her Ph.D. in economics at UCLA.

JENNIFER ARLEN (B.A., Harvard College [magna cum laude]; J.D., Ph.D. Economics, NYU) is the Norma Z. Paige Professor of Law at NYU School of Law and directs its Center for Law, Economics and Organization. An expert on corporate crime, Arlen joined NYU from USC Law School. She clerked for Judge Phyllis Kravitch, Eleventh Circuit Court of Appeals, and was a Visiting Professor at the California Institute of Technology, Harvard Law School, and Yale Law School.

ANTHONY S. BARKOW is Executive Director of the Center on the Administration of Criminal Law at NYU School of Law. He was a federal prosecutor for twelve years in the Manhattan and D.C. U.S. Attorneys' Offices and in Main Justice. He received the Attorney General's Award for Exceptional Service, which is the highest award bestowed in the Justice Department. During his tenure in the government, he tried more than forty cases and briefed and argued more than ten appellate cases.

RACHEL E. BARKOW is Professor of Law and the Faculty Director of the Center on the Administration of Criminal Law at NYU School of Law. She has published more than twenty articles on administrative, criminal, and constitutional law. She has presented her work before the Senate Judiciary

Committee; the House of Representatives Subcommittee on Commerce, Trade, and Consumer Protection; the U.S. Sentencing Commission; judicial conferences; and numerous law schools. She graduated magna cum laude from Harvard Law School, where she won the Sears Prize.

SARA SUN BEALE is the Charles L. B. Lowndes Professor at Duke Law School. She is the author of dozens of articles and the coauthor of three books, including *Federal Criminal Law and Its Enforcement* and *Grand Jury Law and Practice*. Her research has been cited by many courts, including the Supreme Court of the United States. She is the Reporter for the Advisory Committee on Criminal Rules, which drafts the Federal Rules of Criminal Procedure.

SAMUEL W. BUELL is Professor of Law at Duke Law School. He has been an Associate Professor at Washington University and a Visiting Professor at the University of Texas. He is the author of numerous articles on the law governing corporate misconduct. From 1994 to 2004, he served as a federal prosecutor in the U.S. Department of Justice, where he was a two-time recipient of the Attorney General's Award for Exceptional Service.

MARK A. COHEN (Ph.D. Economics, Carnegie-Mellon University) is Vice President for Research and Senior Fellow at Resources for the Future, and Professor of Management and Law at Vanderbilt University. Previously, he served as a staff economist at the U.S. Environmental Protection Agency, the U.S. Federal Trade Commission, and the U.S. Sentencing Commission. His research focuses on enforcement of environmental regulation and the economics of corporate and street crime.

MARIANO-FLORENTINO (TINO) CUÉLLAR is Professor and Deane F. Johnson Faculty Scholar at Stanford Law School. His teaching and research focus on how organizations manage complex regulatory, criminal justice, and security challenges. He served in the Obama White House as Special Assistant to the President for Justice and Regulatory Policy, and in the Clinton administration at the Treasury Department. He grew up near the U.S.-Mexico border and is a member of the American Law Institute.

RICHARD A. EPSTEIN is Laurence A. Tisch Professor of Law at NYU School of Law. He is also the Peter and Kirsten Bedford Senior Fellow at the Hoover Institution, and a Senior Lecturer at the University of Chicago Law

School. One of the most influential thinkers in legal academia, he has written numerous books and articles on a wide range of legal and interdisciplinary subjects and has taught courses across the whole curriculum.

BRANDON L. GARRETT is Professor of Law at the University of Virginia School of Law. His research and teaching interests include criminal procedure, wrongful convictions, habeas corpus, corporate crime, civil rights, civil procedure, and constitutional law. Garrett has published widely on various topics, including DNA exonerations and organizational prosecutions. He graduated from Columbia Law School and clerked for the Hon. Pierre N. Leval of the U.S. Court of Appeals for the Second Circuit.

LISA KERN GRIFFIN is Professor of Law at Duke University School of Law, where she teaches evidence and criminal law and procedure. Griffin graduated from Stanford Law School and has also taught at UCLA, served as a federal prosecutor, and clerked for Judge Dorothy Nelson of the Ninth Circuit and Justice Sandra Day O'Connor of the Supreme Court. Her recent scholarship includes articles on deferred prosecution agreements and dishonesty in federal criminal investigations.

VIKRAMADITYA KHANNA is Professor of Law at the University of Michigan Law School. His interest areas include corporate and securities laws, corporate crime, law in India, comparative corporate governance, and law and economics. He has published papers in the *Harvard Law Review*, *Michigan Law Review*, *Supreme Court Economic Review*, and *Georgetown Law Journal*; is the editor of White Collar Crime Abstracts at SSRN; and has testified before Congress.

Index

www.ingramcontent.com/pod-product-compliance
Lightning Source LLC
LaVergne TN
LVHW101439200926
848483LV00004B/409